Gene Pitney

Gene Pitney

The Singer, The Songs, The Songwriters

DAVID McGRATH

Waterside Productions

Waterside Productions
2055 Oxford Ave
Cardiff, CA 92007
www.waterside.com

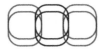

TABLE OF CONTENTS

ACKNOWLEDGEMENTS

This book is only a book because of Gene Pitney. A star; a gentleman; a friend.

This book is a product of the love of music that my mother, Rita McGrath, fostered in me. She introduced me to life, music, and radio. I wish she had lived long enough to see my success with Gene.

This book is only readable because of the proofing, editing, and writing (and listening) skills of my bride, Guida Brown. I am richer than a thousand kings to have her by my side.

This book only became a book because of the kindness of the musical giant Jim Peterik. What a star he is! What a songwriter he is!

This book only got published because of the direction and guidance from Bill Gladstone and Josh Freel from Waterside Productions. Thank you so much.

This book looks so damn good because of the design and layout skills of Paula and Wade West from Westwords Consulting, LLC. They are the best.

This book is so interesting because of the songs written by these extraordinary songwriters and the stories they told. So many enormous talents and musical geniuses.

This book is more compelling to read because of the insights and contributions of Abby Schroeder, who was there from the start. She loved Gene Pitney.

This book was completed because of the encouragement of a number of Gene Pitney aficionados and connoisseurs, including Gary Leveille, Brian Frederick, Glen Ransden, and "Wild" Wayne Jones. I thank them all for their enduring friendship.

This book was somewhat manageable to write because of the efforts of Jeani Berndt, who spent years and years laying out the *Gene Pitney International Fan Club Newsletter* when lay out was nowhere as easy as it is today.

This book is visually interesting because of all the sheet music provided to me from Doctor Tom Petoskey.

This book is far more fascinating and provocative because of the back stories of certain songs shared by: Lynne Pitney, Tony Orlando, Neil Sedaka, Toni Wine, Dick Fox, Marc Almond, Garry Sherman, the Rogers – Roger Greenaway and Roger Cook, Bobby Vee, Roger Atkins, Peter Udell, Brian Hyland, Gerry Bron, Clive Black, Neil Warnock, Tony Macaulay, and David Courtney. Still can't believe I got to talk to all of them.

This book finally became captivating when Lynne Pitney agreed to give us "the last word" on each of Gene's songs. She's in my Hall of Fame of Great Ladies! Thanks for the bacon, Mrs. P.

———————————

I have done due diligence in pursuing and exploring the possibilities for identifying, locating, and contacting the copyright owners and getting appropriate permission for all photos in this book. You are invited to contact David McGrath at Pitneyfan@genepitneybook.com if your image was used without identification or acknowledgment. I tried to find you and couldn't, but I thank you for your wonderful contributions.

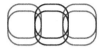

INTRODUCTION

I had to write this book.

Gene Pitney turned my life around personally and professionally. I owe him a huge debt of gratitude, and I hope this is one small payment on that debt. He was a star; he was a gentleman; he was a friend. He was Best Man at my wedding to Guida Brown in 1998; I was a pallbearer at his funeral in 2006.

I enlisted my bride, Guida Brown, with her well-earned degree in journalism, to turn my gibberish into English. She is the best proofreader I have ever met. We wish we had written this book while he was still alive, but we didn't. We thought he would live to be one hundred and sing 'til he was ninety! He didn't. So, instead, we wrote this book in his memory and to remind his family, friends, fellow artists, fans, and ourselves what a star he was, what an impact he had on the music business, and what he did for so many songwriters.

The songwriters' stories are interesting, touching, surprising, and sometimes amusing. We can tell you that each and every songwriter we spoke or shared emails with loved, admired, respected, and treasured Gene. Each one was thrilled and grateful that a star of Gene's stature would record one of his or her songs.

Gene Pitney became my musical hero when I was in eighth grade. That's when Tony Logue, the coolest guy (at least in my mind) at Saints Peter & Paul School on the East Side of Milwaukee, played "Town Without Pity" on the jukebox at Dan's Chicken Pie Restaurant one day after school. He looked at me that afternoon and simply said, "This is a cool song by a cool guy." That day I became a lifelong Gene Pitney fan, both on Tony's "recommendation" and the fact that I quickly discovered Gene's songs spoke to me and all my pimply-faced teenage angst about love, puppy love, unrequited love, lack of love…well…you get it. Little did I know that some twenty years later I would go into business with Gene Pitney and become a part of his fabulous career. Together, we started Gene Pitney Music & Merchandising.

I love music. But, I can't sing, dance, or play any musical instrument. So, the closest I could come to being around music was to be a radio DJ. That's what I did for a living until I moved into the news end of the radio business in 1998.

Through a series of lucky breaks, being in the right place at the right time, and not knowing what I shouldn't do, my dreams came true when I ended up working with some of my musical heroes: Gene Pitney, Peter "Herman's Hermits" Noone, and Dion "Runaround Sue" DiMucci. Guida and I were the team that sold the tour merchandise for these stars. No more; no less. We worked with Gene from 1985 'til 2006. We were with Peter for almost thirteen years, or, as he would say, "Longer than I was with the Hermits!" And, as of this writing we are still out on the road, selling tour merchandise for Dion. Really, does it get any better than that for a kid who was consumed by music in the late 1950s and through the 1960s?

Guida (the other person who turned my life around) and I would create, produce, and sell Gene's tour merchandise at his US shows from 1985 'til the day he died in 2006. We also ran his Gene Pitney International Fan Club, catering to his fans around the world. Incidentally, I'm convinced the ONLY reason Gene kept me around all those years was because he loved Guida. Come to think of it, that's why Peter and Dion kept me around, too!

The frosting on this cake, however, was personal for me. Gene and I became friends. He took me under his superstar wings and taught me the ins and outs of the music business. He allowed me into his personal world, too. We would stay at his home in Connecticut, get to know his family and friends, swim in his pool, and bask in his reflected glory. I just could never have imagined that anything like that could ever happen to ME. Who could?

All through my years at Messmer High School in Milwaukee, during the height of the "British Invasion," I wanted so badly to be part of that excitement and be able to meet and know all those stars who I read about in the British music newspapers and who created the soundtrack of my youth. But, c'mon…other people got those kinds

4

of breaks and had those kinds of jobs with those kinds of stars, not a shy, overweight, self-esteem-less kid from the lower East Side of Milwaukee. It just wasn't in the cards.

Well…maybe it wasn't in MY deck of cards. Apparently, however, God and Gene Pitney were playing with a different deck. To this day – almost every day – I wonder why and how it all came to be. Believe me, much of it had to do with the plain and simple fact that I didn't know what I didn't know about the music business, and I didn't know what I didn't know about approaching a star of Gene's magnitude with a business proposition. I was a dope who was in the right place at the right time with the right star at the right time of his career. And, that star, Gene Pitney, decided to take a chance on this dope. It is still mysterious and magical to me. Talk about "divine intervention." Thank you, God…and Gene Pitney. What a ride it was.

April 5, 2006, will forever be one of the saddest days of my life. My friend, mentor, and hero, Gene Pitney, died in his sleep following a show at St. David's Hall in Cardiff, Wales. His son, Chris, called our home early that morning to break the news to us. I was already at work so Guida had to call me and tell me. My heart broke; I was crushed. I called Gene's wife Lynne later that morning, and we talked, cried, and laughed for a few minutes over the phone. She is one of the great ladies in my life… and not just because she makes me pounds of bacon when we stay at her house! (We still see her on a regular basis.) And, of course, I know the only reason I'm allowed to visit her in Somers, Connecticut, is because she loves Guida. Do you see a pattern?

One of the greatest joys I had while putting this book together was the phone calls with Lynne Pitney, getting her thoughts on Gene's songs. Some surprised me; some made me silently say "Eureka!"; some I marveled at; some made me laugh; all of them made me smile. She is a charming and engaging lady.

To all the songwriters, producers, agents, and singers who talked to me on the phone, then talked to me again on the phone for follow-up after follow-up after follow-up, then answered all my emails, then answered my follow-ups – THANK YOU! Your stories were all amazing and wonderful; some were surprising; some were stunning; all were revealing and illuminating. I love Gene and Peter and Dion – and all of their band members down through the years. I also love the songwriters! What a gift they have to tell all those wonderful stories in about three minutes' time. Their songs make me weep, they make me smile, they bring back fond memories, and they simply make me happy to be alive.

(Left-right) Abby Schroeder, Gary Leveille, and Lynne Pitney.

Lest there be any doubt, I believe Gene Pitney was THE most gifted pop male vocalist of his era. He was the Frank Sinatra of the 1960s. But, as accomplished and brilliant as he was, he still needed the songs. In a remarkable quid pro quo, Gene was lucky to record some of the finest songs written by some of the most fabled and legendary songwriters in the history of pop music. And, those songwriters were blessed to have Gene Pitney record and interpret their works. How fortuitous that he was there and they were there at the same time and place. They created some stunning music and spectacular hit records.

This book is about Gene's songs, the stories behind them, and the songwriters who composed them. As I mentioned, I am not a musician in any sense of the word, so you won't read comments about minor or major keys, key changes, minor chords, crescendos, arpeggios, etc.; I am clueless. I am an average music listener. I love a catchy melody and lyrics that I can relate to in any number of different ways. Tell me a story, and I'll listen to it.

Over the course of writing this book I struck it rich and got to speak to so many of the geniuses who wrote these songs. Along with Gene, they are my musical heroes. I was star-struck talking to the likes of Barry Mason, Les Reed, Burt Bacharach, Hal David, Larry Weiss, Chip Taylor, Jerry "Swampp Dog" Douglas, Phillip Goodhand-Tait, Roger Atkins, Al Kooper, Mark Barkan, Peter Udell, Roger Cook, Roger Greenaway, and all the others.

Another primary player in the Gene Pitney story is Abby Schroeder. She is the wife and business partner of the late Aaron Schroeder, the musical genius who discovered Gene, developed his career, started Musicor Records to showcase him, and was part of the team that found the songs for Gene to record. Abby was there for it all. Abby's input into this book was significant, relevant, and far-reaching. I did four hours of phone interviews with her over the course of a month, and in May of 2021 she reunited with Lynne Pitney at a lunch in Great Barrington, Massachusetts, along with me, Guida, and my trusted sounding board, Gary Leveille, who urged me to organize it. Abby and Lynne hadn't seen each other for over fifty years!

I have led a blessed and successful life working in radio and with some of the biggest music stars of my Baby Boomer generation. However, had that radio career not worked out for me I would like to have been the quarterback for my beloved Green Bay Packers or a songwriter. It's a good thing the radio career panned out because I have no gifts that would have helped me in either of the other two aspirations.

There's a remarkable line from one of ABBA's greatest songs ever, "Thank You For The Music," that sums up songwriters for me: *"But I've often wondered how did it all start? Who found out that nothing can capture a heart like a melody can? Well…whoever it was…I'm a fan. So I say thank you for the music…the songs I'm singing. Thanks for all the joy they're bringing."* (Thanks Bjorn and Benny for all that music!)

Songwriting. What a gift! Thanks to all those who wrote these songs for Gene Pitney. I likely saw two hundred Gene Pitney concerts during the twenty-one years we worked with him. At every show I saw what his music meant to his fans. The tears, the joy, the wonder and delight. Thanks to my friend and musical hero Gene Pitney for singing those songs.

And, some final housekeeping notes: The songs are listed alphabetically just to provide some sort of order. If I had listed them by "best" to "not so best," readers may have disagreed. If I had listed them by top sellers, I would have missed those Philippine sales (with a nod to Peter Noone). So, I took the easiest way and listed them alphabetically.

Additionally, some songs merited more attention than others because I interviewed the writers or I had previously spoken with Gene to elicit his take about a given song – or the story about a given song fascinated and/or intrigued the snot out of me.

We did concentrate on Gene's hits, but when we were able to locate and interview the songwriter(s) for a strong album track or a single that charted poorly, we jumped at it and so those songs are also included here.

Most of these songs are almost sixty years old, as are the memories of the people who wrote them. So, there are different recollections about the same song from the people involved in it. I've had co-writers recall differently how songs they wrote were written and how they were presented to Gene. They usually are variations on a theme, but those different perspectives are at the same time curious and compelling.

Further, unlike his friend Bobby Vee who was a meticulous record keeper and filed away facts about his career fastidiously, Gene was not mindful about the minutiae of his career. It's not that he didn't care; it's more that he was unconcerned about it. I cannot tell you the number of times Gene would say to me in conversations about his career, "I don't remember." Keep that in mind as you delve into this book.

The other thing to keep in mind is that Gene was a great storyteller in all senses of the word, and he had a penchant for swapping out a tertiary fact here and there with favorable self-reflection. I have interviews, written and recorded, with Gene answering the same question from a number of different interviewers with somewhat different answers. Again, just variations on a theme; not dishonesty, distortion, or disinformation.

Knowing all that, you should also know that Gene was a great interview for radio, TV, magazines, and newspapers because he was always personable, amiable, and engaging. He was asked the same questions over and over and over, and he HAD to develop a knack for telling the same story in a fresh and distinctive way each time. That's a gift. Gene had it in spades.

Again, I am not a musician. I don't know a B-flat from a tire that's flat. I know absolutely nothing about music except what I like. Thus you will note the complete lack of analysis of song composition, musicians' abilities, etc. Any comments on that came from the songwriters or Gene.

Most – if not all – of the songs mentioned in this book are available for your viewing delectation on YouTube; even the so-called "rare" songs like The Rolling Stones version of "That Girl Belongs To Yesterday" can be found there.

The quotes in this book are sourced in the text. If a quote of Gene's is not sourced, that means it came from one of the countless conversations I had with him about his songs over the twenty-one years we worked together. While some of those quotes are paraphrased, their content is accurate. I know that because I likely asked him the same questions ten to twenty times and got the same answer each time! I recorded the interviews with the songwriters, producers, other singers, etc. They are all preserved on CDs.

Any factual mistakes, outside of direct quotes or attributions, are mine. There was so much source material to sort through, and I am about as organized as a third grade school field trip run by second graders. If you find a mistake, please let me know at Pitneyfan@genepitneybook.com. If you find what you think is a factual mistake in a quote from a songwriter or other person in this book, again, remember, these memories are now well over sixty years old.

And, the only reason this book is readable is because of the editing prowess and writing and re-writing abilities of my bride, Guida Brown. During the writing process, words, phrases, ideas, and stories just gushed out of my head, and I slammed the keyboard letters as fast as I could to get them on paper before I forgot them. Most of the chapters were in fourth or fifth draft form when I handed them to her…and they were still gibberish. She fixed 'em real good.

She also listened to me rambling on and on…and on…with all these stories in verbal form. Again and again and again. I love songwriters, their stories, and the sound of my own voice! She's a saint.

Speaking of saints, it was my mother, the sainted Rita Frances Gertrude Mary (Naber) McGrath, who fostered my love of music. I cannot remember a morning when there wasn't music coming out of the little green AM radio sitting on top of the refrigerator in our home on Oakland Avenue in Milwaukee as I grew up in the 1950s and '60s. That's where I first "met" all the singing stars of my era. She would also regale me with her favorite 78 rpm records on Saturdays. I still own those 78s to this day.

Because of her I still have great affection and appreciation for the stars of her era: Perry Como, Rosemary Clooney, Tony Bennett, Frank Sinatra, Gene Autry, Frankie Laine, Guy Mitchell, Johnnie Ray, Jerry Vale, Tony Martin, Frances Langford, Dinah Shore, The Four Lads, The Andrews Sisters, Vera Lynn, and all the big bands too numerous to mention.

Also because of Rita McGrath having her radio on every morning as I ate breakfast before school, I became fascinated and enthralled with…radio. By the time I was in fifth grade I knew I wanted to be on the radio to introduce and talk about all those great records that were being played. And that, too, came to fruition. I had, as I like to say, "a long and checkered career" as a radio DJ before transitioning into news at WGTD, a public radio station in Kenosha, Wisconsin. I was blessed to make a fruitful career out of it.

So, Mom, thanks for that little green radio…and…thank you for the music!

Gene with country and pop star Brenda Lee at a rehearsal for the Rock & Roll induction ceremony. She was inducted the same year.

Gene with Isaac Hayes, another 2002 Rock & Roll Hall of Fame inductee.

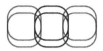

CHAPTER 1:
THE ROCK & ROLL HALL OF FAME

This chapter isn't about the songs Gene Pitney sang; instead, it's about the highest honor a singer can attain: membership in The Rock & Roll Hall of Fame. Gene's songs didn't win Academy Awards; heck, one didn't even make it into the movie! But Gene went one better: in 2002, he was inducted into the Hall of Fame. Here's THAT story.

Gene Pitney, the slender, handsome, tuxedo-clad pop star is sitting at a table in one of the world's most fashionable hotels with a beautiful redheaded lady at his side, awaiting dinner. Less than three minutes after sitting down he is hastily approached by a scruffy male fan – donning long, scraggly hair and clothes that would best be described as grubby – who proclaims that he is Pitney's "biggest fan."

The fan is carrying a book he wants Pitney to autograph. Pitney signs it graciously and listens as the fan tells him how much he enjoys Pitney's hits, especially "It Hurts To Be In Love." The fan is also a musician, and he is telling Pitney, whose hits have topped the charts around the world, what an influence he has been on his band.

What's peculiar about this scenario is that it could have happened in London or Rome, Sydney or New York, Los Angeles or Chicago throughout the 1960s when Gene Pitney was a superstar and the purveyor of pop music's biggest, boldest, and most poignant ballads.

But, in fact, it happened on March 18, 2002, at the Waldorf Astoria Hotel in New York City. The fan was Johnny Ramone of the legendary punk band The Ramones. The beautiful redhead is Pitney's wife of (then) thirty six years, Lynne. The book Ramone asks Pitney to sign is the souvenir book handed out to all attendees at The Rock & Roll Hall of Fame Induction Ceremonies.

While light years apart in musical styles, grooming, and fashion statements, Pitney and Ramone – both inductees into the Hall of Fame that year – bond instantly. Ramone is genuinely and sincerely thrilled to meet his musical idol. However, Pitney, technically is not *thrilled* to meet Johnny Ramone. He is, rather, relieved and gratified.

Relief washes over the now silver-haired Pitney's face when it is apparent that – irony of ironies – Ramone the person doesn't match the image of Ramone the punk star. Johnny Ramone is polite, charming, gracious, and well-mannered. He is an excited fan respectfully gushing over his idol.

Pitney's gratification stems from the fact that in the months leading up to this event, he had been more than hesitant and doubtful about performing at the Hall of Fame Induction Ceremony because he did NOT feel at all comfortable sharing the stage with The Ramones in the jam session that ends every induction ceremony. Their drug-addled, tattooed, anti-social reputation was not his cup of tea. Pitney, long successful at camouflaging a stubborn streak and creating an easy-going public demeanor, did not want to tarnish his "Mr. Clean" image by being linked to these boys anyhow, anywhere, any way.

The real irony, in Pitney's mind, is that now, the leader of that band is standing – awestruck and humble – in front of him, showing a reverence for Pitney's talent that he hasn't seen in years.

"Wow! That was a surprise," Pitney confides to his tablemates as Johnny Ramone walks away with his prized autograph. "A very nice guy," Pitney adds as he settles into his seat to prepare for the festivities.

The group of people congregated at Pitney's table during one of the biggest moments of his career speaks volumes about how he has conducted his professional and personal lives. Pitney needs to cocoon. He has always preferred the safety net and company of family and friends to that of superficial, high-powered show business types.

He has crowded eleven people around his $2,500-per-person table-of-ten. Along with wife Lynne are sons Todd and David. A third son, Chris, couldn't make it. John Shiely, the President and CEO of Briggs & Stratton, a Fortune 500 company based in Milwaukee, Wisconsin, is at the Pitney table along with his wife, Helen, and his sister, Liz Petschel. Chuck and Marsha Rubin, two more business associates-cum-friends of Pitney, are also there.

Rounding out the table is the ever-present husband-and-wife team of Dave McGrath and Guida Brown. McGrath is Pitney's ipso facto chief-of-staff, a fan who became both a personal friend and business partner. He is a handler, bodyguard, PR flack, merchandise hawker, friend, and confidante all rolled into one. Brown keeps them both grounded with her sharp wit, common sense, and business sense.

Pitney, a multimillionaire, who is very protective of his money, has griped – perhaps justifiably – all along about the $2,500 ticket price. While he received two free tickets for the ceremony, he was expected to fork over $5,000 to cover the costs of his two sons being there to see him honored.

"I've got to pay the Hall of Fame $5,000 so they can tell my sons how cool I am?" is the rhetorical question Pitney asked more than once in the months leading up to the Induction. It was more than a run-of-the-mill gripe. Pitney took it as a personal insult.

Shiely, a rock 'n' roll lover, inveterate music collector, and hardcore Pitney fan, is also a multimillionaire. An affable guy with a lot of disposable income, he smoothed everything over by stepping up to pay for the entire table. Shiely's gracious move procured him access to the heart of the event. It also played right into Pitney's frugal hand. Now Pitney could have his "people" there without paying the freight.

Getting Shiely at Pitney's table was easy. Pitney, the international singing star, and Shiely, the international businessman, had known each other for a number of years. Shiely had hired Pitney to perform at two Briggs & Stratton-funded events in Milwaukee. Pitney was more than happy to have someone as worldly, sophisticated, and likeable as Shiely around him at an event like this. Gene considered him a friend.

Pitney had McGrath make up the guest list for his table and turn it into the Hall of Fame. The Rock & Roll Hall of Fame Foundation, which runs the Induction event with an iron fist, will do virtually anything like this – of minor importance – that an inductee asks. Requests of more significant weight are handled much differently and with less evenhandedness.

Who would be sitting at his table was very important to Pitney, because even though he was a key player at the event and would be in the spotlight, he was still very uncomfortable. Because of his lifestyle choice to live in and work from Connecticut instead of one of the major show business cities, Pitney withdrew from music's inner circle a long time ago.

He is an outsider in his own mind and in reality. He has acquaintances in the entertainment community who are performers, but they are not really his friends. There would be no show business small talk or idle star chit chat for Pitney this night. He would not be working the room.

His tablemates, as described before, were family, friends, and business associates, none who surpassed him in show business fame. That is also part of the Pitney psyche. He prefers to be the straw that stirs the drink in social and/or business situations.

Because of his massive success early in life, Pitney is now accustomed to being the center of attention. When he's not, he will either drift from a conversation or completely check out of it.

As dinner is served, just about everyone at every table is craning his or her neck to see who else is there. Unfortunately, it is not a star-heavy event. There are a lot of record company and music business executives, but outside of the other inductees (Isaac Hayes, Brenda Lee, The Talking Heads, Tom Petty and the Heartbreakers, and The Ramones) and those stars who were chosen to induct them (Jewel, Alicia Keyes, Darlene Love, Eddie Vedder, Brian Setzer, and Jakob Dylan) there is only a smattering of other celebrities in the room.

Among them are Fred Schneider from the B-52s and Richard Belzer, the comedian-turned-actor (*Homicide: Life on the Streets, Law & Order: Special Victims Unit*). Legendary wall-of-sound producer Phil Spector, who worked with Pitney early in both of their careers, is also there. Their paths, unfortunately, do not cross at this event. Tommy Shaw from Styx and Damn Yankees is in the crowd, as is Matchbox Twenty's Rob Thomas.

Inductee Tom Petty, with his wife and kids, and a few members of his band, The Heartbreakers, occupy the table immediately adjacent to Pitney's. But, the two stars, both huge in their own eras, though sitting only six feet apart, never meet.

Part of that is due to Tom Petty being completely engrossed with his family and almost completely blasé to the event and all the to-do around it; part of it is Petty's ever-present, hulking bodyguard making people wary; part of it is Pitney's reluctance to mingle. He can be hail-fellow-well-met but only on-demand. Small talk and idle chatter are not his long suits.

One of Pitney's classic entreaties to McGrath before any meet-and-greet is "Don't let me be the last one in the room." He is a hit-and-run kind of guy, both with people in the business and with fans. Now you see him; now you don't. It's a style that has served him well both personally and professionally. It functions superbly as a barrier to anyone bearing down on him, looking for any kind of relationship via a conversation, and it has made him a more enigmatic star than any of his peers. For Pitney, that's a win-win.

The Induction ceremony, which will be shown on VH-1, is shot out of order. The two-hour long program shown on TV has been edited from a night of performances and speeches that dribbled on for over four hours.

Each artist is assigned a handler by VH-1 to expedite matters, making sure the star is in the right place at the right time. About fifteen minutes after the show is underway, Pitney's handler takes him and McGrath to the "artist holding area" adjacent to the stage.

Because this event is held at a hotel and not a TV studio or regular performance venue, there is no backstage area, per se. Pitney is led through a kitchen where workers are clanging pots and pans and chatting noisily with each other. Most are Hispanics in their early twenties. They are completely clueless that the meticulously dressed and groomed man gliding past them is a remarkable recording artist who has sold close to fifty million records around the world since 1961 and tonight is being given one of the highest awards his industry has to offer.

It is not in their width and breadth of knowledge that he is a former teen idol who once sang at the Academy Awards and in command performances for the Queen of England. These boisterous workers epitomize that intriguing phenomenon of being in a room with someone who is famous but not knowing who he or she is. Pitney, a legitimate rock and roll icon, is just one more obstacle for them to navigate while getting their jobs done in their kitchen.

Those who think of show business as all glitz, glamour, fame, and fortune would

be stunned to see both how Pitney is unnoticed and ignored – and that the trail through the kitchen is via a greasy floor as slippery as an ice rink.

As he makes his way gingerly across the expanse of the kitchen, he holds onto McGrath and somewhat jokingly says, "I can't afford to fall down and get dirty because I only brought this tuxedo!"

Turning the corner and heading to the door that will take him out of the kitchen and into the holding area, Pitney encounters Paul Shaffer and his band, the CBS Orchestra, from *The Late Show with David Letterman*. They are huddled in another slippery section of the kitchen, rehearsing the background vocals for Brenda Lee's songs.

Pitney had rehearsed both that morning and the day before with Shaffer and the band. He feels completely comfortable about his performance tonight at the Induction ceremony because of Paul Shaffer's abilities and command of the situation. Shaffer, a diehard Pitney fan, gives Pitney a quick "Hey Gene" and gets right back to making sure his troops know exactly what they are going to do on stage with "Little Miss Dynamite."

The "artist holding area" is to the left of the stage and not hidden from the view of the audience. As a matter of fact, the tables on the ballroom floor are only fifteen to twenty feet away. A small, simple rope marks the area off. There is a break in the action on stage as Pitney and McGrath are dropped off by the VH-1 handler with instructions to "stand by."

While Pitney is in the holding area waiting to perform and The Ramones wait to be inducted, Dee Dee Ramone approaches McGrath and says: "Johnny (Ramone) said that you work for Gene Pitney. I love Gene Pitney. Would you introduce me?"

McGrath introduces Ramone to Pitney, and the two vastly disparate men talk for a few minutes. Ramone, who has a quasi-naïve presence and comes across almost child-like, is very nervous as he talks to Pitney.

"You know, Gene, a lot of people think we're assholes because of the music we do and the way we look," he says. "But we grew up in the '60s, and we all love you and Del Shannon and Bobby Vee. And, people should be able to hear it in our tunes. The influence is there."

Pitney, not really knowing what to say as Ramone fusses over him, smiles, nods, and thanks him. He's more taken aback by Ramone's fidgety mannerisms than by the admiration he has for Pitney's talent. Soon, the brief conversation is over; Ramone makes his way back to his seat, and Pitney watches Brenda Lee perform.

Sadly, Dee Dee Ramone, whose real name was Douglas Glenn Colvin, died three months later, on June 5, of an apparent accidental drug overdose, in Los Angeles.

As Ramone walks away, McGrath spots Brian Setzer, the former leader of the Stray Cats, sitting at a table about twenty feet from where Pitney is standing. Setzer is a huge Gene Pitney fan who did a cover version of "Town Without Pity" with his big band.

McGrath points him out to Pitney, and Pitney does something completely out of character. Never confident of who might know him or remember him and who might not, Pitney rarely approaches other performers. But, this time, he doesn't hesitate. "I'm gonna go over and say 'Hi' to him," Pitney says matter-of-factly.

Pitney thanks Setzer for covering the song, and they trade some small talk for about a minute, then Pitney returns to his spot in the holding area. Setzer can't contain himself. Less than thirty seconds later, a grinning Setzer walks over to Pitney, shakes his hand again and says, "That was so cool that you came over to say 'Hi' to me. I've wanted to meet you for a long time. I think you're great!"

Moments later, Pitney follows Brenda Lee on stage with a light but tight version of "Hello Mary Lou" and a breathtaking performance of "Town Without Pity." And, as Pitney is performing his bravura version of this Academy Award-nominated song from the Kirk Douglas film, who do you think is singing along the loudest in the audience? Brian Setzer!

Shaffer and his band have recreated Pitney's recorded versions of these songs virtually note-for-note, only the pacing is quicker. At the aforementioned Sunday rehearsal, Shaffer painstakingly worked with his band, the back-up singers, and the added string players to make the arrangements and performances sound like an exact copy of Pitney's original Musicor 45s.

On that stage, in front of his peers, Pitney is in total command. While most of the assembled multitude is evidently here to see the reunion of The Talking Heads and the inductions of Tom Petty and the Heartbreakers and The Ramones, Pitney lets them know that he is still alive and well – just in case anyone wondered.

Confidently striding onto the stage, he wows the somewhat jaded crowd with a voice that can still blow plaster off the walls. For his six minutes in the Hall of Fame-performing spotlight this night, Gene Pitney dominates the stage. Pitney makes it absolutely clear to everyone in the Waldorf Astoria ballroom that he has lost none of his gift. He was and still is one of the most magnificent pop singers of all time. As is his special wont, Pitney effortlessly accomplishes what he wanted to do this night: prove that he is still a vital, vibrant, contemporary performer. Bowing, waving, and beaming, Pitney leaves to a long standing ovation.

Gene at rehearsal before the Rock & Roll Hall of Fame induction.

He is immediately led to the press area for fifteen minutes of photos and questions, then back to his table to enjoy the rest of the evening. He will be led back to the stage about thirty minutes later for the official Induction.

Darlene Love, who inducts Pitney into the Hall of Fame, was not his first choice, second choice, or third choice – or any choice to do the honors. The Hall of Fame Foundation – most likely its director, Susan Evans – selected her.

Pitney had suggested producer Phil Spector or songwriter Burt Bacharach, both intimately involved in his early success. Both names fell on deaf ears. No reason was ever given. Perhaps Spector's embarrassingly drunken misbehavior during his own induction into the Hall of Fame in 1989 had soured Hall officials on the eccentric producer. Perhaps Bacharach was not hip enough or cool enough for the event. Or, perhaps he wasn't available. No one at the Hall of Fame Foundation was ever considerate enough to tell Pitney why his suggestions were not heeded. But, clearly someone in power at the Hall of Fame Foundation desperately wanted Love to do the Pitney Induction. And, whoever that was, he or she won out.

Love was the singer on the Pitney-penned rock classic "He's A Rebel." Paul Shaffer always refers to the song as the "National Anthem of Rock 'n' Roll." In a 2003 *USA Today* article, music critic and author Ken Barnes called the song "the ultimate manifesto for pop music's misunderstood, non-conformist bad boy archetype, with a titanic Darlene Love guest vocal and a rip-roaring sax solo raising the intensity."

After a VH-1-produced video introduction that is a recap and synopsis of Pitney's career, Love is introduced to induct him. She seems uncomfortable reading the trite induction speech that was obviously written for her. While, at two minutes and fifty three seconds, it certainly doesn't ramble on aimlessly and seemingly forever as did Eddie Vedder's dissertation on The Ramones, it also doesn't have the passion, enthusiasm, and authenticity that Vedder's did. It comes across as very sterile when everyone hoped it would be heartfelt.

"Good evening. Gene Pitney was one of rock 'n' roll's first teen idols. Don't just take my word for it: ask Marianne Faithfull or any other female artist on tour with Gene. Gene really had a way with the females.

"But Gene had far more than just solid good looks. He possessed a strong, unique, and highly identifiable voice that set him apart and made him one of the greatest vocalists in rock 'n' roll.

"A talented musician, Gene was invited by The Rolling Stones to play on their first UK

album. The Stones and Gene met while on tour in England, which is also how The Crystals first met Gene. At one of these gigs Gene played a song he had recently composed – 'He's A Rebel.' We recorded the song, and it became The Crystals' first #1 hit.

"It must have been somewhat bittersweet for Gene because while 'He's A Rebel' sat at #1 on the hot charts, Gene's own record – 'Only Love Can Break A Heart' – languished behind at #2. (She turns to Gene offstage) Sorry Gene!

"A prolific songwriter, Gene not only wrote many other hits but also gave Ricky Nelson one of his biggest smashes, 'Hello, Mary Lou,' penned 'Rubber Ball' for Bobby Vee, which was also a #1 hit in England for Marty Wilde, and wrote 'Today's Teardrops' for Roy Orbison.

"Gene had no problem recording songs by other talented writers and was a big song supporter of the Brill Building. In fact, his #1 hit, 'It Hurts To Be In Love,' was written by then unknowns Helen Miller and Howie Greenfield, who later co-wrote most of Neil Sedaka's hits.

"Gene's dramatic vocal delivery made him a natural for movie soundtracks in an era when Hollywood was reaching out to new artists. His songs for the silver screen include 'Town Without Pity' and '(The Man Who Shot) Liberty Valance.'

"Gene must also be recognized for his pioneering country music crossover efforts and his duets with Melba Montgomery and the legendary George Jones.

"From his early hits '(I Wanna) Love My Life Away' and 'Every Breath I Take' to the classic 'Twenty Four Hours From Tulsa' right up to his 1990 #1 UK smash 'Something's Gotten Hold of My Heart,' a duet with Marc Almond from Soft Cell, Gene remains active in the business.

"This is especially true on the live circuit with US gigs and annual tours of the UK, Australia, and Italy.

"With such a vast list of accomplishments and a life dedicated to music, it is with great pride and considerable honor that I induct my friend of more than forty years – GENE PITNEY! Welcome to the Rock & Roll Hall of Fame."

The surprising aspect of the Love/Pitney inductor/inductee pairing is that the two singers had NEVER met before this night. She had to approach Pitney's table earlier in the evening to introduce herself to the man who had written the biggest hit of her life.

With all the people whom Pitney actually knows in the business who were a part of his success, the question begs to be asked: Why was Darlene Love chosen to induct him?

Pitney's unscripted acceptance speech is relatively short – one minute and forty five seconds. While most of the other inductees thank family and friends for their long-term love and support, there is no mention of either in Pitney's remarks. He does, however, thank Paul Shaffer and the band! (Pitney was very pumped working with Paul Shaffer's "Late Show" band and a "string section from heaven," as he called them. He said that the strings on "Town Without Pity" that night gave him goose bumps.)

"Thank you very, very much. First of all, I would like to say a big 'thank you' to all the people that have stuck with this. This was my eighth nomination (applause and laughter) – so there were a lot of nominations and along the way a lot of rejections. So, I appreciate the people that hung in there – and we finally got here.

"And, I would like to say a big 'thank you' to a special group of people that I think are particularly important to me – to have been able to allow me to leave my songs at a quality level that I still perform at today, almost forty years later – and these are the songwriters that have created pretty much the body of my entire work. (applause)

"I'd like to tell you some of the people; I'm talkin' about Goffin and King…and Mann and Weil…and Burt Bacharach and Hal David and some of them that Darlene just mentioned.

"But I think those people have probably been the most important in allowing me to carry on and get here to this point today.

"And, I would like to say a big 'thank you' (he turns around)…he's gone right now…but to Paul Shaffer and some magnificent musicians. (applause)

"When it comes down to this night, and we're up here performing these songs underneath your critical gaze, he's the guy that really puts it together, and I'd love to have that band with me on the road!

"Thank you very much. Thank you."

Pitney's seeming dismissal of his family might come as a surprise to the casual observer, but to those who know him well, this is SOP, standard operating procedure. There has always been a Grand Canyon-like divide between Pitney's professional life and his personal life. Without fail, in interviews Pitney talks about Pitney the entertainer. While he will talk about his other business projects away from show business, there are only rare references to his family and home life. Only in his Fan Club newsletter do fans get a glimpse into his personal life. Even there it is very superficial.

Pitney is simply an extraordinarily private person. As a matter of fact, over the course of his forty-plus years in show business there have been less than a handful of outsiders whom Pitney has allowed to cross from his professional life into his private life.

He does not have any deep, dark family secrets to hide. His wife, Lynne, is beautiful, gregarious, and fun to be around. His three sons, Todd, Chris, and David, are amiable and successful in their career paths. The only interesting curiosity in his personal life is the distance he has always maintained from his own brothers and sisters. But, there are millions of families around the world that share this not out-of-the-ordinary phenomenon.

While this spin is not intentional, it does, nonetheless, play right into Pitney's mesmerizing image. He has always been an enigma: a dark, brooding, loner who shies away from fans, publicity, and the show business community. He's the small-town boy in the big-time world of entertainment.

The long Monday night trails into Tuesday morning before the Induction Ceremony begins to wind down following the usual train wreck of a jam session. Pitney, who is never comfortable on stage as anything other than a soloist, plays along and does an unrehearsed duet with Love on "He's A Rebel" and then suffers through a painful two takes of "Take Me To The River" that drove much of the crowd out of the room.

At the Sunday rehearsal, Pitney could only rehearse the "He's A Rebel" duet with Shaffer because Love was at a church service. But, again, completely out of character, he was game to do the duet with Love, possibly – probably – just for the novelty of the situation. Without fail, the last thing Gene Pitney wants during a performance is a surprise. Pitney subscribes whole-heartedly to the "if-it-ain't-broke-don't fix-it" philosophy of putting together a show.

While his critics will tell you that he has done virtually the same show over and over for the last thirty years, they also have to add that his performance is always peerless.

Pitney comes off the stage after the jam session, engages in some chitchat with his tablemates, and shares some final goodbyes before heading back to his room with his wife, Lynne. No parties for him. They are just not his style. Pitney has never been a schmoozer, and he's not about to become one now.

Retreating to a posh, comfortable hotel room is, however, a bit too anti-climactic for his two young sons, Todd and David. They have invitations to a post-Hall of Fame party being thrown by Warner Brothers Music and they have gotten wind of – and directions to – Phil Spector's annual party.

As pop star Pitney settles in to enjoy the quiet solitude of his luxurious Waldorf Astoria suite (provided by the Hall of Fame), the young tuxedo-clad Pitney boys, who are both handsome enough to easily pass for pop stars themselves, trundle off into the early-morning darkness of New York City to find some noisy fun and do the celebrating that their dad just doesn't care to do anymore.

Text of the VH-1 Synopsis of Gene Pitney's Career for the Hall of Fame Video

"Gene Pitney came on the scene in the early '60s when bland teen idols had given rock 'n' roll a bad name. Pitney was a singer of staggering emotional power. He filled the Top 40 with thrilling anguish.

"He was also a gifted musician. On his first hit, '(I Wanna) Love My Life Away,' he played most of the instruments himself and overdubbed his voice numerous times.

"A standout composer, Pitney wrote hits for Ricky Nelson and Phil Spector's Crystals. He played on the first Rolling Stones album and brought his version of a Jagger-Richards song ('That Girl Belongs To Yesterday') to the charts before the Stones had an American hit.

"Gene Pitney transformed the everyday torments of youth into timeless trauma. Heartache has rarely been so heavenly."

Gene catching up on British fan mail.

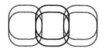

CHAPTER 2:
BACKSTAGE (I'M LONELY)

Lyrics by Willie Denson and Music by Fred Anisfield

Fun Fact: This iconic hit had lyrics written by a full-time postal worker who would later win millions of dollars in a state lottery. The music, on the other hand, was composed by a man who may have suffered from serious mental illness. Oh dear!

Gene Pitney said: "How could I pass on THAT song…and THAT story?" He had bigger hits than "Backstage (I'm Lonely)," but this is THE SONG that his legions of hard-core fans really identify with and attach to him.

Long before Austin Powers was known as "The International Man of Mystery," Gene Pitney truly lived up to that moniker. Pitney was an enigma to his fans, to his friends, and, in many respects, to his family. And it was songs like this that cultivated that image. There was always a puzzling and almost ardent need for his fans to embrace the mystery that seemed to be Gene Pitney. Songs like this satisfied that need. Privately he was mystified by it; publicly he gave the fans what they craved.

"A thousand hands applaud tonight…I sing my songs, my star shines bright…I stop and smile, I take my bow…I leave the stage and then somehow…Backstage I'm lonely…Backstage I cry…you've gone away, and each night I seem to die a little…

"Every night a different girl…Every night a different club…And yet I'm lonely all the

time…When I sign my autograph…When I hold an interview…Can't get you out of my mind."

Pitney sang it like he meant it, but it was actually a million miles from the truth in his life. The lyric is vivid and theatrically dramatic; some have written that it is "breathtakingly melodramatic." Many fans thought it mirrored Pitney's off-stage life, but not so much. It was a charismatic and harmless charade. "Yeah, I was lying a lot when I sang that song," Pitney explained countless times with a chuckle.

But, it was the image his fans wanted to have of him. And he fed it to them – at least on his records – over and over. From time to time he was labeled "The Prince of Pain" in fan and music magazines because of his myriad songs of lost love, unrequited love, and broken hearts. During the height of his recording career it was not something he tried to debunk. He knew how to find those songs that appealed to lovelorn teenagers with raging hormones who were yearning for new love or pining for lost love. Better

Gene meeting Britain's Princess Alexandra at a show in London. She is the cousin of Queen Elizabeth II. Her husband, British businessman Sir Angus Ogilvy, is in the background between them. The man smiling to her right is Welsh comedian, actor, singer, and television presenter Harry Secombe.

yet, he knew how to sing those songs for those kids who were hastily "crashing into love" on a regular basis.

So many legendary songwriting teams wrote songs for Pitney, including Burt Bacharach and Hal David, Barry Mann and Cynthia Weil, Gerry Goffin and Carole King, Barry Mason and Les Reed, and Roger Cook and Roger Greenaway. The most atypical team, however, was the pair who wrote this swashbuckling-yet-forlorn song that helped define the sound of Gene Pitney: Willie Denson and Fred Anisfield.

Denson, who crafted the memorable, despair-filled lyrics of this story of the singer who is a winner in his career but a loser at love was born and raised in Columbus, Georgia. In 1957, at the age of 21, he headed to New York to pursue his dream of being a songwriter. In an email interview, his wife, Ann, said "Willie was writing songs in high school. It was a dream and a hobby of his to come up with hit songs for artists."

To keep food on the table for his family while chasing that dream, he took a night-shift job at the US Postal Service so he could write and pitch his songs to publishers during the day.

Willie finally hit it big in 1961 when The Shirelles took "Mama Said," a song he co-wrote with the legendary Luther Dixon, to #4 on the *Billboard Hot 100*. In a 1996 interview, Willie Denson said his mother inspired "Mama Said." He said she was "always happy, always smiling."

Willie, under the names Wee Willie Denson and Denny Denson, also had a short-lived recording career on two small record labels.

Luther Dixon had also co-written "Tonight's The Night," "Boys," and "Baby It's You" for The Shirelles and "16 Candles" for The Crests. And, while The Shirelles also recorded a number of other Denson-Dixon collaborations, it's unknown how Denson and Dixon met and hooked up as a songwriting team.

Even with "Mama Said" in the *Billboard* Top 10 and being played on every Top 40 and R&B radio station in the country, Willie did something quite unusual. He kept his night job. "My dad continued working at the Post Office to support the family while writing music," his son Derron Denson wrote in an email interview. Willie worked at the Post Office for over 30 years, until he retired in 1995. Ann Denson added, "We don't believe he considered himself a celebrity."

In 2001, Willie made headlines of a different sort. He won $3 million in the Georgia lottery – more than he ever made from writing a couple of iconic hit songs in the 1960s! Following his death from lung cancer at the age of 69 in 2006, his daughter Danette Powell commented on her dad's big lottery win: "Winning didn't change him a bit. There was no difference."

Fred Anisfield, who wrote the imposingly flamboyant melody to "Backstage (I'm Lonely)," is a mystery man. He was born in Washington Heights, New York, in 1935. Like Willie Denson, Anisfield, too, had a short-lived recording career, putting out two singles on Scepter Records (as Freddy Anisfield). This is likely where he met Willie Denson, who was working at the label with The Shirelles.

Anisfield apparently was a bit of an odd duck. One well-known songwriter who wrote a few songs with him recalled in an email interview, "He also had a chemical imbalance that caused a nervous breakdown once a year. A couple of them were very colorful. I remember seeing him walking up and down Broadway dressed like a rabbi reading the Old Testament; another time he showed up at a publisher's office wearing long underwear and a winter topcoat. He was never violent. I remember having to take him to Creedmoor Psychiatric Center Hospital in Queens once. I also remember us going to the movies to see *From Russia With Love*, and when James Bond's love interest came on the screen, Freddy gasped rather loudly 'GEVALT!' He did finally eventually get himself under control with proper meds."

Fred Anisfield died in 1982 at the age of 47.

Unfortunately, Willie Denson's widow Ann said that she never met or knew who Fred Anisfield was, doesn't remember how the two songwriters got together, who came up with the idea for "Backstage (I'm Lonely)," or how the song got to Gene Pitney.

Enter Luther Dixon…again. In 1966, he was writing songs for and producing The Platters for Musicor Records, Gene Pitney's label. It was Dixon who got his "Mama Said" writing partner's song "Backstage" in front of Musicor owner Art Talmadge who then presented it to Pitney.

Pitney recalled Art Talmadge calling him on the phone to pitch the song to him. "Art was a pretty laid-back guy," Pitney explained, "but he was jumping through the phone when he called me about 'Backstage.' He said, 'You gotta do this one, Gene. This has your name written all over it.' I think he just read the lyrics to me. So, I didn't hear that melody until I got to New York. How could I pass on THAT song? It had it all: dramatic lyrics, a melody that just grabbed your ears and wouldn't let go of them, crashing cymbals, resounding horns, and THAT story! Loved it."

Gene took THAT story: *"what good is fame…it's just a game…I'd give it all to be the same… Backstage….I wait now…hoping I'll see…your smiling face…waiting there backstage for me-e-e-e…"* to #4 in the UK in March 1966. In the US it peaked at #25 on the *Billboard Hot 100* in May 1966. Those chart results reflect the fact that at this point Gene was a legitimate superstar in England while his career was starting to trail off in the US.

On "Backstage" Pitney under-employed the broken-hearted sob in his voice that he used so often and so well on his records. That tactic makes his already distinctive voice really jump off this record when he harmonizes with himself on the chorus and a few parts of the verses.

This tear-jerker should be considered a masterpiece because of Pitney's reticence to be schmaltzy while still delivering a thunder-and-lightning vocal. Imagine what a Sammy Davis, Jr. or Celine Dion would have done to this song. Pitney laced it with passion

Gene with longtime friend and Music Director Maurice Merry at a Gene Pitney International Fan Club Convention in London. Howard Matthews, a Pitney friend, fan, collector, and expert, is in the background.

without being overly dramatic. While the record was loaded with melodrama, his quasi-reserved delivery warded off the possibility of the record becoming maudlin or sappy. Not everyone agrees with this assessment. See the factoid below.

Favorite Lyric: *"Out on that stage I play the star…I'm famous now I've come so far. A famous fool I let love go…I didn't know I'd miss you so."* Willie Denson knew that life isn't about "stuff"; it's about relationships. A wise man was Willie Denson.

Factoid: Gene co-produced this record with Stan Kahan to make sure those "crashing cymbals and resounding horns" made it onto the record.

Factoid: Fred Anisfield could write melodies with the best of them. He also wrote the very catchy melodies and the lyrics to "Where Did The Magic Go?" on *The Gene Pitney Story* album as well as "Lonely Drifter," which was a track on Gene's 1967 *Just One Smile* album and the B-side to Gene's 1968 single "Billy, You're My Friend." And, Anisfield wrote the kingly music and the masterful lyrics to "Conquistador," which appeared on the 1966 US album, *Backstage (I'm Lonely)* in the US and *Nobody Needs Your Love* in the UK.

Factoid: "Backstage (I'm Lonely)" was recorded first by singer/TV star/movie star James Darren in 1963. Surprisingly, no one in Willie Denson's family ever heard of James Darren or his subdued and less dramatic version of the song. "We don't know anything of James Darren," said Willie's son Derron. "My dad had plenty of *Billboard* posters and articles, but we haven't seen or heard of James Darren." By the way, Gene never knew of the Darren version of the song until long after his own record was a hit.

Factoid: Not everyone loves this record. For example, well-known author Richie Unterberger, who is also a reviewer for the online website AllMusic.com, offered this measured review: *"It could be argued that 'Backstage' takes Pitney's schtick to ludicrous extremes and to a degree with which the listener might find it hard to empathize. Sure, it's tough doing all those shows to adoring crowds, doing interviews, and seeing all those girls, isn't it, Gene, especially when you're making more in a week (at least in 1966) than many of us see in half a year? But as a mini-pop operetta, it's well done and enjoyable to hear."*

Factoid: The success of "Backstage (I'm Lonely)" coupled with his other UK hits in 1966, "Princess In Rags," "Nobody Needs Your Love," and "Just One Smile" earned Pitney the #17 spot on the *Best-Selling Artists of 1966* according to *Music Week*, the longtime trade paper of the British music industry. That placed him ahead of The Rolling Stones, The Seekers, and Elvis Presley that year.

Factoid: A number of other artists would have liked to have had a crack at this song. In a 1999 interview for the *Gene Pitney International Fan Club Newsletter*, legendary crooner Jack Jones said he wished that he had gotten "Backstage" to record first. Petula Clark echoed that sentiment in a 2000 *Gene Pitney International Fan Club Newsletter*. "I'm still mad that he found 'Backstage' before I did! I love that song. What a great show business song. It must be thrilling still to sing that song in concert. It's such high drama." Country music star Narvel Felts said in a 2000 *Gene Pitney International Fan Club Newsletter*, 'Backstage' really jumps out at me. It's easy to relate to because I'm in that position, too."

Factoid: Lifelong Gene Pitney fan, British glam rocker Marc Almond, who duetted with Gene on the 1989 remake of "Something's Gotten Hold of My Heart," which went to #1 in the UK and several European countries, recorded "Backstage" on his 2007 album *Stardom Road* as a tribute to Gene. He also wrote a new verse for the song:

Another town, don't know its name
An empty feeling, just the same
A silent drive, another show, to a lonely hotel room I'll go
At times like these I miss you so

Almond explained why he wrote the new verse in an email: "I took the liberty of writing that opening verse myself to set the scene. I was trying to give the album a biographical story. I just listened to it again and forgot about it until you reminded me; it still sounds good after all this time. I was thinking of Gene when I sang that song as a tribute, thinking of his death in a hotel room after a show. Touring can be lonely, different towns and hotels. Gene's death before his time made me think of him alone and far from his home and family. It was a real shock."

And, the last word goes to…Lynne Pitney: "Absolutely loved it. Loved the drama and the grandeur. One of my favorite songs that Gene did. I loved the way Gene sang it. What always struck me about this song was how much Gene loved performing it on stage. It's the one that really got his adrenaline running. I would have loved this song by anybody, but, having said that, you really had to have the right voice to carry it off! Actually, I just LOVE sappy songs (*laughter*)!"

BLUE ANGEL

BY ROGER COOK

RECORDED BY

GENE PITNEY

ON BRONZE RECORDS BRO 11

PUBLISHED BY COOKAWAY MUSIC LIMITED

25p

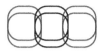

CHAPTER 3:
BLUE ANGEL

Lyrics and Music by Roger Cook

Fun Fact: Oddly enough, the other 1960s star that Gene Pitney was always compared to, Roy Orbison, also recorded a song titled "Blue Angel."

Gene Pitney said: "I don't know why, but I really liked this song when Roger played it for me on his ukulele. But, I didn't expect it to be a hit."

With the exception of Australia, where "Blue Angel" went to #2 in 1974, this song wasn't a hit. It did spend four brief weeks in the UK chart, peaking at #39 in 1974. But, like a few other Pitney non-hits, it became a favorite at concerts outside the US where the fans turned it into a bit of a singalong.

"Blue Angel" is the story of a human tragedy. Pitney sings the song from the viewpoint of a childhood friend of a young woman who leaves their hometown to seek success in the music business. She joins a band, setting out to make it big. But, as so often is the case, her career never takes off.

To a way too jaunty melody, Pitney tells her doleful story in Roger Cook's succinct words, *"How many years since you took off with your guitar…joining a band and singing sad songs 'round the bar."*

And, it gets worse. The hometown childhood friend ends up with a drug addiction and has to turn to prostitution to make ends meet. *"Now the gentlemen of Soho buy your kindness and your smile. And your flesh is just a souvenir of London for a while. But I know what keeps you going what you spend your money on. Some pusher man from hell has got you hooked on all that's wrong. And a pretty dress don't cover up your eyes. And I won't forget the emptiness I found in your disguise."*

Pitney sings her story with candor and frankness – sometimes a bit too stridently – but always laced with warmth. "My first impression, before we went into the studio, was that this was really just an album track," he said. "There wasn't too much to do with this type of song but to sing it straight away. Roger produced it, and I thought we made a pretty good record. But, compared to some of the other songs we cut for that album, I didn't think it was a strong single."

The album he referred to is *Pitney '75*, released on Bronze Records in the UK. That album included the stunning Phillip Goodhand-Tait song "Oceans Away," a captivating version of the Paul Williams song "Waking Up Alone," and a splendid cover of "Tryin' To Get The Feeling Again" that gives Barry Manilow's version a run for its money.

Gerry Bron, who owned Bronze Records, said in a phone interview that culling a first single from the *Pitney '75* album was a struggle. "Gene didn't want 'Blue Angel' to be the first single," Bron said. "And he didn't want one of the covers to be a single either. He really pushed for 'Oceans Away.' I didn't dislike 'Oceans Away.' After all, I produced it. But it was 1974, and I felt something a little edgier, like 'Blue Angel,' would have been more successful for Gene."

Roger Cook, who wrote the song and produced it for Pitney explained where the odd feel of the song came from. "It was based on a kind of 1930s German feel," he said in a 2021 phone interview from his home in Nashville. "Think 'Cabaret' and those free-wheeling pre-World War II days in Berlin. I had the idea to put four or five banjoes on the record to make it sound like one of those old banjo bands of the 1930s. I think it worked!"

Cook did add that he was disappointed it wasn't a Top 10 hit in England. "I really thought it was such a catchy song and Gerne had the right vibe on it."

Gerry Bron slipped into the business side of show business when he talked a little bit about the financials of *Pitney '75* and how record sales of "Blue Angel" eventually ended up paying for the entire album. "Hitting #39 on the UK singles charts isn't really a hit, is it? We sold a decent number of singles, and it led to OK sales on the album. But, thank God for the fans in Oz. They embraced 'Blue Angel' and made it a huge hit in Australia, and that's where I recouped my investment."

Without getting into details, Bron said his investment in the *Pitney '75* album was "significant but not colossal." "Look, when you worked with Gene you were working with the ultimate professional. He was never late for a recording session. He was always prepared for every session. And, unlike so many other artists, Gene was so good he could get a song done in one or two takes. That meant we weren't burning up expensive studio time."

Thirty years later, in 2004, this song still mystified Pitney. While sitting in his home studio one day listening to "Blue Angel," he said, "The first time I heard the basic track

Catching up on more British fan mail.

Author Dave McGrath telling Gene that Little & Large (Syd and Eddie) wanted more money to open on his UK tour. Just kidding! Gene loved them. Photo courtesy of Sue and Brian Dench.

that Roger had put together for the song I thought it was a polka! When you think of Roger and his writing partner Roger Greenaway, you think of sophisticated songs like 'Something's Gotten Hold of My Heart' or 'You've Got Your Troubles.' The lyrics for 'Blue Angel' are dark, but they are sophisticated. Why he set it to this melody and this track is still a mystery to me. It is not the height of sophistication. I think this could have been a huge hit for The Fortunes or maybe The Hollies ten years earlier. It kinda sounded like that Hollies song 'Stop, Stop, Stop' I thought."

The song became an almost required part of his set list for every post-1975 UK and Australian show. His fans loved this song. There is a break in the song, after the third verse, where he goes into a string of *la-la-la-las*, and this is where audiences always chimed in. He loved and encouraged it. "I thought it was a good bond with the audience. They could be background singers on a song with me, and I didn't have to pay them!"

Favorite Lyric: *"And I can bless my good fortune, I came through it fine. Oh oh blue angel you will always be a good old friend of mine."* Roger Cook rewriting the evergreen "There but for the grace of God go I." Each of us knows a childhood friend or two who, through bad genes, bad choices, or bad breaks, ended up in a life of despair, but we still accept them as that *"good old friend of mine."*

Factoid: Roger Cook said, "Gene Pitney was a real hero of mine. He was such a very nice man; he was so easy to work with. Just a very mild-mannered and sweet man. And, always a smart dresser."

Factoid: This song was produced by Roger Cook at George Martin's AIR Studios at 214 Oxford Street in London.

Factoid: Pitney bought the rights to all of the Bronze Records recordings from Gerry Bron. Todd Pitney, Gene's son, digitally remastered all of the songs at Gene's home studio in Somers, Connecticut. Those remastered songs appear on the Castle Music CD *Gene Pitney: Blue Angel/The Bronze Sessions.*

And, the last word goes to…Lynne Pitney: "It's such a sad song with such a catchy melody. This was another one of those songs that I thought really wasn't a good fit for Gene. But, his fans loved it. He would always do it on his British tours because they loved to sing along with it. I'm not sure he really liked it that much, but he knew it was important to his fans, and that was important to him."

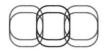

CHAPTER 4:
BLUE GENE

Lyrics and Music by Chip Taylor

Fun Fact: Before Chip Taylor wrote such pop classics as "Wild Thing" for The Troggs (1966), "I Can't Let Go" for The Hollies (1966), and "Angel of the Morning" for Merrilee Rush (1968) and Juice Newton (1981), he wrote the title track to Gene Pitney's 1963 *Blue Gene* album.

Gene Pitney said: "This song really puzzled me. I had to sing a song about me?"

Chip Taylor was a budding 23-year-old songwriter in 1963 when, out of nowhere, he was asked by Aaron Schroeder, Gene's manager, to write the title song for Gene's soon-to-be-recorded fourth album, *Blue Gene*.

"I had a very good relationship with Aaron," Taylor wrote in an email interview. "I liked him a lot. He was one of the first New York publishers to publish my songs. He called and told me that Gene was going to be recording his next album, *Blue Gene*, and asked if I would try to write a song titled 'Blue Gene.'"

A commission to write the title track for the next album of a rising pop superstar would seem to be a daunting task for an unproven songwriter. Chip Taylor, though, took the challenge in stride. He remembered writing the song at his parents' house, where he was living, the day after Schroeder asked him to do it. Thinking back on how problematic or challenging it was to write a song as specific as this, for a singer with that singer's name in it, Taylor said, "I didn't find it especially hard. But, that being said, I don't think it was a great song. It was not as inspired as most of my songs were. Probably because it had to be so specific."

Garry Sherman, who would become one of Pitney's favorite arrangers, arranged this song. Taylor wasn't overly fond of the finished product. He said it didn't have the same feel as the demo that he had done himself. "I recorded the demo with my guitar, an upright bass, and percussion," he explained. "I liked the feeling of THAT recording.

"Gene's recording was more drum-influenced. I would have rather it sounded more like my recording, but I was flattered that Gene liked it enough to record it. I thought he was such a special artist, but I wish I liked the song more."

In a casual conversation about this song, Pitney recalled he was more than a bit surprised when it was presented to him. "I knew Aaron wanted to call the album *Blue Gene* as a play on the words 'blue jeans'…you know, the pants. I didn't know that he had asked someone to write a song called 'Blue Gene' until I heard the demo."

He did admit that he likely rolled his eyes when he heard the song. "It's actually a very nice little song, but, c'mon, I was supposed to sing a song about myself? I was still pretty young and early on in my career, so I just did it. It ended up being a pretty good record. Garry Sherman prettied it up. I think we rehearsed it once and got it in the first take. I do remember, however, hoping that Musicor would not select it as a single. I was just afraid of what the reaction would be to my singing a song about myself."

In spite of the song's somber title and glum girl-breaks-boy's-heart-storyline Pitney's vocal on this song is very breezy and light-hearted. It is one of the most casual vocal performances Gene ever committed to vinyl, almost the complete opposite of how he usually sang and how he usually sounded. Pitney gave this jaunt through dejection and self-pity an almost "I-don't-care" flavor and attitude. He sang it as if the protagonist was saying "She broke my heart, and I'm supposed to be broken up, but I'm really not. This is all for show!"

Both Pitney and Taylor are regarded as giants in their respective fields now, but, in 1963, the fledgling young songwriter, Taylor, and the promising young singer, Pitney, ended up being two ships passing in the night. According to Taylor, "I wasn't in Aaron's office that often, and I don't think Gene was either, but I'm not sure of that. So,

I might have said hello to Gene once or twice. I know I did have huge respect for his songwriting. I loved 'Hello Mary Lou.' And, again, I thought he was a magical, one-of-a-kind singer."

Surprisingly, even though he had written the title track for one of Gene's personal-favorite albums, Taylor said he never pitched Gene another song to record. "I don't think I ever thought I wrote a song that fit him. I was writing mostly country songs at the time. Aside from that, I respected his writing, and I was probably shy about trying to write for him. Plus, I rarely tried to write songs for specific people. I just wrote songs that felt good to me and hoped they would get published and the publisher could find a good artist to record them."

As of this writing, Chip Taylor is still writing and performing. Visit his website: www.trainwreckrecords.com for the latest.

Favorite Lyric: *"Those ruby red lips…those little white lies…that golden light…a love so bright…just seemed to fade from your eyes."* Very nice turn of a phrase in the first two observations; very wistfully sorrowful conclusion in the last observation. Well-played Chip Taylor.

Factoid: Chip Taylor, whose real name is James Wesley Voight, is the younger brother of Oscar-winning actor Jon Voight, and that makes him Angelina Jolie's uncle!

Factoid: This was one of two songs recorded by Gene that had his name in the title. The other, "Gene Are You There," was written by Janette Tidwell. That song is profiled in this book, too.

And, the last word goes to…Lynne Pitney: "I know this song only because I loved the *Blue Gene* album. And I really loved the photo of Gene on that album. He's wearing that blue sweater and it was shot in very soft light. It's such a romantic cover! I always wondered if he felt silly recording a song with his name in it. I never asked."

The song / record on which "Gene Are You There" is based.

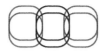

CHAPTER 5:
GENE ARE YOU THERE

Lyrics and Music by Janette Tidwell

Fun Fact: This is one of two songs that Gene recorded with his name in the title. Unlike "Blue Gene," the title track of his 1963 album, this song was NOT written specifically for him. Gene sorta wrote it for himself – just sorta.

Gene Pitney said: "I kept hearing this sweet melody that just drifted around in my head for days before I knew I had to record this song." That song turned out to be "Gene Are You There."

One day in 1971, in the New York offices of Musicor Records, Pitney came across an obscure record by an obscure artist that caught his ear, and he concocted a pretty clever idea. The record was "Jeannie Are You There" recorded in 1970 by Judy Kester, a little-known country singer signed to Musicor. Gene decided to rewrite the lyrics and change the title. His 1971 version of the song became "Gene Are You There." Clever!

Janette Tidwell, who wrote "Jeannie Are You There," also wrote and co-wrote songs that were recorded by the likes of George Jones and Tammy Wynette. In a 2019 phone interview, she recalled how Gene hatched his plan. "He asked Kelso Herston, who had produced the Judy Kester record, to call me and ask if he could rewrite some of the lyrics and re-title it 'Gene Are You There.' I agreed on the spot. I was thrilled that the guy who sang 'Liberty Valance' wanted to do my song. I couldn't believe my luck."

In Judy Kester's version, the Jeannie of the song is the young daughter of a blind father who's *"never seen the moonrise or the sunset in the west...and he's never seen the dawning of the spring..."* In Pitney's rewrite "Gene" is the boyfriend of a blind girlfriend – or maybe they are husband and wife. Pitney recorded the song in London in 1971, employing the same Herston-produced backing track used by Judy Kester.

Backing up a bit, it appears that Musicor Records, now under the control of Art Talmadge and Pappy Daily who had forced Aaron Schroeder out of the label he founded, had somewhat high hopes, either for the original song "Jeannie Are You There" or for the singer Judy Kester, and decided to use a lot of resources. Kelso Herston, a well-respected producer and guitarist from Muscle Shoals, Alabama, had been signed to a multi-artist production deal by Musicor. Judy Kester was one of the label's new artists that he was set to produce. Herston didn't come cheap. He was legendary for his session work with Jerry Lee Lewis, Johnny Cash, Dolly Parton, Slim Whitman, and George Jones. He eventually went on to become president of United Artists Records/Nashville and Capitol Records/Nashville.

In spite of what appears to be a lot of effort and expense on Musicor's part, Kester's career lasted about two-and-a-half minutes – the length of "Jeannie Are You There."

After the Judy Kester record flopped, Musicor evidently wanted to cut its losses. What happened with the Pitney version of the song is puzzling, at best; half-baked and shortsighted, at worst.

Gene's career was flagging in 1971, and he likely thought building his name into a song was a clever promotional ploy to get radio programmers' attention. The label also came up with a promotional ploy of its own: Musicor promoted the song in fan magazines as being written by "a blind fan of Gene's." Janette Tidwell isn't blind, and she didn't write the song specifically for Gene.

Presumably, Musicor looked at the Pitney record simply as an opportunity to amortize the production costs of the Judy Kester record. It appears the label decided to drop only a few dollars in trade magazine promotion, more or less to throw a bone to their fading star, instead of putting in an honest and genuine effort to sell some records based on Pitney's stature.

At this point in his career, Pitney wanted out of Musicor. His friendship and business relationship with Aaron Schroeder had floundered and died when Pitney threw in with Talmadge and Daily over Schroeder. Now his relationship with Talmadge and Daily was faltering, too.

Gene was never reticent to point a finger of blame: "We were in business together, I thought, but it seemed like I was the only one looking out for me at that point. When I quit getting into the Top 10, Musicor looked at me as a liability. To them I was overhead. I couldn't wait to get out."

"Gene Are You There" got a UK release in 1972 on the British-based Pye International label, but it was buried on the *New Sounds of Gene Pitney* album. Pitney was still touring the UK on a regular and successful basis and still having mid-level chart success there with his records. Tours sell records, and, since "Gene Are You There" was Pitney's idea from the outset, it's a wonder he didn't arbitrarily – and promptly – put it in his UK shows that year. But, he didn't.

In 1977, when Pickwick Records put out the 24 *Sycamore* album in the UK, it included "Gene Are You There." This time, Pitney put the song into his UK show.

Rodney Collins, formerly a journalist with Record Mirror who went on to BBC Radio 1 and 2 and Radio Luxembourg in the 1970s, wrote the liner notes for that Pickwick album. Rodney now hosts a show called Gene Pitney and Friends that is heard on a number of stations around the world. He reported, "Gene said 'Gene Are You There' was the most requested non-hit song on his 1977 UK tour." (You can join Rodney Collins' Gene Pitney at 24 Sycamore Facebook group for all the details on his Gene Pitney and Friends radio show.)

Collins also noted that "Gene Are You There" had never been considered for release as a single from the aforementioned 1972 Pye album. "I worked at Pye when Gene moved from EMI Stateside to Pye, and I do not recall any discussion with Gene when he asked for this track to be a single." That may reflect the enigma that was Gene Pitney; this was a song that was quite close to his heart, yet he didn't lobby for its release as a single in the UK where he was still a star and it could have been a hit.

By 1971, with the onset of the so-called "second British Invasion" of heavy metal and progressive rock bands like Led Zeppelin, Mott The Hoople, T. Rex, Uriah Heep, and others, pop stars like Gene Pitney were an afterthought in the music industry.

Contact proofs from a 1962 shoot in manager / producer Aaron Schroeder's New York office.

That having been said, "Gene Are You There" was a first-rate Pitney record. But, by his own doing, Pitney's steadfastly loyal British fans were never given a chance to buy this record and put it in the charts because they never heard it on the radio.

In hindsight, that is most unfortunate because Gene really took care of business with this song. His tender, almost delicate, rendition of the song is spellbinding. In the hands of any other singer, this is a routine I-love-her-and-she-loves-me song. But, Pitney's understanding of the delicate nature of the story brings out a gracefulness in his vocals that is beyond elegant. He chose to subdue his powerful voice and allowed it to take a back seat to the sweet, sweet story he is telling.

There is a school of thought that believes that putting his name in the title of the song was unorthodox and unquestionably self-serving. Maybe. More likely "crafty" is what it was. Rewriting, retitling, and recording "Gene Are You There" was not an egotistical miscalculation by Pitney. He found a song that fit the Pitney mold: a melodramatic story that he could tell with that seductive voice of his. And how propitious that the horn- and string-filled Herston track sounded like it HAD been done with Pitney in mind. Pitney could have legitimately anticipated a hit with this record.

Truth be told, had it been written and recorded five or six years earlier, when he was red hot and more relevant, his gentle rendition of this strikingly lovely melody and wistful lyrics would have earned him a hit. Sadly, the lack of commitment to him by Musicor Records was a missed opportunity. Had Pitney pushed harder for "Gene Are You There," it could possibly have become the hit that erased the painful memory and cruel fact that 1968's "She's A Heartbreaker" was his last US Top 20 record. Likewise, had he flexed a little star-power muscle in the UK, he could likely have scored a Top 10 with this one.

Favorite Lyric: The whole song! One of the sweetest songs ever written!

Factoid: This wasn't the first time Pitney had recorded over a track that had been produced for another artist. Most famously, he recorded his 1964 smash "It Hurts To Be In Love" over the track that was produced for Neil Sedaka's never-released version of the song. Also, Gene used all the tracks that had been used by The Platters when he recorded his 1969 Musicor album *This Is Gene Pitney Singing The Golden Platters of The Platters.* (Is that the longest and most cumbersome album title in pop music history?) Musicor Records had acquired those masters when they signed The Platters to the label in 1967. Gene said if you listen closely to some of the tracks you can faintly hear the voice of the group's lead singer, Tony Williams. He explained Musicor wanted to rush the album out just to get product on record store shelves and didn't bother to completely wipe Williams' voice off all the tracks.

Factoid: By 1970, after Aaron Schroeder had been pushed out of Musicor, Art Talmadge and Pappy Daily were running the day-to-day operations of the label. Daily had come out of Texas where he had co-founded Starday Records and discovered country star George Jones. Daily began signing country performers like his old friend Jones and B-list (by then) star Melba Montgomery to Musicor. He also signed Judy Kester.

Factoid: Kelso Herston, who produced the Judy Kester version of this song that Gene then adapted for his use, was both a gifted musician and music executive. This is what was written about Herston when he was inducted into the Alabama Music Hall of Fame: "Kelso Herston, a Florence (Alabama) native with over forty successful years in the music industry, is the consummate 'Music Man,' playing on sessions for over two hundred different artists, producing over fifty top recording artists, publishing over one hundred songs, and being responsible for over five thousand nationally-acclaimed jingles." Herston went on to become the president of United Artists Records/Nashville from 1963-1967 and the president of Capitol Records/Nashville from 1967-1972.

And, the last word goes to…Lynne Pitney: "I never realized that the girl in this song was blind! I never got that from the song. It's a beautiful song that just didn't get the attention it should have gotten. This was a time when Musicor wasn't really backing Gene anymore, and it didn't get any radio play. I remember Gene being pretty irritated with Musicor at the time. It fell by the wayside. A pity."

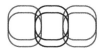

CHAPTER 6:
HALF HEAVEN-HALF HEARTACHE

Lyrics by Aaron Schroeder, Wally Gold, and George Goehring and Music by George Goehring

Fun Fact: Someone changed the lyrics to this song, but no one knows who did it!

Gene Pitney said: "It's a great song. If you can hit the notes the song will sell itself. When I'm doing it live on stage it just has all the ingredients." That's how he explained his love for this song to WWUH Radio host "Wild" Wayne Jones in an on-air interview.

"Half Heaven-Half Heartache" was one of Pitney's all-time favorite songs to sing in concert. This breathtaking song of melancholy never failed to bring down the house at his live shows. From the plaintive song's quiet and serene – albeit heartbreaking – beginning to its dynamic and vibrant ending, it allowed Gene to display – almost flaunt – his near-operatic range.

"George Goehring created this melody, which is stunning in its simplicity," Pitney explained. "So, because I'm not concerned about hitting certain notes or pushing my range, I can sink my teeth into it and really sell it. I love this one."

However, he added that he wasn't fond of how the song ended in falsetto. "Not my idea," he explained. "It was either Aaron or Wally who wanted a little flourish at the end, so I gave them that." Pitney disliked it so much he never sang the falsetto part of the song in his live shows later in his career.

With his elegant vocal on this song, Pitney spoke to the heartbreak of unrequited love. *"My arms reach out for you…I kiss you tenderly…but when you touch my lips…you're kissing him not me."* The minimal backing track on the verses of "Half Heaven-Half Heartache" allows us to hear all the anguish in his voice, and when he hits the string-filled chorus, that voice of anguish plunges into such despair that even the lush violin arrangement can't hide it.

This song was recorded during the same session as "Only Love Can Break A Heart." If you listen to the two songs back-to-back you'll hear Pitney using the same hushed style on both of them. He was in a special place that night.

George Goehring, who wrote this unforgettably haunting melody that lingers with you long after you've heard the song, was only 19 years old when he left his hometown of Philadelphia to look for musical success in New York in the mid-1950s. The aspiring songwriter got a job playing piano in nightclubs. He was in show business! That late night job in the smoky nightclubs of New York City sustained him for five years as he pursued his real dream: writing hit songs.

"I'd play in the clubs all night, grab a few hours sleep, write songs, and then run around all day to the publishers in the Brill Building, trying to sell my songs," he explained in a September 2001 issue of the *Gene Pitney International Fan Club Newsletter.* Eventually he was offered a job as a staff writer with Joy Music for $75 a week. "I was thrilled," George said. "It's what I always wanted to do."

Goehring started to see some success. He had a small hit in 1957 when The Platters recorded "The

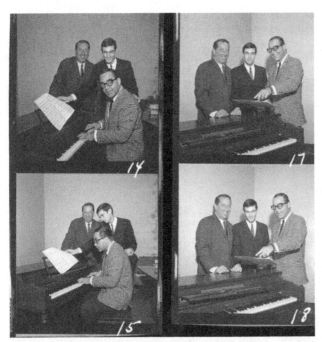

Photo outtakes from a session with Musicor Records co-owners Art Talmadge (left) and Aaron Schroeder (right).

Mystery of You," but, it was Connie Francis who changed his life and set his career in motion. She was the most famous female pop singer in the world in 1959; he was an unknown songwriter. She entered George Goehring's world and decided to record a song he had written with lyricist Edna Lewis. It turned his world upside down.

"Connie lived down the street from me," the friendly Goehring recalled, "and I was at her house one day pitching songs. I played 'Lipstick On Your Collar' for her. She changed my life with five words, 'Okay, I'll take this one.'"

"Lipstick On Your Collar" hit the charts in 1959 and became one of her biggest hits. George Goehring was on his way. While this song was his "big break," he says that having Gene Pitney record his song "Half Heaven-Half Heartache" was "the biggest thrill of my life."

Here is the full interview with George Goehring that was published in the September 2001 *Gene Pitney International Fan Club Newsletter.*

Question: How did the Gene Pitney-George Goehring connection come about?

George: I was writing a lot of songs with Aaron Schroeder and Wally Gold at that time, and Aaron was handling Gene at the time. Aaron said, "Let's write a song for Gene along the lines of Roy Orbison's 'Crying.' Something that builds. This song was written backwards. I already had the tune in my head. I had the hook first – the 'Half Heaven-Half Heartache.' The three of us actually wrote the lyrics together to fit the tune. When we gave it to Gene he flipped over it right away, so we knew we had something. It was so exciting for me because Gene was/is my favorite male singer. You can imagine what a thrill that was for me as a songwriter.

Question: How did the song come together?

George: The melody came first, and for a long time all we had was the title. We knew "Half Heaven-Half Heartache" was a great idea, but what did it mean? What was the concept? What was the "heaven," and what was the "heartache"? Was she cheating on him? Or was her love running hot and cold? We tried several opposites, but none seemed to work. Then, I remember walking to Aaron's office one day thinking "Maybe they're still together, but she's still thinking of another love." Then the line hit me: *"Can't you forget that other love you knew?"* It worked perfectly as the melodic line after the title. When I got to Aaron's office he said, "That's it!" And we developed that idea. I remember Wally Gold and Aaron piecing together the words to the opening strains like a marvelous jigsaw puzzle, you know, *"My arms reach out for you…"* For the second phrase we originally had *"Within your angel eyes a world of dreams I see…yet I keep wondering if they're for him or me. Will it always be Half Heaven-Half Heartache…"* To this day I still don't know who changed that to *"Within your angel eyes a world of dreams are there…yet I keep wondering if they are mine to share. Oh it's just not fair…"* The first time I heard THOSE lines was when I first heard the recording. I never did get around to asking whose lines they were. For some reason I thought they might be Gene's lines. Another line was changed earlier in the song, too. They're gutsier than what we had, and it got away from too much "E" rhyme.

Gene: It wasn't me! I don't know who changed the words.

Question: Where did the extraordinarily pretty hook for this song come from? Did it just pop into your head one day?

George: I sat down at the piano one day, and I just found it. That's how it happens sometimes. But, sometimes you can be walking down the street and a tune will hit you, too.

Question: Were you at the recording session for "Half Heaven-Half Heartache"?

George: I didn't get to the session, but I'll never forget the first time I heard Gene's record because it was one of the highlights of my life. Aaron sat me down in a chair and

first played "Only Love Can Break A Heart," which was recorded at the same session. Then he played "Half Heaven-Half Heartache." I just about fell off the chair. I will never forget that. That was one of life's marvelous highlights for me, as you can imagine.

Question: How did you find out the song would be released as a single?

George: Actually it was Burt Bacharach who told me that I had "the next Gene Pitney single." I really didn't

Gene meeting French singing star Charles Aznavour.

52

think it was going to come out as a single because Gene was on a roll with Bacharach-David songs like "Only Love Can Break A Heart," "(The Man Who Shot) Liberty Valance," and "True Love Never Runs Smooth." I was in the Brill Building one day and Burt Bacharach and Hal David were already in the elevator, and Burt simply said to me, "You've got the next Gene Pitney single; do you know that?" It was like winning the lottery because every songwriter wanted Gene to record his or her stuff.

Question: When did you first meet Gene?

George: I first met Gene at Aaron's office when the song was climbing the charts, and we kind of celebrated. We sat in Aaron's office, and Gene thanked me for writing the song, and I thanked him for singing it.

Question: How did you feel about Jane Olivor recording the song as a duet with Gene for her *Love Decides* CD?

George: Jane Olivor happens to be my favorite female singer, so you can imagine what it felt like to hear her sing my song with Gene! It was like a double feature! I think if it had come out as a single it would have been a monster hit.

Aaron Schroeder discovered and managed Pitney and founded Musicor Records. Schroeder wrote more than 2,000 songs, including 17 recorded by Elvis. The biggest hit he ever wrote for Presley, "It's Now or Never," he co-wrote with Wally Gold, another of the co-writers of "Half Heaven-Half Heartache." The melody of "It's Now or Never" was borrowed from "O Sole Mio," an Italian standard.

According to the book *Behind the Hits* by Bob Shannon and John Javna, Schroeder and Gold wrote the lyrics to "It's Now or Never" in about a half an hour. The song hit #1 in countries all over the world and was Presley's best-selling single ever: more than 20 million records were sold. Wally Gold was quoted in the book as saying, "Aaron wrote other hits; I wrote other hits. "But a song we finished in 20 minutes to a half hour was the biggest song of our careers."

Some of Schroeder's other hits for Presley included "Stuck on You," "Good Luck Charm," another song co-written with Gold, and "A Big Hunk O' Love." Frank Sinatra, Nat King Cole, Roy Orbison, and many other artists also recorded Schroeder's songs.

Aaron Schroeder died in 2009 at the Lillian Booth Actors' Home in Englewood, New Jersey, where he lived the last few years of his life. He was 83. The cause was complications of Alzheimer's disease.

Wally Gold also co-wrote Lesley Gore's #1 hit "It's My Party." Gold, Schroeder, and Don Costa wrote Duane Eddy's "Because They're Young," the theme song for the 1960 movie starring Dick Clark, Tuesday Weld, and Doug McClure. Gold later became a producer at Columbia Records where he produced albums for Tony Bennett, Jerry Vale, and Barbra Streisand. While working for music mogul Don Kirshner in the 1970s, Gold discovered the band Kansas.

Wally Gold died from colitis in 1998 at the age of 70.

As of this writing, George Goehring lives in Delray Beach, Florida.

Favorite Lyric: *"My arms reach out for you…I kiss you tenderly…but when you touch my lips…you're kissing him not me…why must it be…Half Heaven…Half Heartache…"* As Don Everly wrote (and The Everly Brothers sang), *"It makes me cry…to see love die… so sad to watch good love go bad."* Yup!

Factoid: If you want to hear this song sung using the original lyrics – before they were changed for the Gene Pitney record – find the Ral Donner version on YouTube. He recorded this song first in 1961.

Factoid: Schroeder and Gold also co-wrote "Take Me Tonight," "Those Eyes O' Liza Jane," "Carrie," and "Time and The River," all of which Pitney recorded. In fact, Pitney loved "Take Me Tonight" so much that he recorded it twice. The original was recorded in 1961 on Musicor Records, and he re-recorded it in 1975 for Bronze Records.

Factoid: International singing star Jane Olivor recorded her version of "Half Heaven-Half Heartache" as a duet with Gene at his home studio in Somers, Connecticut, in 2001. "I'm the biggest fan of Gene's in the whole world," she said in an interview for the *Gene Pitney International Fan Club Newsletter.* "My producer, Steve Addabbo, had always liked the song, and he knew someone who knew Gene, and before you knew it, we were on the phone with Gene setting it up." As a teenager growing up in Brooklyn, Olivor idolized Gene. She said she DID have butterflies in her stomach as she approached his house in Somers, but she needn't have worried. "Gene was great," she confirmed. "He was an angel. He worked very hard, and he couldn't do enough for us. It was just a great, fun, and awesome experience. It went by extraordinarily fast.

I don't even remember how many takes we did. I was just so caught up in being there and recording with Gene Pitney."

Factoid: In a 2003 article in the British newspaper *The Guardian* about songs that changed peoples' lives, singer Suzi Quatro said this: "I was 11 or 12 and visiting my extremely rich girlfriend's house for a sleepover. I ended up in her basement kissing her older brother for seven hours – nothing else, honest, just kissing – and in the background, over and over again on repeat, was...yes, you guessed it, Gene Pitney's 'Half Heaven-Half Heartache.' Years later I met Gene at a TV show, told him the story, and his reply was: 'You wouldn't believe how many times I've heard that story.'"

Factoid: Country star Narvel Felts said in a 2000 *Gene Pitney International Fan Club Newsletter* interview that "Half Heaven-Half Heartache" is a song he would have loved to record. "That is really just a great record. And, I think Gene's performance on it is stunning. I just wish I had been there to watch him record that one!"

Factoid: In 1962 George Goehring bought his mother a transistor radio for Christmas. When she opened it on Christmas Eve and turned it on, "Half Heaven-Half Heartache" was being played by radio station WIBG in Philadelphia. George said, "The family looked on in disbelief. I'll never forget the expressions on their faces. I think my father thought I had the thing rigged to play that song."

Factoid: In 2009, Rod MacDonald released a version of "Half Heaven-Half Heartache" on his album *After The War*, featuring its composer, George Goehring, playing piano.

Factoid: At a 2005 show at The Kravis Center in West Palm Beach, Florida, Pitney stopped the show to introduce songwriter George Goehring, who was in the audience, to the crowd. He thanked George for writing the song and added, "Please write me another one!"

And, the last word goes to...Lynne Pitney: "This one is the BEST! He has the voice of an angel on this record. 'Half Heaven-Half Heartache' is a tremendous song. I just love his tenderness in this song. For so many people this is their favorite song that he ever sang. I can see why. Your heart just melts when he sings those lyrics, *'Why must it be Half Heaven-Half Heartache.'* You just want him to win THAT girl! It is absolutely in my Top 5."

An early Gene Pitney promotional photo.

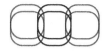

CHAPTER 7:
HELLO MARY LOU

Lyrics and Music by Gene Pitney and Cayet Mangiaracina

Fun Fact: Gene Pitney had to settle a copyright infringement lawsuit with a Catholic priest named Cayet Mangiaracina over this song.

Gene Pitney said: "I had that phrase 'Hello Mary Lou, goodbye heart' in my head. I just knew if I could wrap a song around it I had a winner. I knew that the song was there… if I could get to it." This 1961 Ricky Nelson hit is one of Gene Pitney's most successful copyrights as a songwriter. It also became more than a bit of a thorn in his side.

Nelson was at the zenith of his TV and pop idol musical fame and popularity when he recorded and released his durable version of "Hello Mary Lou." When it was released on Imperial Records (as a double A-side single with "Travelin' Man") writing credit on the record was given solely to Pitney. Nelson's single soared into the Top 10, and the publisher of the similarly titled song "Merry, Merry Lou" took notice, and, like a bat out of hell, said "Not so fast." Champion Music, a subsidiary of Decca Records, sued for copyright infringement, and eventually a settlement was reached.

With a nod to the legendary radio broadcaster Paul Harvey, now the rest of the story. The song "Merry, Merry Lou" was written by Cayet Mangiaracina in 1954 and recorded in 1957 for Decca Records by his band, The Sparks. Bill Haley and His Comets also recorded the song for Decca in 1957 but changed the title to "Mary, Mary Lou."

Abby Schroeder, who managed Pitney with her husband Aaron, handled copyright issues for their record label, Musicor Records, as well as for all of their artists and all of their music publishing companies. She said it was easier and cheaper to give Mangiaracina co-credit on "Hello Mary Lou" than to fight it out in a costly court battle with Decca Records.

"Anytime somebody writes a song and maybe it sounds like someone else's but they say they never heard the other song, they're not lying. Gene may never have really heard it, but maybe it was playing somewhere and he was there. But, in a legal sense, there is the possibility that Gene had heard it somewhere simply because it was available to be heard. And when it comes to copyright infringement, it's very difficult to prove that you didn't take it if it sounds a lot like it."

In her heart of hearts, she doesn't believe Gene did anything sly or malicious. "You know, he may have heard it once somewhere or something like that, but the songs are remarkably unsimilar except for a note or two."

Gene chose to never talk about the issue after the out-of-court settlement. He likely felt insulted and cheated. Rightly so. As Abby Schroeder already mentioned, the similarity in the songs is beyond minor and vague. That court-imposed shared copyright cost him well over a million dollars in royalties over the years.

Schroeder added, "Gene was very mad about that, but there was no way he could have won. It would have cost a fortune to defend in court. We talked him into settling because we knew it could have been financial devastation for him. He never got over it."

In a 1986 TV interview with Red Robinson in Vancouver, Canada, Gene explained how he wrote "Hello Mary Lou." "I sat in my little 1935 candy apple red Ford coupe strumming my guitar while parked at a place called Walker's Reservoir. It was about seven or eight miles from my house in Rockville, Connecticut. I would always park in this one spot that overlooked the water. That calmness allowed me to clear my head of everything else that was in it and think of songs to write."

And, he said in interview after interview, "There was no real Mary Lou. It just rhymed with I love you!" His favorite memory of this song is the first time he ever heard it on the radio. "I was in Philadelphia with my promotion man promoting my own record, and all of a sudden Ricky Nelson comes on with 'Hello Mary Lou,' and I damn near fell out of the car! I never pictured him as the guy who would take that song. My manager, Aaron Schroeder, knew everybody, and somehow he got that song in front of Ricky. It's a fun song, and Ricky made a great record of it, but to this day I'm still not sure how it became such a big hit. What a moneymaker that has been for me over the years."

Cayet Mangiaracina's music career was short-lived because he became a Catholic priest with the Dominican Order around 1957. After being awarded co-writing credit for "Hello Mary Lou," the royalty checks started rolling in. In a 2021 phone interview, Father Cayet said his mother got a few of the first royalty checks, but, once he was accepted into the religious order, every single check after that has been mailed to the headquarters of the Dominican's southern province in New Orleans. "As a Dominican I took the vow of poverty so I can't own anything. "

Gene on a promotional radio visit with an unidentified DJ.

Quarterly checks from BMI pay music royalties to songwriters when their songs are performed publicly, and the ones to Father Cayet have ranged from a few thousand dollars all the way up to one that was $90,000. He added, "They all go to further our mission to preach the Gospel of our Lord. It was a gift from God, and I thank him every day."

To this day, Father Cayet says he had nothing to do with the lawsuit that not only has paid off handsomely for his religious order but also made him a good-sized footnote in the history of rock 'n' roll. "I had just entered the order and was in my first novitiate year in Winona, Minnesota," he explained. "That's where I suddenly got papers to sign because this thing was in the courts. I was in my 20s and didn't know what was going on, so I signed the papers and sent them back in.

"I didn't know who Gene Pitney was at the time, and I wasn't that concerned about any of it as I was just starting my ministry. Gene and I never spoke during the time that song was being litigated."

"Hello Mary Lou" is an iconic record in the history of pop music because of who sang it and when he sang it. And, it is simply a fun little song to sing. No more. No less. Pitney was always very fond of Nelson's record. "I loved it," Pitney always said. "The version he did was almost exactly the same as the demo I did on the song. I don't think I had a cowbell on mine though (*laughter*). His record was pretty much the way I thought it should be arranged and produced."

Ricky Nelson's version of "Hello Mary Lou" as well as Gene's own version and all the other cover versions listed in the factoid below are remarkable because

Contact proof sheet from the *Pitney '75* photo session.

the singers all took the same approach to this song. It has pretty mundane lyrics set to a rambunctiously fun and catchy melody, and all the artists sang it with the authentic joy that defined and exemplified rock 'n' roll in the 1950s and early 1960s.

Favorite Lyric: *"You passed me by one sunny day…flashed those big brown eyes my way… and ooh I wanted you forever more."* While there are other female charms that also entice men, it's the eyes, always the eyes, that catch their attention. Especially if the woman is looking at the man with either a furtive glance or a long second look. Men see it; they want it; they need it. They want those big brown eyes flashing their way, even if it leads to nothing else but a minor flirtation. Men crave female attention. Pitney went on to prove that point with every single line that followed this one in this song.

Factoid: Some surprising acts have covered "Hello Mary Lou," including Led Zeppelin. It was released on their live album *How the West Was Won* in 2003. It was from a live performance at the LA Forum in 1972. Also dipping into the Pitney catalogue were Creedence Clearwater Revival, Brownsville Station, New Riders of the Purple Sage, and The Statler Brothers. For the Statler's version, Gene picked up *The Music City News 6th Annual Songwriters Award for Best Traditional Upbeat Song* in 1986 in Nashville. Author David McGrath accepted the award for Gene on a nationally-televised TV special.

Factoid: The great Sam Cooke also recorded a very good R&B version of "Mary, Mary Lou" in 1958.

Factoid: Cayet Mangiaracina's name has an interesting history. Cayet is his mother's maiden name. His father's parents came from Sicily and, in Sicilian, his last name literally translates as "the grape eater." "Mangia" means eat, and "racina" is grapes.

And, the last word goes to…Lynne Pitney: "I loved it; everybody loved it. And, everyone, when they hear it, can sing along with it. It's such a joyful song. Gene was always grateful that Ricky Nelson recorded this song. And, everybody wants to know who Mary Lou was!"

I MUST BE SEEING THINGS

(AND HEARING THINGS)

Words and Music by
AL KOOPER   BOB BRASS   IRWIN LEVINE

As Recorded By GENE PITNEY On Musicor Records

75¢

SEA-LARK ENTERPRISES, INC.

A. SCHROEDER MUSIC CORPORATION

Sole Selling Agents: CPI   CIMINO PUBLICATIONS INCORPORATED
479 Maple Avenue   Westbury, L.I. N.Y.

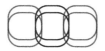

CHAPTER 8:
I MUST BE SEEING THINGS

Lyrics by Bob Brass and Irwin Levine and Music by Al Kooper

Fun Fact: This dazzling Pitney heartbreaker was written by the same team that cranked out the pop smash "This Diamond Ring" for Gary Lewis & The Playboys.

Gene Pitney said: "To this day I think Musicor should have released Jimmy Radcliffe's demo version of this song instead of my recording. His version was that good." Pitney was singing power ballads long before the hair bands of the 1970s and '80s knew how to spell those words. Al Kooper, of the songwriting team of Kooper-Brass-Levine, tells the story about how "I Must Be Seeing Things" found its way to Gene.

In a phone interview, Kooper said, "We were under contract to Aaron Schroeder's publishing company Sea Lark Music and always had the 'inside' information as to when Gene would need new material when he was getting ready to record a new album. When it was time for him to record we would pay attention to that. Everything we then wrote was written for him. We simply concentrated on writing songs for Gene."

In general, Kooper said that he wrote the melodies for all of their songs that Gene recorded because neither of his partners played any musical instruments. The aforementioned New York session singer Jimmy Radcliffe sang on most of their demos.

"We got to know what kind of songs Gene liked or needed, but we also knew that

Gene didn't mind moving out of his comfort zone from time to time. So, we could write a song like 'The Last Two People On Earth' (a song about nuclear destruction) and feel comfortable pitching it to him."

Kooper expounded on that song and how he thought Gene handled it. "I loved it," Kooper said. "It was an iffy song because of the subject matter," he admitted. "We knew it would be a tough one to do…to sound believable. But I thought Gene and the producer got a very nice, mysterious sound on it. I loved that Gene 'got it' and that he consented to do it because I thought it was great for him."

Gene Pitney was the master at selling torment and agony. "I Must Be Seeing Things" had those characteristics in spades, and Pitney, as Kooper said, put the "S" in star with his hypnotically larger-than-life vocal on this record. It has been said time and time again that you always knew a record was a Gene Pitney record right off the bat because his voice was so unique and his interpretive style so rare. This song is further proof of that.

Pitney explained that this was the height of his career and he was constantly touring, so when it was time to get into the studio to record, Aaron Schroeder and Wally Gold from Musicor Records usually had twenty to thirty songs for him to listen to. "They both had great ears and knew what I liked and what would fit my style.

"Once you're commercially successful and consistently in the Top 10, songwriters start to write specifically for you and your style. When you look at the writing credits on my first three or four albums you'll see the same songwriters' names popping up. So, when Aaron would tell me this song or that song came from so-and-so, I knew what to expect. It made it easy for me to pick the songs I wanted. I'm also pretty sure Aaron and Wally only presented me with songs that they liked and had already agreed on."

As mentioned, the demo for "I Must Be Seeing Things" was done by Jimmy Radcliffe. Radcliffe had also been signed to a Musicor Records recording contract by Aaron Schroeder because Schroeder and his wife, Abby, liked Jimmy personally and professionally. Radcliffe had done the demos for the Gary Lewis hit "This Diamond Ring," Manfred Mann's "Pretty Flamingo," and countless songs written by the likes of Ellie Greenwich, Bacharach and David, and Leiber and Stoller that went on to be hits.

"Jimmy had great integrity on his demos," Gene recalled. "Sometimes they were better than the records that made the charts. When I heard his version of 'I Must Be Seeing

Things' I turned to Aaron and said, 'Why don't you release this?' Aaron said, 'It's too good of a song to give to a demo singer. This song needs you.' I loved it right away. I wasn't sure it could be a hit because it was a simple little song. That's why I dressed it up on the last couple of lines."

"I Must Be Seeing Things" is a soap opera-like saga of romantic betrayal. You can hear the heartbreak in Pitney's voice in every single word and every single note, from his crushing opening line where he sounds like he's whispering to a friend…or talking quietly to himself, *"Isn't that my girl…and…is that my best friend…out there walking much too close together,"* to his pleading and brokenhearted closing line, *"I must be seeing things I thought I'd never see…I must be hearing things you made a fool of me…I must be seeing things and hearing things…OH NO…I need you SO…oh please don't GO-O-O-O-O-O-O!"*

Kooper said "I Must Be Seeing Things" was crafted to include everything a Gene Pitney record needed. In his words, "It had love, lost love, heartbreak, and betrayal. What a fucking song we wrote for him."

He also said that the take-no-prisoners ending of the song with Pitney soaring on "OH NO," "SO," and "GO" was the singer's idea of how to end the emotionally-charged song. "That was NOT us. We just kept repeating the chorus. Gene made it his own."

In his memoir *Backstage Passes & Backstabbing Bastards*, Al Kooper wrote, "When other artists were not 'appreciating' our songs, it was always Pitney who'd take one of our teen traumas and tack it onto an album or make it the flip side of a single, just so we could eat. When 'I Must Be Seeing Things' hit the charts it felt good to be doing something to repay Gene's kindness for recording various 'gems' of ours like 'The Last Two People on Earth,' 'Don't Take Candy From a Stranger,' and 'Hawaii.'" (Kooper and Levine also wrote "She's Still There" on Gene's *Looking Through The Eyes of Love* American album.)

In spite of the fact that Gene Pitney was at his peak in 1965, "I Must Be Seeing Things" stalled at #31 on the *Billboard Hot 100*. Kooper recalled, fondly and gratefully, how that didn't matter to him. "I was just glad he did it and it made the Top 40. We weren't in the Top 40 very much considering all the stuff we had out there."

Gene Pitney defined pop royalty for male singers in the era of The Beatles, Rolling Stones, and The Dave Clark Five, and he will always hold a preeminent place in the annals of pop music. By 1965, though, the British Invasion was taking its toll on male American pop stars like Bobby Vee, Bobby Rydell, Paul Anka, and others. Still, why "I Must Be Seeing Things" did not become a huge hit in the US is baffling and perplexing. It really is a quintessential Gene Pitney record. But, as usual, his legions of British fans still adored everything Gene was putting out in that era, and they sent this song to #6 in the UK.

"I Must Be Seeing Things" debuted at #78 on the *Billboard Hot 100* on February 27, 1965. Just one week later Gary Lewis and the Playboys hit #1 with "This Diamond Ring." Both songs were written by the Kooper-Brass-Levine songwriting team. Unfortunately, these two back-to-back hit records would be the end of their pop chart success due to drugs – Kooper loved his marijuana – and the changing musical tastes of both the record-buying public and Al Kooper.

Gene working out a melody in manager / producer Aaron Schroeder's New York office.

The American kids had abandoned their homegrown teen idols and had passionately – maybe even fanatically – embraced the English stars of the British Invasion. Al Kooper was abandoning what he called "Clearasil-ically-composed pop music" (ouch!) in favor of jazz and blues-rock.

Kooper and Irwin Levine would write a couple more songs together before going their separate ways and embracing different songwriting styles.

After his songwriting trio broke up, Kooper concentrated on performing as well as writing. He played the organ on Bob Dylan's groundbreaking "Like A Rolling Stone" single. He met blues guitarist Mike Bloomfield at that recording session and much later recorded the Super Session album with Bloomfield and Stephen Stills. Kooper would move on to join the urban blues band The Blues Project before splitting off to form Blood, Sweat and Tears. One album later he left BS&T to do session work with The Rolling Stones, Jimi Hendrix, and The Who.

In the early 1970s Kooper moved to Atlanta where he discovered Lynyrd Skynyrd and produced the band's first three albums on his own record label, Sounds of the South. Kooper produced the two hit singles "Sweet Home Alabama" and "Free Bird" for the band.

Having moved to England in 1979, Kooper ended up producing David Essex as well as playing on and producing three tracks on George Harrison's *Somewhere in England* album. He played on Harrison's smash "All Those Years Ago" with Harrison, Paul McCartney, and Ringo Starr.

Irwin Levine stayed true to his pop roots and virtually owned the record charts in the early 1970s as he single-handedly propped up Tony Orlando's recording career by co-writing hits including "Tie A Yellow Ribbon Round The Ole Oak Tree," "Candida," "Say, Has Anybody Seen My Sweet Gypsy Rose," and "Knock Three Times." Levine also cranked out The Partridge Family hit "I Woke Up In Love This Morning."

Regarding all of Levine's success AFTER the Kooper-Brass-Levine team broke up, Kooper said, "I thought it was great, and I was very proud of him. I was glad that he did that." But, Kooper did admit to some professional jealousy about the success, "A little…yeah. Irwin wanted to write pop hits. He was talented. At any point in time I would have gone back and written a song with him. I recall fondly that period of time when we wrote together. We wrote some really good songs."

Irwin Levine died in 1957 at the age of 58 from kidney failure.

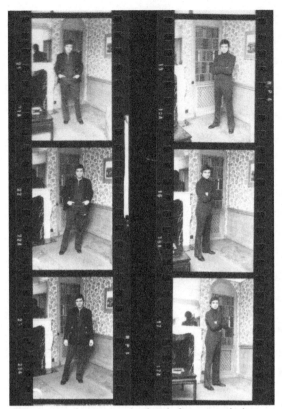

According to Kooper, Bob Brass left the music business "in favor of a comparatively honest blue-collar job at the Fulton Fish Market" in New York. Kooper said Brass had died but wasn't aware of the circumstances.

Al Kooper, now in his 70s, is still alive and well as of this writing, although numerous back surgeries have left him not as mobile as he would like to be. He is retired from the music business and lives in Somerville, Massachusetts. He has stayed active in music in many different ways through the years, from movies to TV to teaching.

Figuring out where to put his hands for a casual photo in his home in Somers, CT.

Favorite Lyric: *"Isn't that my girl? And is that my best friend? Out there walking much too close together… and it don't look like they're talking about the weather."* Discount the obvious grammatical problem but take into account that the songwriters fit "together" and "weather" in a rhyming scheme about deception and lost love! This line in the Pitney record, as puppy love-ish as it seems, produces such a monumentally vivid, tormenting, and heartbreaking visual. Classic teen anguish. Bravo Kooper-Brass-Levine!

Factoid: On his relationship with Gene, Al Kooper said this: "Gene and I were pretty close. I thought he was great. We were similar in a lot of ways: keyboard players, songwriters, and…I was there the day he first walked in to see Aaron Schroeder. Bob Brass and Irwin Levine weren't. I was a big fan from that first day that I saw him in Aaron's office. We just got along great. As a matter of fact, he sent me an email a week before he died. From the road…from England. He said that he had a health problem, and he didn't know what happened to him, and then he just changed his shoes and that seemed to solve the problem. And a week later I heard he died."

Factoid: Al Kooper's early musical career included a stint as a fourteen-year-old guitarist for The Royal Teens, a group that had future Four Seasons singer/songwriter Bob Gaudio on piano. The group had a #3 US hit with the novelty song "Short Shorts" in 1958.

Factoid: There are only a few cover versions of "I Must Be Seeing Things." One was done by a group called The Waking Hours in 2002, and there were two French versions under the title "Mes Yeux Sont Fous" (English translation: "My Eyes Are Fools"). One was by the French pop superstar Johnny Hallyday, and the other was by the great orchestra leader Paul "Love Is Blue" Mauriat.

Factoid: Al Kooper played on the demos that ended up becoming Pitney's first Musicor album, *The Many Sides of Gene Pitney*. He played guitar because he hadn't made the transition to keyboards yet. He did not play on the "I Must Be Seeing Things" session but was in the recording booth.

Factoid: Kooper-Brass-Levine HATED the Gary Lewis version of "This Diamond Ring." In his memoir Kooper wrote, "We were revolted. They'd removed the soul from our R&B song and made a teenage milkshake out of it. This was disgusting." Kooper-Brass-Levine had written it in hopes that The Drifters would record it, but the group passed on it.

Factoid: Some of the best writing about the early days of Gene Pitney's career is in the aforementioned Al Kooper memoir *Backstage Passes & Backstabbing Bastards: Memoirs Of A Rock 'n Roll Survivor*, which is available on the internet. His recollection of being in Aaron Schroeder's New York office the day Gene walked in for his audition with his future mentor (Schroeder) is mesmerizing. The book really is a must read.

And, the last word goes to…Lynne Pitney: "I just love listening to Gene's voice on this song. I loved the way Gene told the heartbreaking story…and that ending, wow! It's what Gene called a "Bravo" ending. He told me he did it in just two takes. He always said the Italian fans loved those dramatic songs; at his shows in Italy they'd yell, *"Br-r-ravo Peetney!"* I loved this one!"

A 1960s promotional photo.

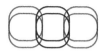

CHAPTER 9:
(I WANNA) LOVE MY LIFE AWAY

Lyrics and Music by Gene Pitney

Fun Fact: This record was not meant to be a single. It wasn't even meant to be released.

Gene Pitney said: "This is one of those songs that just came to me out of the blue. There was no real inspiration. I wrote it at the piano. Melodies came easy to me on the piano, so that's where a lot of my writing was done. I guess I just started thinking about the four seasons and how I could tie that into some sort of love song. Bingo. It flowed pretty quickly. I had it written in about an hour or so. The recording process took a lot longer."

Pitney says he started writing songs right after high school, during the time he was going to school to study electronics. But, he doesn't remember much about it. "I don't remember why or where I started to write songs. I loved music all my life. I started a band in high school, Gene & The Genials. I really didn't have any plans on becoming a performer...none at all. In those early days I had serious stage fright. The band was for the fun of it and the girls."

This song was the first song that he wrote and had a hit with himself. "I wrote it, I sang it, and I played most of the instruments on it. I did all the overdubbing, too. It was quite the experiment. And, I paid for it, about $30. You know the old saying,

'Necessity is the mother of invention.' I had no money for a professional demo with a full orchestra, but what I did have was talent. I could play piano, guitar, and drums, so I could keep costs down by doing it all myself. I only had to bring in a bass player. I've been credited as being an innovator, but it simply came down to the fact that I had no money!"

This song is 1:58 of simply joyful and pristine pop music. Pitney's exuberance on this song is addictive. It's not much more than a charming little ditty, but it's one that you just want to sing along with every time you hear it. As he rejoices in this upbeat high school-type love letter to whomever the lucky girl is, Pitney puts realistic, almost instinctive, excitement into his vocal.

Here's how Pitney produced "(I Wanna) Love My Life Away" for $30: First he recorded the lead vocals and piano; then he played that tape back and played guitar and sang harmony along with it onto another tape; after that, he added the drums, the bass guitar, and then any additional backing vocals, always going back and forth between the two tape recorders. After a couple of false starts and trial and error recordings, the finished product was put together in about six hours.

At the time, Pitney was on a songwriter retainer with Aaron Schroeder, who was trying to build a publishing company without a big budget. "(I Wanna Love) My Life Away" was really recorded as a demo to pitch to other singers.

But, Schroeder, who managed Pitney and would create Musicor Records just for him, had a better idea. In an interview with WWUH Radio host "Wild" Wayne Jones, Pitney said, "It was Aaron Schroeder who listened to it and had the insight. He said 'I think this can be a hit record.' It was a long, long grind; I did every record hop, every TV and radio interview I could. It became a hit."

Abby Schroeder also recalled the events that started Pitney's hit-making career. "Gene had a manager in Connecticut named Marty Kugel. He would tell Gene to go to New York and just walk in and out of publishing houses and see if he could get a record deal. When Gene came to us, Aaron was very interested because of the way he sang. Aaron thought Gene had star potential. Gene had just one of the most wonderfully different sounds in the recording industry. We were thrilled to get him some attention and help him make a name for himself.

"Aaron took him down to Allegro Sound Studios in the basement of the 'Irving Berlin

Building' at 1650 Broadway to cut that record. Actually, Aaron produced it. A guy named Charlie Brave ran the studio and engineered most of the sessions. It was reasonable and convenient. It was a great first record for Gene."

Gene Pitney was not yet twenty-one years old when he pulled all this off. He was endowed with talent, wisdom, and astuteness that belied his youth. Aaron Schroeder, a music-business veteran, had the acumen and foresight to see what a talent Pitney was and what a star he could be. The coupling of these two creative giants created a hit machine that churned out one splendid hit after the other in the early 1960s. Equally important, Pitney was able to withstand the eventual onslaught of the British Invasion that derailed the careers of so many other American pop stars. Ironically, while British bands and pop stars were ruling the American charts in the mid-1960s, Pitney was dominating the British charts.

Favorite Lyric: *"I'll keep you warm in the winter…give you cool, cool kisses in the summertime…walk by your side in the autumn…and in the spring bells will chime."* Teenagers are complicated. They don't know anything, but they think they know it all. They think love is as simple as these lyrics because they haven't been married and raised families. That's the point of this song. When you're a teenager love SHOULD be this simple. Brilliant!

Factoid: "(I Wanna) Love My Life Away" was Gene Pitney's first chart record. Released in 1961, it peaked at #39 on the *Billboard Hot 100*.

Factoid: Country singer Jody Miller, who had a huge country hit with "Queen of the House" in 1965, recorded this Pitney classic in 1978. It only made it to #67 on the *Billboard Hot County Singles* chart.

And, the last word goes to…Lynne Pitney: "This is the first song of Gene's I ever heard on the radio. I was driving in a car with some friends, and it came on and I said, 'Oh my God! Listen…that's Gene!' And, they're going 'What? Huh?' I clearly remember hearing that song for the first time. It just jumped out of that car radio. I was so proud of him. Of course no one knew how big a star he would become. It was just so exciting to hear a record by someone you knew on the radio."

FOXWOODS CASINO

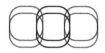

CHAPTER 10:
IF I DIDN'T HAVE A DIME
(TO PLAY THE JUKEBOX)

Lyrics and Music by Bert Russell and Phil Medley

Fun Fact: This is a song Gene wanted to be a hit, but DJs flipped the record over instead and played "Only Love Can Break A Heart."

Gene Pitney said: "This is one of those songs that was perfect for the time that it came out. It was sweet and simple and told a story that spoke to the kids who were buying my records."

Early in his career, Pitney always had this song in his live show. But, as he racked up more and more hits through the 1960s, it often fell by the wayside because of time limitations on the package shows where he usually topped the bill. After the hits stopped and he made his living touring, he had the luxury of doing an eighty-minute performance, so he added it back into the show because he loved to sing it.

"It was always a fan favorite," Pitney said. "Look, they know what they like, and it's my job to sing that. And I love this song, too, so it was a win/win to put it back in the show."

The unfortunate component of this song for this book is that everyone involved in major roles in creating this record is now dead. With the exception of some comments Pitney made for his Fan Club newsletter in the early 1990s, no interviews were possible.

The songwriters were Phil Medley and Bert Russell. Medley died from cancer in 1997 at the age of 81. Russell died in 1967 at the age of 38 from heart failure. Chuck Sagle, the arranger and musical conductor for the record, died in 2015 at the age of 87 from a stroke. Aaron Schroeder, the owner of Musicor Records and co-producer of the record, died from a rare form of dementia at the age of 83 in 2009. Wally Gold, the other co-producer, died from colitis at the age of 70 in 1998. Gene Pitney died of natural causes in 2006 at the age of 66 while on tour in the UK.

Pitney's delicately nimble vocal sells this simple "what if" story of a guy who wonders what might have happened if he didn't have a dime to play the jukebox. Of course he wouldn't have ended up dancing with the dreamy girl with "ruby lips and golden hair" who just happened to be "standing there beside the jukebox." And this romance would not have blossomed.

It's an effortless vocal, and that's what makes this song work so well. It doesn't get in the way of the imagery of the song. As you listen to Pitney describe what seems like a scene in a romantic one-act, boy-meets-girl play, the mental images play out in full color. This song was tailor-made for Pitney. He added a wistful tone to make it an even more fairytale ending.

Medley and Russell tell a very feasible story here. They set it up, they let it play out, then they gently and subtly explain, in hindsight, that if that lucky guy didn't have a dime...to play the jukebox...he would have lost the chance of a lifetime. That's the moral of this story: *"Oh, oh love songs that they sing wouldn't mean a single thing...even though you're standing there...ruby lips and golden hair...if I didn't have a dime and I didn't take the time...to play the jukebox."*

Chuck Sagle's arrangement and orchestration is eloquently understated, again staying out of the way of the lyrics' imagery. The Schroeder-Gold production thoughtfully defers to the Pitney vocal and the Sagle arrangement.

Pitney loved this record and really wanted it to be a hit. It was the B-side of "Only Love Can Break A Heart."

"That song ('Only Love Can Break A Heart') really worried me," Pitney famously once said. "Up to that point I hadn't really done anything that slow. When I went to

Concert photo courtesy of British fan Howard Matthews.

promote it at radio stations, I tried to get the DJs to play the other side, 'If I Didn't Have A Dime.'"

Pitney's effort paid off a little bit. "If I Didn't Have A Dime" got enough airplay in some radio markets that it charted on the *Billboard Hot 100*, peaking at #58 in October 1962. Of course, it lost that race with destiny to the A-side, "Only Love Can Break A Heart." That magical record would soar to #2 in November of 1962 and became Pitney's biggest US hit.

The songwriters Bert Russell and Phil Medley were known to everyone in the music business in New York, including Aaron Schroeder. Schroeder was the one who brought "If I Didn't Have A Dime" to Pitney's attention. Schroeder's wife, Abby, said in a 2021 phone interview that "Aaron instinctively knew what songs were right for Gene. Gene didn't 'hear' a song as fast as Aaron did. Then Aaron and Wally would twist his arm and convince him what was good for him. This was a great song for Gene, and he did a pretty charming job on it."

Bert Russell's real name was Bertrand Russell Berns, and he wrote and/or produced songs under the names Bert Russell, Bert Berns, and Russell Byrd. His songwriting

credits include "Twist and Shout," "Piece of My Heart," "Here Comes the Night," "Hang on Sloopy," and "Everybody Needs Somebody to Love."

Philip Medley co-wrote "Twist and Shout" with Bert Russell. The song was made famous by both The Isley Brothers and The Beatles. Medley also wrote "A Million to One" and co-wrote "Killer Joe," recorded by The Rocky Fellers, The Rivieras, and The Kingsmen.

Gene during a 1960s recording session in New York.

Chuck Sagle is credited with discovering Carole King. Other stars he worked with included Neil Sedaka, Tony Orlando, Bobby Darin, Barry Mann, The Del-Vikings, Joni James, Clyde McPhatter, The Diamonds, Roy Hamilton, Jack Jones, Link Wray, Sal Mineo, Lenny Welch, LaVern Baker, The Arbors, and The Manhattans.

Favorite Lyric: *"Now with every sweet caress oh, my darling how I bless...that little jukebox."* This is impeccable personification, and it is the perfect touch as the key element to telling the short story that is "If I Didn't Have A Dime." The jukebox was the matchmaker here. Mr. Russell and Mr. Medley may not have realized how brilliant they were!

Factoid: Fans from around the world who visit Gene Pitney's gravesite at the Somers Center Cemetery leave dimes both on his headstone and the grave's accompanying bench. It's a poignant reminder of what his music meant to them.

Factoid: Bert Russell was the founder of BANG Records. He started the label in 1965 with three executives from Atlantic Records: Ahmet Ertegun, Nesuhi Ertegun, and Gerald "Jerry" Wexler. The first letters of their names: Bert, Ahmet, Nesuhi, Gerald formed the label's name, BANG Records. Neil Diamond, Van Morrison and The McCoys all had huge hits on BANG Records.

And, the last word goes to...Lynne Pitney: "What can I say? This is such a sweet, sweet song, and Gene knew exactly how to sing it. There was no one like him. His songs will live on. This song follows me around for days after I visit him at the cemetery because of all the dimes that his fans leave there. It's always so touching. I'm so grateful for the kindness of his fans. He loved them all."

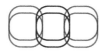

CHAPTER 11:
I'M GONNA BE STRONG

Lyrics and Music by Barry Mann and Cynthia Weil

Fun Fact: After seeing Pitney perform at the 1964 San Remo Song Festival in Italy, a very impressed Frankie Laine said to him: "I got a song for you, Kid." That song was "I'm Gonna Be Strong."

Gene Pitney said: "I thought this song needed to be poignant without being hysterical."

The path to the New York recording studio to record "I'm Gonna Be Strong" began on the Mediterranean coast of Liguria in northwestern Italy. Pitney was one of a number of American teen idols who performed at the famous San Remo Song Festival in Italy in 1964. Appearing that year, in addition to Gene, were Paul Anka, Frankie Avalon, Bobby Rydell, Ben E. King, Little Peggy March, and Nino Tempo & April Stevens. The legendary Frankie Laine also performed that year and, as Gene recalled, "He became the accidentally-on-purpose chaperone of the American delegation."

In January 1964, when the festival took place, Frankie Laine was already fifty years old and old hat to anyone buying records then. But, Pitney said, this group of American pop stars respected him for the career he had and for the talent he was. "At that point, Frankie had been performing for twenty years or so, and we all went to him for advice," Pitney pointed out. "Paul Anka was the most natural performer of all of us at that point, but even he went to Frankie with questions. Frankie liked Paul a lot. They were always talking.

"I remember one night we were all at dinner with Frankie, and I was sitting between him and Paul. I had performed 'E Se Domani' that night at the festival, and apparently Frankie was kinda blown away by it because he complimented me quite a few times. At one point, he leaned over to me and said, 'I got a song for you, Kid.' He told me about this record he had cut the year before for Columbia Records that went nowhere. Never even made it into the Top 100. It was 'I'm Gonna Be Strong.' He said 'It could be a classic if you do it right. Columbia has no idea what to do with me. That's why my version was such a dud.' I made a mental note to seek out the song when I got back to the States."

At this point in his career, Pitney was on the brink of becoming an international star. In mid-to-late 1963 he broke into the UK market with "Twenty Four Hours From Tulsa," which spent almost five months in the charts and peaked at #5 in November of that year. He would kick off 1964 with this appearance at San Remo, his first of four, and another British smash, "That Girl Belongs To Yesterday," written by Mick Jagger and Keith Richards of the then still-fledgling Rolling Stones.

1964 ran the rising star ragged with tours everywhere. Pitney knew he had to hit the road at home, in the UK, and in Italy to promote the worldwide release of his records. But, he also had to make time to get into the studio in New York to keep recording and producing music.

After San Remo at the end of January and the beginning of February, there was one show in Sydney, Australia, in April as he tried to break into that market. Next up, twenty-three one-nighters in fourteen states between June and September on The Dick Clark Caravan of Stars tour. He had to break away from the Dick Clark tour for one show in Italy in August, and he ended the year with a triumphant tour of the UK in November and December. By the time he got to the UK, his fourth British hit of the year, "I'm Gonna Be Strong," was sitting at #2.

Pitney recalled that year this way: "Exciting, yes, but chaotic. This was long before singers like me were treated like stars. We were riding and sleeping in buses and staying in cheap hotels every other night. You HAD to be young and excited about what you were doing to put up with it."

In all that touring chaos, finding new material and finding the quality time needed to get it recorded always weighed heavily on him. "This was an era when songs raced up and down the charts in eight to twelve weeks," he recalled. "So, we had to sort through hundreds of songs to find the twelve that we wanted for an album, AND we had to make sure at least four of them were strong enough to be hits. I was doing that at the same time I was on the road singing, doing radio and TV shows, meeting fans, and hanging with the other singers on the tour. It was draining both physically and mentally."

After he got back from San Remo he tracked down the song that Frankie Laine had told him about, "I'm Gonna Be Strong." Thinking back with a chuckle, Pitney recalled, "I couldn't find it at a record store. I phoned my manager, Aaron Schroeder, and told him about it."

Abby Schroeder, Aaron's wife and business partner, found the Frankie Laine record. "I went to every secondhand record store I could find in Manhattan, and I finally found it," she recalled.

At first listen, Pitney wasn't sure. "When I found out that it had been written by Barry Mann and Cynthia Weil I knew it had to be a good song. But, Frankie's version of it was not good. Not because of him. It was just the wrong arrangement for the song, and it seemed like it was produced in a rush. But, I knew there was a great song in there.

"I listened to it over and over, and one day it just came to me. Frankie's version sounded almost too cheerful. That's why it didn't work. This is a song about a guy whose girl is dumping him. There had to be despair but also some pride. So, I started walking around for a few days singing it at different tempos until I landed on the one I wanted. It wasn't a hard song to record. We got it done pretty quickly."

Pitney explained that "I'm Gonna Be Strong" was recorded at the tail end of a session at Bell Sound in New York that was squeezed in before he headed out on the Dick Clark summer tour. "It was the last song we recorded that night before we ran out of time when the union guys would have gone into overtime. Gary Geld and Peter Udell, the guys who produced the record for me, wanted me to add harmonies to it. I didn't think the record needed them. We were at an impasse and up against the clock, so we all decided to sleep on it and go back in the next morning for another playback.

"So, we all went back to Bell Sound early the next morning to hear what we had done. They played the song back for me, and I was satisfied at how well it had come out. I still didn't think it needed harmonies, but Gary and Peter did, so we compromised. That's why there is only harmony on the second half of that song. When I sang the ending harmony that moves up to THAT note on the last word, 'cry,' they told me that I hit a D above a high C as I climbed!"

In a 2021 phone interview, Garry Sherman, who arranged the song in spite of what the Musicor label indicates, said, "I wrote that ending just for Gene because I knew he had a beautiful high C. There was no one else like him in pop music at the time. The other thing you should know about Gene Pitney was he was so good, so talented, all the songs that I arranged for him we usually got in two or three takes."

Pitney owned this song from the tense and hushed opening lines to the false bravado of the closing lines. His straightforward delivery belies the storyline on purpose. As in Roy Orbison's "Crying," the listeners are left hanging for the resolution of this crisis of love until the very last lines…where we get tricked. Gene imbues the song with a

Gene putting the final touches on a song.

sense of loss even as he tells off the little darling who is leaving him. Then, when she presumably slams the car door and walks out of his life, what does he do? He breaks down and cries. Somehow Gene Pitney made that all make sense. He really earned his fan magazine title of "The Prince of Pain" on this one. As only Gene Pitney could, he made a remarkably unremarkable vocal remarkable.

"He really did," agreed Garry Sherman. "He was a unique and extraordinary singer. He always knew, emotionally, how to sing a song, what it called for. Some arrangers would offer suggestions to artists on how to sing a song. Mitch Miller was famous for doing that in the 1950s. I never did that with Gene because my name wasn't Burt Bacharach (*laughter*)!"

At this point in Pitney's career, Aaron Schroeder and Wally Gold were producing most of his songs. This hit got away from them because apparently Pitney was in a mood. In a 2021 phone interview, Peter Udell explained that he and Gary Geld produced the record as a favor to Pitney. "Gary and Gene were friends. They were just simpatico. They had known each other for a year or so. I think Brian Hyland introduced them to each other. Gene wanted to get this record done and thought Gary was the guy to do it. It seemed to us at the time that Gene and Aaron Schroeder were at each other's throats, and Gene was just doing what he wanted to do."

Udell did recall something extraordinary that happened at the studio before the song was recorded. "Gene knew how he wanted to do the song, but he asked to have Barry Mann and Cynthia Weil come in and show him how they envisioned the song. Songwriters were rarely invited to recording sessions just for that reason: artists and producers always had their own vision of how a song should be. Songwriters weren't paid too much deference in those days. I think Gene did it just to stick it to Aaron a bit."

Even though they were aware something was amiss, Udell said he and Geld decided to stay away from the tiff between Pitney and Schroeder and just produce a great record for them. "We really wanted to work with Gene. Just about everybody did. We just asked for producer and arranger credits on the record, and we waived our royalties. That's what was done a lot back then. We didn't really feel any tension at the session. Nothing really tricky about it. Gene was great to work with. I think we got it in two or three takes."

Garry Sherman was one of Pitney's favorite arrangers. They were also very close friends, and Sherman would later serve as the Best Man at Pitney's wedding to Lynne Gayton. Sherman got his standard fee for arranging the record but, as a favor to Pitney, agreed to allow Geld and Udell to be listed as arrangers on the record.

"Look, Peter and Gary were friends of mine," Sherman said. "At that point I had more work than I could actually take, so it was fine with me. Peter and I are still friends. Gary died a while ago."

As for the harmonies being on only the last half of the record, Udell didn't disagree with Pitney's explanation, but he explained it more definitively. "We wanted the harmonies to help take the song to its dramatic ending," he said. "We certainly didn't think Gene's vocal needed any help. His singing was pitch perfect, note perfect, and faultless. Adding the harmonies just enhanced the dramatic build up to that astounding ending. No pop singer of that era but Gene Pitney could have done that.

"And, by the way, Mann and Weil didn't write that ending that way. My partner Gary Geld was a musical genius. He was brilliance personified. He and Garry Sherman wanted Gene to show off his voice and do something special at the end that would set this record apart from anything else on the radio. Gene was happy to oblige."

In a 2021 phone interview, Brian Hyland confirmed Peter Udell's recollections of how he and Geld got the "I'm Gonna Be Strong" gig. "Gene and I were always roommates when we did those *Dick Clark Caravan of Stars* tours," he explained. "We just had great fun together. I think Gary came to a couple of those shows, and I introduced him to Gene, and they just hit it off. Gene must have then reached out to him. Doesn't surprise me. Gary Geld was a brilliant songwriter who could do pretty much anything with any song in a studio, sometimes at a moment's notice. I can see why Gene would have wanted someone like him for that record. It sure was a great record."

Earlier, Pitney was quoted as saying he was "satisfied" with his vocal on this record while listening to the studio playback. Truth be told, he felt it was one of his best vocals ever. He reflected on the song for Chicago Tribune columnist Bob Greene in a 1997 interview. "What a song. The last phrase in the song, *"...how I'll break down and cry..."* how the notes change within that last word. All these years later I still get goosebumps every time I sing that song." Sometimes he jokingly anguishes over that last phrase. "Nowadays when I sing that song in concert, thirty years later, and I have to go for that note, I think to myself, 'Why was it so easy back then?' And, I'm always grateful that I can still hit THAT note. As they say in Australia, 'Good on ya, Gene.'"

Favorite Lyric: *"When you say it's the end I'll just hand you a line...I'll smile and say*

Gene appearing on *Connecticut Bandstand* on WNHC-TV in New Haven, Connecticut.

don't you worry I'm fine...And you'll never know darling after you kiss me goodbye...How I'll break down and cry." Heartbreak hidden in and camouflaged by conceit. It just doesn't mix well nor end well, does it? Pitney made that perfectly clear when he wrung out fifteen seconds of pain and torment on the last word *"cry-y-y-y"!*

Factoid: It has been said that Frankie Laine's record is "the marching band version" of "I'm Gonna Be Strong."

Factoid: Barry Mann and Cynthia Weil also wrote Gene's 1965 hit "Looking Through The Eyes of Love." And, just to remind you of their vast and meaningful contribution to pop music, here is just a partial list of some of the great songs they have written: "On Broadway," "Blame It On The Bossa Nova," "Only in America," "Walking in the

Rain," "You've Lost That Lovin' Feeling," "We Gotta Get Out of This Place," "(You're My) Soul and Inspiration," "Kicks," "Hungry," "Rock and Roll Lullaby," "Just Once," "Somewhere Out There," and "Here You Come Again."

Factoid: Frankie Laine's lackluster 1963 version of "I'm Gonna Be Strong" was produced by Terry Melcher and arranged by Jack Nitzsche. Melcher, the son of movie star Doris Day, would later go on to produce most of the hits for Paul Revere & The Raiders and the first two albums by The Byrds. But, in 1964 he was still wet behind the ears and had no idea what to do with Frankie Laine's record. In the book *Maybe I'm Doing It Wrong: The Life & Music of Randy Newman*, authors David and Caroline Stafford say this recording session was also fraught with anxiety and jitters for the young Melcher because of Phil Spector. They wrote, "Terry was romantically involved with Jackie DeShannon, who'd been providing some background vocals. Ominously, Phil Spector also had the hots for Jackie. Just as the session was about to begin, Phil slipped into the control room…sat himself down and glared at Terry for six hours." Later on, Jack Nitzsche would have a long list of musical accomplishments, including co-writing the iconic British Invasion hit "Needles and Pins" for The Searchers. His co-writer was Sonny Bono. Nitzsche also co-wrote the Oscar-winning song "Up Where We Belong" from the 1982 film *An Officer and a Gentleman*. His co-writer on that song was his then-wife, singer Buffy Sainte-Marie. Nitzsche was also part of the famed studio musicians group The Wrecking Crew; he was one of the co-architects of the Phil Spector "Wall-of-Sound"; and he played keyboard on a number of Rolling Stones songs, including "Paint It Black."

Factoid: Terry Melcher and Bruce Johnston of The Beach Boys were the creators of the one-hit wonder group The Rip Chords that had a Top 10 hit in 1963 with "Hey Little Cobra." Melcher's last big hit as a producer was "Kokomo" for The Beach Boys in 1988.

Factoid: Cyndi Lauper recorded a stunning version of this song…twice: first in 1980 when she was in the band Blue Angel, then she re-recorded it in 1994 under her own name. She was not as reserved as Gene Pitney was in his hit version!

Factoid: As songwriters, Gary Geld and Peter Udell wrote three hits for Brian Hyland: 1961's "Let Me Belong To You" and 1962's "Sealed With A Kiss" and "Ginny Come Lately." The pair also wrote the Gary Lewis hit "Save Your Heart For Me." Through the mid-1960s they also penned a number of other songs that showed up on Pitney albums, including "I Can't Run Away," "I'm Afraid To Go Home," "Down In The Subway," and "If Mary's There." Udell said that was Pitney returning the favor for their producing "I'm Gonna Be Strong" free of charge!

Factoid: Brian Hyland recorded "If Mary's There" and "I'm Afraid To Go Home" first. "They used my track of 'I'm Afraid To Go Home' for the Pitney record," he explained. "So, that's me playing the 12-string guitar on a Gene Pitney record!"

Factoid: In 1971, The Carpenters hit paydirt with the Geld-Udell composition "Hurting Each Other." It had been previously recorded by Jimmy Clanton and Ruby & The Romantics.

Factoid: Both Geld and Udell were theater-struck as kids, and their dream was to write Broadway musicals. Eventually they did. They were twice nominated for Broadway's *Tony Award*: in 1970 for their music and lyrics as part of "Best Musical" nominee *Purlie* and in 1975 for "Best Score" for the music and lyrics they wrote for *Shenandoah*.

Factoid: After a long and extraordinarily successful career as a musician, arranger, composer, and orchestrator on many hit records in the early 1960s as well as Broadway shows and movie soundtracks, Garry Sherman returned to his first career, sports podiatry. As of 2021, at the age of 88, he still maintains a full-time practice in New Jersey.

And, the last word goes to...Lynne Pitney: "This was such an enormous hit for Gene. It's such a recognizable song. Everyone knows it. But, this song always scared me. When I would watch him perform it live at shows I would sit there and just clench my teeth or hold my breath just waiting for him to hit those last magnificent notes. I always knew he was gonna do it, but I just wanted to make sure. I just wanted to always help him get those last few notes...and he always did it. He was always so proud of this song. I am, too."

Gene in concert in 1962. (Photo credit: Al Fedu / Connecticut Life)

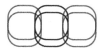

CHAPTER 12:
(IN THE) COLD LIGHT OF DAY

Lyrics by Larry Weiss and Scott English and Music by Larry Weiss

Fun Fact: The songwriting team that penned this vastly under-valued gem would go on to solo careers where they would separately write two of the biggest hits in the history of pop music: "Rhinestone Cowboy" and "Mandy."

Gene Pitney said: "It was such a perfect fit for my image. Yeah, I loved this one a lot. I was really disappointed it wasn't a Top 10." Larry Weiss and Scott English, who would later rise to superstardom in their profession, played a small part in Gene Pitney's career in 1967 with their song "(In The) Cold Light of Day." This really is the most gut-wrenching, heart-breaking song Gene Pitney recorded in his long career of gut-wrenching, heart-breaking songs. It seems like it could have come right out of his diary.

Pitney's trip from a plaintive pledge of love to a passion-filled pleading is twenty-eight seconds of pure vocal magic in the opening stanza: *"I've offered you all I have just to spend my life with you. (Just to be with you). But someone's got a claim on me; these few hours will have to do. So hold me tight, let's make this night last forever."*

Was it a night of passion and love between a single man and "the one who got away" or maybe a married guy who started some playful flirting that led to the realization that she was the one he really wanted to grow old with? We don't really know, but this was the kind of provocative story that Gene Pitney knew how to tell so very well.

"I don't remember how the song got to me or how it was presented to me," Pitney recalled, "but I'm glad I got it. Talk about melodrama! I don't remember, but if someone asked if this song was written for me, I would have to say yes."

Remarkably, co-writer Larry Weiss said the song was NOT written specifically for Gene. "I was just writing songs, hoping to get someone to record them," he said in an email interview about the song that Pitney recorded in 1966. "I don't remember how 'Cold Light of Day' got to him, but getting Gene Pitney to sing my song was a THRILL!"

"(In The) Cold Light of Day" was another archetypal – almost stereotypical – Gene Pitney love song. But, it was not a somber song about lost love like "I'm Gonna Be Strong" or a crestfallen song about broken-hearted love like "Only Love Can Break A Heart" or a pissed-off song about unrequited love like "It Hurts To Be In Love." This was an emotional song about verboten love…not completely unfamiliar territory for Gene Pitney. You remember "Twenty Four Hours From Tulsa"? That, too, was about a one-night stand. It certainly is never stated in "Twenty Four Hours From Tulsa" that the guy was married or otherwise committed to whomever the "dearest, darling" Dear Jane letter was written to, but that is certainly the insinuation.

"(In The) Cold Light of Day" came out close to the end of Gene's hit-making years, and, in the brutal terms of the music and radio industries, it was a "stiff." One of the real mysteries of the music business is how a record becomes a hit…or why it doesn't. Surprisingly, this perfect Gene Pitney recording of a perfect Gene Pitney song never even charted in the US.

The exceptionally fickle American record-buying public seemed to have moved on from Gene by then. If Pitney's label, Musicor Records, did a first run of 100,000 copies of the record, it's likely that 99,000 of them are still boxed up in a warehouse somewhere. But, because Pitney had long-lasting star power and far more devoted fans in the UK, "(In The) Cold Light of Day" spent six weeks in the charts there in March of 1967, peaking at #38.

Even though the song didn't work out for Gene, "(In The) Cold Light of Day" would prove to be the harbinger for bigger and better things on the horizon for the writers, Larry Weiss and Scott English.

Prior to having Pitney record "(In The) Cold Light of Day," the pair had written "Help Me Girl," which was a medium-sized hit for both The Outsiders and Eric Burdon (former lead singer for The Animals) in late 1966.

They finally got that first big hit that all songwriters want and need when the Chicago-based band The American Breed took the Weiss-English song "Bend Me, Shape Me" all the way to #5 on the *Billboard Hot 100* in late January 1968. Incidentally, that song was first recorded by the aforementioned band, The Outsiders.

But, even bigger things awaited them. In 1971, Scott English would co-write (with Richard Kerr) and record another

An early 1960s promotional photo.

heartbreaker of a song titled "Brandy." English's record hit #12 in the UK. Three years later, in 1974, Barry Manilow would record that same song, retitled as "Mandy," and take it to #1 in the US and Canada, #4 in Australia, and #11 in the UK.

Originally, English wasn't thrilled with all the changes Manilow made in his version of the song. The songwriter did, however, soften his stance later on telling a number of interviewers that once the checks started coming in he told Manilow that "I ended up loving you for buying me houses."

Why the title change? In 1974, Clive Davis, the head of Manilow's record label, Arista Records, suggested Manilow cover the Scott English song "Brandy." However, in the three years between Scott English's 1971 hit version of the song in England and Manilow's 1974 recording, the band called Looking Glass had hit #1 in 1972 with their record "Brandy (You're A Fine Girl)." Manilow, therefore, changed his title to "Mandy" to avoid confusion. "Mandy" became Barry Manilow's first US #1 and set him on the road to superstardom.

Contact proofs from a wooded photo shoot.

Larry Weiss took a bit longer to hit the big, big time. Eight years after penning "(In The) Cold Light of Day," Weiss wrote a seminal song about a singer struggling to get a break in the music business. He first put that song on his own album in 1974. His record label put it out as a single, and it got a little radio airplay, but it languished none-theless. Then, Glen Campbell heard the record on the radio. That song was "Rhinestone Cowboy."

In an interview with Bart Herbison of the Nashville Songwriters' Association, Weiss said, "Glen heard it and flipped. He literally pulled off to the side of the road and flipped." Weiss added that Campbell immediately went to his re-cord label, Capitol Records, and said he wanted to record "Rhinestone Cow-boy" as his next single.

Campbell recorded it in 1975, and the song soared up the charts, hitting #1 on the *Billboard Hot 100* on Sep-tember 6, 1975. It stayed in the charts for twenty-three weeks. In an inter-view for a documentary about Manuel Cuevas, the man who designed Glen Campbell's performance outfits, Weiss explained that he had long wanted to write such an iconic song.

"It was an aching for me that I wanted to have a great song," he said. "I had hits before, but I didn't feel I was writing on the level of creating what they call a 'copyright' or an 'evergreen.' I felt it was time for me to have that." Larry Weiss certainly accomplished that goal with "Rhinestone Cowboy."

In 2019, Bruce Springsteen did a cover version of "Rhinestone Cowboy" in his *Western Stars* documentary.

Scott English died in England on November 16, 2018, at the age of 81.

Larry Weiss is still alive and active as of this writing. Read all about his career on his website: www.rhinestonecowboy.com.

Favorite Lyric: *"So clock on the wall…please don't tick at all…just stand still."* Wow! Talk about being in the moment. Who hasn't been here either with the one you love or the one you shouldn't be with?

Factoid: Because of his connection to Gene with this song, Lynne Pitney said that Scott English offered "Brandy" to Gene first. "They wanted Gene to record it, and he said no. He just didn't think it was going to be a hit."

Factoid: Scott English is a cousin of songwriter Mark Barkan who wrote "Pretty Flamingo." It was originally titled "Flamingo," and Gene Pitney was the first artist to record the song. It was Manfred Mann who had the international hit with it, retitled as "Pretty Flamingo." Barkan also wrote a few other songs Gene recorded, including "Not Responsible" and "The Ship True Love Goodbye" (co-writer).

Factoid: "(In The) Cold Light of Day" was co-produced by Gene Pitney and Stan Kahan. Kahan also wrote songs under the name Bob Elgin. He co-wrote the 1961 hit "A Hundred Pounds of Clay" for another singer named Gene: Gene McDaniels.

Factoid: Larry Weiss also wrote "Weaving In and Out of My Life," which Gene recorded for his 1971 Musicor album *Ten Years Later.*

And, the last word goes to…Lynne Pitney: "I remember we were in England, and he had just recorded it, and he was on a TV show to perform it. Well, they go to a commercial break or something, and he's standing there ready to go, and all of a sudden he comes running over to me and asks, 'What's the first line?' This is the kind of song Gene could sink his teeth into. He loved this song, and so did I."

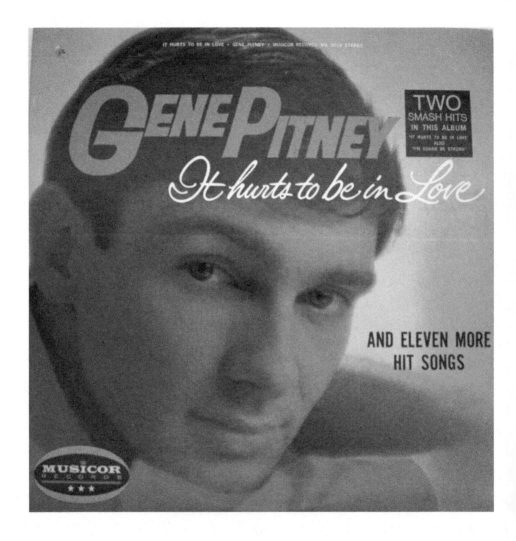

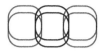

CHAPTER 13:
IT HURTS TO BE IN LOVE

Lyrics by Howard Greenfield and Music by Helen Miller

Fun Fact: In 1964, Gene Pitney "stole" this song away from Neil Sedaka who had recorded it first. Well, that's Pitney's version of how this hit came to be! Intrigue? Chicanery? Mix up? There is a lot going on with this record.

Gene Pitney said: "It was a complete steal!" There are many different stories floating around in cyberspace of how Gene Pitney ended up recording "It Hurts To Be In Love." They are all variations on a theme. Almost sixty years later, this is what we know: Neil Sedaka recorded it first. Gene Pitney recorded it second. Sedaka's record got shelved, but Pitney's record became a huge hit. The story about why Sedaka's version didn't get released is where the backstory gets muddled and convoluted.

Pitney gave his first-person account in a number of interviews over the years. Pitney recalled in an interview on WOLZ Radio in Fort Myers, Florida, "I went into the publisher, Don Kirshner at Screen Gems/Columbia Music, and I was looking for songs for a session. He played me a demo recording – actually it was a master – of Neil Sedaka, and it sounded great! I told him, 'That's a hit. Why doesn't he put that out?'"

Pitney then went on to explain why Sedaka didn't release the song: "Neil had just moved from label to label, and, to make a long story short, the producer at the new label didn't want to put out something that had been recorded without him. So, they went in and recorded new material, and they just shelved this thing. I asked Kirshner if I could use the track; they gave me the actual track that Sedaka had used. I learned the song exactly as Neil sang it. I even got the same girl to do the answers, Toni Wine, and we recorded it. That's me singing Neil Sedaka. He was my inspiration."

Legendary artists' agent and manager Dick Fox, a close personal and professional friend of Sedaka, responding to an inquiry about the song, wrote this in an email, "Neil and I have spoken about this song about a hundred times. The story that Neil always tells is that he had recorded the song, but his publisher didn't want to release it as they didn't have the publishing for the song. Gene got hold of Neil's record, took Neil's voice off, and took the exact record, arrangement, production and put his voice over Neil's track and, of course, had a big hit with it."

In his book *Always Magic In The Air*, Ken Emerson told the story this way: "(Tony) Orlando heard (Helen) Miller play another song that she had written with (Howard) Greenfield, a ballad entitled 'It Hurts To Be In Love,' and urged them to speed it up to a rock 'n' roll 4/4. When they followed his suggestion and made a demo at a stomping tempo, Sedaka was eager to cut the song even though it had been promised to Gene Pitney. Sedaka recorded his voice 'right over their demo' he recalled. His wife, Leba, and teenage writer Toni Wine, whom Kirshner had recently signed, added hand claps. But Sedaka's contract with RCA stipulated that he record in RCA's studios, where he was unable to recapture the demo's excitement."

Having recorded his voice over the Sedaka track that RCA rejected, Pitney ended up with a giant hit in 1964 that kept him in the charts after his parting with Burt Bacharach and Hal David. Emerson wrote that losing this record was crushing for Neil Sedaka. "Sedaka, in his view, missed a chance at a comeback."

There are at least four versions of Sedaka's recording of "It Hurts To Be In Love" available on CDs and on YouTube. "Takes 1, 2, and 3," as they are represented on the Astro Records release *Neil Sedaka In The Studio Volume 2 1958-1962*, are awful. There is fourth version where the musical track is more powerful and Sedaka's voice is double-tracked, and it is quite good. Razor & Tie Records issued that version in 2009 as part of the anthology release *The Definitive Collection*. That's the track that Pitney had used. You listen and decide who did the definitive version. As of this writing, they're all up on YouTube.

Pitney's vocal on this unyielding tale of unrequited love was far more indignant and far more red-blooded, All-American-male than Sedaka's. Sedaka's version lacks angst and emotion; Pitney's version is loaded with resentment, apprehension, and misgiving.

In this story of unwanted affection, Pitney pours his heart out over the legendary Gary Chester's drums, which sound like a heart getting ready to explode from dejection and hopelessness. Pitney tells his ungrateful lover in very well-enunciated and no uncertain terms, *"It hurts to be in love…when the only one you love…turns out to be someone…who's not in love with you…"*

It's probably not fair to compare the voices of Sedaka and Pitney on this song on an apples-to-apples basis. Sedaka was, in this phase of his career, a guy singing teeny bopper-oriented songs in a teeny bopper-oriented style. And, he was very successful at it. With his first hit – "(I Wanna) Love My Life Away" – already under his belt, Pitney was a couple of years beyond the teeny bopper stuff, and he had swerved into an almost Frank-Sinatra-of-his-generation persona with songs like "Only Love Can Break A Heart," "Town Without Pity," and "Half Heaven-Half Heartache." He sorta became the adult in the room.

It's evident when comparing the two recordings that Pitney's passionate and unrestrained vocal is what was needed to bring this record to life. Sedaka's single track demos are spiritless and unconvincing. He almost sounds exhausted. Sedaka did come close to getting it right on the double-tracked version.

Ironically, even in the years Sedaka was struggling to get discovered, he and his vocals took it on the chin a lot. Here's Ken Emerson quoting Sedaka in the aforementioned book *Always Magic In The Air*: "Pitching songs to Atlantic (Records), Sedaka tried in vain to interest (Jerry) Wexler and Ahmet Ertegun in his potential as a performer. 'I used to make demos, and they would say "Who's the girl on the demo?"' Sedaka said."

In a 2004 interview, Tony Orlando reiterated the Ken Emerson version of the story, adding some details about his suggesting a different take on the song. Again, he explained that the first time he heard the song it was a semi-ballad. "I was walking through Screen Gems/Columbia Music, and in the office I see Helen Miller, Jack Keller, and Howie Greenfield, and they say 'Listen to this song.' And they play 'It Hurts To Be In Love' for me like a ballad. They were doing it like 'Soldier Boy' by The Shirelles.

"So, I say 'Why don't you guys do this like the old Solitaires song 'Walking Along.'

You know, like Frankie Valli did 'Sherry.' To this day, I don't think Gene Pitney knows who changed the rhythm of that song! It might have made the difference!"

"It Hurts To Be In Love" co-writer Howard Greenfield grew up in the same Brighton Beach, New York, apartment building as Neil Sedaka and was Sedaka's longtime collaborator. Some of the massive Top 40 hits they wrote together included: "The Diary," "Oh Carol," "Stairway To Heaven," "Calendar Girl," "Little Devil," "Happy Birthday Sweet Sixteen," "Next Door To An Angel," and the pop classic "Breaking Up Is Hard To Do."

Greenfield was also a writing partner of Jack Keller for a few years. The two of them scored some huge hits including "Everybody's Somebody's Fool" and "My Heart Has A Mind of Its Own" for Connie Francis and the absolutely luxuriant Jimmy Clanton hit "Venus In Blue Jeans."

Greenfield's co-writer on "It Hurts To Be In Love," Helen Miller, was a bit of an enigma and a very atypical songwriter for the 1960s era. Prior to co-writing this hit for Pitney, she wrote the melodies for "Foolish Little Girl" (again with Greenfield) by The Shirelles, "Charms" by Bobby Vee, and "Make Me Your Baby" by Barbara Lewis.

In spite of a vast age difference, Toni Wine, who does the female vocals on this record, became close friends with Helen Miller. Wine was seventeen, and Miller was forty one when they worked together on this Pitney hit.

According to Wine, Miller lived on Long Island and worked in New York and led two separate lives that never intertwined. "She was 'old' already when I first met her," Wine said. "When I was a teenager she was already married and lived out on Long Island with her husband. Her husband was not in the business, and they led a very quiet life out on Long Island. Then she had a whole other life in the city when she would come in to do her music. She was a brilliant songwriter; she was a very aware kind of woman who was a great songwriter. She wrote with a lot of people. She really didn't talk to a lot of people about herself. She loved R&B. She was an R&B writer as well as a pop writer. She played piano with the best of them, chain smoked cigarettes, and she was a riot. She was a GREAT lady. She had a lot of interesting friends. She picked and chose her friends, and I was lucky to be one of them. And even though I was much younger, my mother allowed me to stay with her two and three nights if I was going to be doing her demos. I loved her."

Howard Greenfield died of AIDS in 1986. He was only 50 years old.

Helen Miller died in Florida in 2006 at the age of 81.

Favorite Lyric: *"It hurts to be in love…when the only one you love…turns out to be someone…who's not in love with you."* Howard Greenfield laid his cards on the table in the opening line. If you've ever had a secret crush on someone, loved someone from afar, or, maybe, loved someone you shouldn't, there is nothing you don't understand about this line.

Factoid: Since Pitney used the same track that Sedaka had used, Neil Sedaka always points out, proudly, that he is playing piano on the Pitney hit!

Factoid: Toni Wine, who did the female vocals on both Sedaka's and Pitney's recordings of "It Hurts To Be In Love," would later be the female half of The Archies who took "Sugar, Sugar" to #1 in 1969 by selling some six million copies. Ron Dante, who also fronted The Cufflinks ("Tracy"), was her male partner in The Archies. He later went on to produce and sing on a number of Barry Manilow albums.

Factoid: Toni Wine, as of this writing lives in Nashville, still tours as a back-up singer and keyboardist with Tony Orlando.

Factoid: Helen Miller and Howard Greenfield also wrote the 1963 Johnny Crawford hit "Rumors."

Factoid: Helen Miller would also co-write another big Gene Pitney hit, "Princess In Rags," with Roger Atkins.

And, the last word goes to…Lynne Pitney: "This was one of the first songs I remember Gene recording where he sang harmony with himself. I love that harmony. Gene really liked this record because it was a bit of a departure from the big, sad ballads he was known for. He liked the different sound it gave him. This is a great record, but I think that harmonizing made it even better. He did a great job 'copying' Neil Sedaka!"

Gene and Lynne leaving the Church of San Giovanni Battista in Ospedaletti, Italy, following their wedding on January 28, 1967.

Gene and Lynne (Gayton) were high school sweethearts. She also appears on "I've Got Five Dollars and It's Saturday Night."

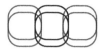

CHAPTER 14:
I'VE GOT FIVE DOLLARS
AND IT'S SATURDAY NIGHT

Lyrics and Music by Ted Daffan

Fun Fact: Gene Pitney & George Jones: The Most Promising Singing Group in the *18th Annual Billboard Country Music Poll* in 1965! Say what?

Gene Pitney said: "Truth be told though, I might have been just a little bit scared of George!" Pitney always remembered fondly that George Jones would call him "My little pal." "I don't think he knew who I was, and I know he couldn't remember my name… ever," Gene recalled. Gene also fondly remembered what George told him at the Nashville recording session for this song: "Let's kick some ass on this one." That they did.

This song was written and originally recorded in 1950 by Ted Daffan. It took six years to find a home with country star Faron Young, and he took it to #4 on the *Billboard* country charts in 1956. About 10 years later, in 1965, the song found a new home with Gene and country legend George Jones when they recorded it as a duet. It became a big country hit for them, peaking at #16 on the *Billboard* country chart.

"This was the kind of song you could just have fun with," Pitney explained. "It's your standard country music drinkin' and partyin' song. You can't screw it up."

Maybe…maybe not. Surprisingly, George Jones had previously recorded "I've Got Five Dollars and It's Saturday Night" in the 1950s. Pitney recalled that record company owner/record producer Pappy Daily reminded Jones that he had done so, and Jones said, "I must have been drunk and walked through it cuz I cain't remember it at all."

Pitney said that's when Jones decided to make amends. "Little Pal," he said, "let's show them what this song SHOULD sound like. I'm ready if you are. Let's kick some ass on this one." Both singers offered up spirited vocals, and neither tried to outdo the other. Pitney even added a little bit of a country twang here and there on his vocals. They did, indeed, record the definitive version of the song.

Gene Pitney rarely ventured too far afield from the comfort of his musical wheelhouse in his recording career. "She's A Heartbreaker" was an instance where he did and shouldn't have. It was a disastrous attempt at doing an R&B-flavored rock 'n' roll record for him. On the other hand, country music agreed with Pitney. His unique voice and splendid articulation were a perfect fit for the country genre of the 1960s.

For example, if Burt Bacharach's horns, strings, and piano on Gene's "Twenty Four Hours From Tulsa" had been exchanged for a steel guitar, maybe a mandolin or flamenco guitar, it would have been easily accepted as a country record as superb and as relevant as Marty Robbins' "El Paso." "Twenty Four Hours From Tulsa" likely would have gone to #1 on the country charts with the "Dear Jane" narrative of that song. Those were the essential elements of country music's biggest hits during that decade: steel guitar, mandolin, and plaintive lyrics.

The Pitney-Jones pairing came about when Jones, who was looking for a label after parting ways with United Artists, was signed to Musicor Records in 1965 by his longtime friend Pappy Daily. Daily had co-founded Starday Records in Texas and had discovered and signed Jones in the mid-1950s, starting him off on his propitious, if checkered, career.

Daily and Art Talmadge, who had been A&R (Artists & Repertoire) men and producers at Mercury Records, had snapped up a controlling interest in Musicor Records from Aaron Schroeder just prior to the Jones signing. A & R is the division of a record label that is responsible for finding talent and then leading the artistic and commercial development of those recording artists. An equally important facet of the job is to act as a liaison between the artist and the record label.

Gene Pitney's entrance into the country music field was more of a Musicor contrivance than anything else. In a remarkably shameless – but farsighted – cross-promotion plan meant to expand both Pitney's and Jones' fan base and expand and extend the label's existing catalogue without searching out and signing new talent, Musicor had the two superstars record a pair of duet albums which spawned "I've Got Five Dollars and It's Saturday Night" and a few lesser country hits. Oddly enough, it garnered the unlikely duo a top country music award as well.

Figure this one out: George and Gene won the award for "Most Promising Singing Group" in the *18th Annual Billboard Country Music Poll* in 1965! Yup…they beat out Ernest Tubb and Loretta Lynn, Roy Drusky and Priscilla Mitchell, Johnnie and Jonie Mosby, and…drum roll, please…George Jones and Melba Montgomery! Meanwhile, they had to settle for second place in the "Favorite Singing Group" category behind The Browns but ahead of Flatt and Scruggs, The Wilburn Brothers, and Carl and Pearl Butler.

In 1992 Gene talked with his longtime friend, Wayne Jones, on WWUH Radio in Hartford, Connecticut, about working with George Jones and their unlikely pairing. "That's one of the better things that [Musicor] did," he mentioned. "It was purely a ploy by the record company to create more product with the people they had on the label. George was signed to the label, but he was recording purely country stuff, and I was signed to the label recording purely pop stuff. Art Talmadge had the idea, 'I wonder if these two guys can sing together.'

"George and I talked about it afterwards and laughed about it. George was frightened of singing with someone like me, and I was frightened of singing with someone like him. It went so easy; we just gelled together so well.

"George was a wild man. I knew him when he was in the middle of all that stuff, and I remember having an insurance physical. I was sitting down having lunch with two guys from the insurance company, and they said that they had just gone down to see George on his ranch. He was out with his Cadillac in the field. He got mad at a horse, and he chased the horse in his Cadillac and ran the car over a culvert or something and destroyed the undercarriage and just left it there and went into town and bought another one. That's the way George was.

"I watched him on a special about a year ago. It was George Jones and Randy Travis. Randy's a terrific artist, but when George sang a song you could just tell the difference. Maybe you gotta live it to be able to sing it. All that experience and all those rough times. There is no man in country music who can bend a lyric the way that George Jones can. It was really a privilege for me to be able to work with the guy."

Recalling how he prepared for the session with Jones, Pitney said he quickly realized he was going to have to do things Jones' way. "George and I met with Pappy Daily at a motel near the recording studio to look over songs for the album and feel each other out, you know? How should we do this? Who's gonna take lead on which songs? Keys, arrangements, et cetera. I realized very quickly that George was bound and determined to do things his way. He was not gonna change his phrasing or style to suit mine. And, since he and Pappy were longtime friends, I was the one who was going to change to fit into what George wanted to do. And it worked out great. In the studio our voices blended beautifully. George and I had no problems at all. None. Of course, George could be very intimidating. There were some days when I wasn't sure what was gonna happen."

Pitney also clearly remembered the photo shoot for the album covers for the Nashville recording sessions. "Pappy Daily wanted to put me in cowboy clothes for the pho-

tos," Gene remembered with a chuckle. "I had no intention of wearing that kind of outfit, but Pappy was the co-owner of my record label, so I had to handle it prudently. I talked to George about it. He told me he didn't care what I wore and nobody else should either. That was George. A famous nonconformist. He also had a bit of a temper. So George cooked up a scheme utilizing both of those

The power trio of Musicor Records: Gene flanked by co-owners Art Talmadge (left) and Aaron Schroeder (right).

traits. He went to Pappy acting all incensed about putting me in cowboy clothes. He told Pappy, 'I'm the fucking country star here, not that little pipsqueak pop singer. Put him in pipsqueak clothes, Pappy, or I ain't doing the photos. Got it?'

"The next day Pappy and I went to a nearby men's stores and got me my 'pipsqueak' outfit consisting of a red shirt and light blue pants. It's the best we could do under the circumstances."

Another issue that had to be decided was billing. Was it going to be George Jones & Gene Pitney or Gene Pitney & George Jones? "I don't know how that was settled," Pitney admitted. "All I know is that Art Talmadge, who came from more of a pop music background at Mercury Records, wanted me to get top billing. Pappy, who had a long country music background and was George's friend, wanted George on top. We know who won, but I don't know what went into that decision. I would have been happy either way. Had I been asked I probably would have said George should be top billing. He earned that with his long career."

Musicor put out two albums featuring Pitney and Jones: *George Jones & Gene Pitney* and *It's Country Time Again.*

Since the George and Gene pairing had worked out so well for Musicor, the label then had Gene record a duet album with another label mate, Melba Mont-

Gene in a performance on an early UK tour.

gomery. She had recorded a number of duets with Jones down through the years, including their 1963 smash "We Must Have Been Out of Our Minds," which she had written. The duet albums Pitney recorded with both Jones and Montgomery were sheer – if unwitting – prescience on Daily's part.

While the duet albums and singles were relatively successful in country music circles, the pop music industry, by and large, ignored them. That lack of recognition and acknowledgement denied Musicor, Daily, and Talmadge the respect and credibility that they deserved for the trailblazing concept of pairing up pop and country megastars. Dying in 1987, Pappy Daily didn't live to see the burst of popularity that star duets would have in the 1990s. Talmadge, who died in 2006, had to be galled by it.

Songwriter Ted Daffan has three other country classics to his credit: the seminal "Truck Driver's Blues" and two much-covered country anthems of unrequited love, "Born to

An early mock up of Gene's *Only Love Can Break A Heart* album released in 1962.

Lose," which Pitney recorded solo, and "I'm a Fool to Care," a duet. Both recordings are on the *George Jones & Gene Pitney* album. Daffan died in 1996 at the age of 84.

Favorite Lyric: *"I gotta work next week but that's alright…I got five dollars and it's Saturday night…"* Well, that sums up the "Great American Weekend," doesn't it? And, to prove it, over thirty years later Loverboy had the same perspective with a slightly different point of view in their hit "Working for the Weekend": *"Everybody's working for the weekend…everybody wants a little romance…everybody's goin' off the deep end… everybody needs a second chance."*

Factoid: Lynne Gayton, Gene's girlfriend at the time, did the handclaps on the song and participated in the famous *"Heys!"* that started the song off then punctuated each verse. She and Gene married in 1967.

Factoid: Pitney and Jones performed a very fun live and lively version of the song in 1965 on Jimmy Dean's ABC-TV show with Dean doing the *"Heys!"* Gene was highly animated as he coached Dean on when to come in with a *"Hey!"* Dean looked like he was having the time of his life. George Jones looks like he's trying to have fun and play along, but he really comes off as nonplussed if not bewildered.

Factoid: Country music star Narvel Felts said in a 2000 *Gene Pitney International Fan Club Newsletter* interview, "I always thought that Gene's voice was very well suited to sing country music, and if he had decided to go in that direction he would have been a very successful country artist. I thought it was very refreshing to hear Gene Pitney on country radio stations. I thought George Jones was a lucky man that Gene would duet with him. If Gene hadn't been a pop star I'm sure he would have been a BIG country star. He was that good. Plus, Gene had the instincts to pick great material."

And, the last word goes to…Lynne Pitney: "I'm on this record, and I never received a penny for it *(laughter)*! But, I probably got dinner. We were in Nashville with Pappy Daily, George Jones, and Melba Montgomery. We were all just clapping our hands and yelling 'Hey!' for that record. It's the best record ever *(laughter)*!!! It's a fun record. It just makes you feel good. And, don't forget, I was on it! When you listen to George and Gene and how their voices just blended together even though they were so completely different, they did a really, really good job. Gene was thrilled to record with George Jones."

♪ust One Smile

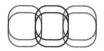

CHAPTER 15:
JUST ONE SMILE
and NOBODY NEEDS YOUR LOVE

Lyrics and Music by Randy Newman

Fun Fact: Pitney struggled to make sense out of both of these songs composed by Randy Newman, who would go on to win multiple Academy Awards.

Gene Pitney said: "When I heard Randy Newman's demo of 'Nobody Needs Your Love' I thought to myself 'This is NOT a good song.'" And he said this about "Just One Smile," another Randy Newman composition: "My producer hated it; my arranger hated it; and my record company hated it." These songs both ended up being massive hits for him in England. Pitney's American fans, however, were shortchanged. "Nobody Needs Your Love" was never released in the States. "Just One Smile" barely cracked the Top 40. More on that lamentable turn of events later.

Long before Randy Newman got his first Oscar nominations in 1981 for "Best Original Score" for the movie *Ragtime* and "Best Original Song" for "One More Hour" from that same movie or his first Grammy Award in 1984 for "Best Instrumental Composition" for "The Natural" from the Robert Redford movie of the same name, he wrote these two pop songs that caught Gene Pitney's ear. Pitney took Newman's song "Nobody Needs Your Love" to #2 in the UK in the summer of 1966. He immediately followed with "Just One Smile," which was released in late 1966 and went to #8 in the UK in early 1967.

To say the trailblazing Pitney jumpstarted the career of the then-23-year-old Randy Newman would be an understatement. With those two monster hits, Pitney handed him the keys to open the doors to a fascinating and intriguing career as a singer/songwriter. To be fair, the great Cilla Black had the first UK hit with a Randy Newman song when she took the not-so-pop-ish and now-forgotten "I've Been Wrong Before" into the UK Top 20 in 1965.

There are no ifs, ands, or buts about it though, it was Gene Pitney who was the key player in establishing Randy Newman in the music industry. Newman was under contract as a songwriter to Aaron Schroeder, Pitney's manager and mentor, in the mid-'60s and that's how his songs got to Pitney.

Pitney often philosophized about the genesis of those two giant UK hits, "Just One Smile" and "Nobody Needs Your Love." "That was the time when Randy was finding his way as a hit songwriter," Pitney explained. "Singers and bands at the start of their careers, when they are fighting for success, have to work harder to get noticed. They're creatively hungry, and they're out to show the world they can do it. That is often when they crank out their best work. Songwriters are no different. I remember how I agonized over my early songs and how hard I worked, knocking on door after door in New York, trying to get someone to like them and appreciate them.

"Whatever was driving Randy emotionally in 1965 and 1966 drove him to write some phenomenal songs. There was something going on in his life that drove him to write the heartbreaking songs that I got. I can only describe them as sorrowful, but they struck a note with British teenagers, didn't they?"

Pitney told "Wild" Wayne Jones from WWUH Radio in Hartford, Connecticut, that Newman's demos for these songs were pretty primitive. "He wouldn't go into a studio, and he would only make the demos with him playing piano into a tape recorder."

In a 1999 *Gene Pitney International Fan Club Newsletter*, Pitney said "Just One Smile" was a tough song to turn into a hit record. "I knew the song was there somewhere, but Randy's demo completely hid it because of the way he recorded it. But, I was determined and saw it through. When the orchestra started to play the arrangement and everything fell into place, I was very relieved."

NOBODY NEEDS YOUR LOVE
WORDS AND MUSIC BY RANDY NEWMAN

RECORDED
BY

GENE
PITNEY

ON
STATESIDE
RECORDS

3/-

JANUARY MUSIC CORPORATION. NEW YORK
A. SCHROEDER MUSIC PUBLISHING CO. LTD.,
15, BERKELEY STREET, LONDON. W.1
SOLE SELLING AGENTS: CAMPBELL CONNELLY & CO. LTD., 10, DENMARK STREET, LONDON. W.C.2

Again, talking to Jones, he added, "I knew that if I could sit down and live with that thing long enough I could get out of it what I heard. I found a common note that threaded through the entire chorus. To me, it's one of the best songs I ever recorded."

He explained it in a little more detail in a 1993 interview for *Goldmine Magazine* with writer Dawn Eden. "I had to fight so hard to get a Randy Newman song called 'Just One Smile' done," Pitney told her.

"Randy Newman used to make these horrible demos," Pitney continued. "He was a very eccentric guy, and they couldn't get him into the studio, so he would always do his own demos on a tape recorder at home. When he did them, he would leave several bars in between each line of the song, and it stretched everything out so bad.

"I heard 'Just One Smile,' and I kinda lived with it. I got it down pat on the piano, and I started to condense it because I knew there was something there, and everybody hated it. The producer hated it. The arranger hated it. Everybody tried to talk me out of it, and I put my foot down, and I said, 'No. There's a great song here somewhere.'"

Thank goodness he did lay down the law. "Just One Smile" MAY be Pitney's magnum opus.

Over an opening guitar being bleakly strummed as it lurches into a doleful piano, Pitney sublimely coaxes us into his story of lost love and abandonment. Before long, listeners are in the middle of his heartbreak and pain and shaking their heads that any-one could dump this remarkably sensitive lover. They are cheering – almost begging her – for that "smile" for him. For Gene…because he is selfless in the face of romantic treachery. *"All I've had has been taken from me…now I'm cryin' and tears don't become me…Just one smile…the pain's forgiven."*

Nobody did heartbreak better than Gene Pitney. Nobody. Nobody should have tried. Gene Pitney was the king of the hill. He earned his "Prince of Pain" moniker with every little note he sang in this song. Pitney was also the poster boy for elegance in the 1960s, from his always clean-cut and dapper "look" to his memorable choice of songs – like "Just One Smile" – to his glorious voice. In the world of 1960s pop music male singers, he was peerless.

Newman proved too elusive to be caught for an interview about "Just One Smile" and "Nobody Needs Your Love." These songs are discussed, albeit briefly, in the Randy Newman biography *Maybe I'm Doing It Wrong: The Life & Music of Randy Newman* by David & Caroline Stafford.

Condescension for pop music flows from the pens of these authors like lava from a furious volcano. They choose to ignore that, like movies and TV shows, oftentimes pop songs require the suspension of disbelief. Otherwise the standard two-and-a-half or three-and-a-half minute pop song would not exist. If shortcuts and dubious or debatable imagery weren't employed by the songwriters, all of their songs would end up being Herman Wouk novels on vinyl.

In their 2016 book they wrote, "'Nobody Needs Your Love,' never released in the US, went to number two in the UK. It is a song of stirring misery – at this stage in his career Randy seemed incapable of writing a song about anything except exquisite torture. *'Why can't it be like before? Don't you need me anymore?,'* Gene sings, and *'if you don't want me I don't want to live.'* Journalist Tony Parsons described the record, with some accuracy, as a 'suicide note,' but then again, Gene Pitney could have made 'Happy Birthday To You' sound like a cry for help."

A suicide note? Really? Point missed. "Nobody Needs Your Love" is actually a love letter to a lost love. He's been dumped, and Pitney backs into his pledge of love with the simple-but-heartfelt phrase *"…nobody needs your love more than I do…"*

Certainly Pitney takes angst to a new level here, but that's what makes this record so terrific. The sadness in his voice is palpable. He wants her back; he needs her back. *"If you care about me…please don't leave without me…"*

"When I first heard Randy's rambling demo," Pitney recalled, "the melody was there, but it wasn't there." Pitney was right. Other singers have tackled this song but missed a lot of the melody.

Newman's elementary melody doesn't distract from the agony-filled lyrics. It would be fair to say the melody is a bit melancholy. It would also be fair to say it is not gloomy and that it actually pulls the listener into this story because it is so pretty and so pleasant. A nice touch on Newman's part. And, lest there be any doubt, it needs to be reiterated: Nobody did heartbreak better than Gene Pitney. Nobody. Nobody should have tried.

As for "Just One Smile," the authors of the Newman biography wrote: "'Just One Smile' is the plaint of a crushed soul, so reduced in self-esteem that the glimpse of a single smile is all he dare ask of his faithless lover (*'…one little dream to build my world upon…'*); or, to put it another way, it's the scream of the 'bottom' in a co-dependent SM relationship. Either way, you listen and, even as your heart aches with empathy for the poor unfortunate's plight, the sensible part of your brain is thinking 'you need to end this relationship and get out of the house. No second thoughts. Just do it. Now, I know that's hard, but I'm going to give you some phone numbers of organisations that can offer you counselling and practical advice.'"

Good night nurse! "Just One Smile" is a 2:46 pop record, not a PhD dissertation on love. The Staffords are more than a little full of themselves here, trying to prove how brainy they are. Instead, they come across as snarky.

Fortunately, some common sense prevailed in this book when Randy Newman summed up this chapter of his career in a very pragmatic fashion. "When I wrote 'I've Been Wrong Before,' 'Just One Smile,' and 'Nobody Needs Your Love' my publisher at the time, Aaron Schroeder (also Gene Pitney's manager), was so happy, because they were songs with hooks and it looked like I would go on to earn some money. But I didn't continue doing it.

"I'm not saying that I could have written millions of hit songs if I decided to; that's a talent I may not have. Burt Bacharach has it; he knows where the gold is. When Bacharach gets his hook, he knows it's there. I've come to appreciate him."

Most of Pitney's records were released in the UK on the Stateside label (stylized on the record label as $tateside). Owned by EMI, Stateside's sole purpose was to license and release American records, from many different labels, in England. It was a great business model. Stateside cherry-picked the records it wanted to release, then made them hits in the UK.

Stateside was able to do this for three reasons: major label money, major label moxie, and, because England is about the size of Alabama. The size of the country made marketing, promotion, and distribution quite easy compared to doing it in the US. Not all of the records they licensed were hits, but most of them were.

Musicor Records, under the ownership and leadership of Aaron and Abby Schroeder, was pretty much a mom-and-pop operation. They just couldn't compete with the major labels like RCA Victor, Columbia, Capitol, et al. According to Abby Schroeder, Stateside could push a good record into the British Top 10 by spending about $5,000 in promotion. "We didn't have $5,000 to spend on promoting one record," she said in a phone interview. "Even if we did – how do you spread $5,000 across fifty states to make any kind of splash?"

It's unclear who chose not to release "Nobody Needs Your Love" in the US. Abby Schroeder, who is a huge Randy Newman fan, doesn't remember. As for "Just One Smile," she said, "There was just no money in the budget to push it." Schroeder does admit that Pitney acted as his label's de facto promotion department through his non-stop touring at home and abroad. "And, Gene was always on the phone doing radio and print interviews, and he did every local and national TV show he could. He was a workhorse."

Randy Newman's stock-in-trade likely was never going to be writing pop hits, as was mentioned earlier. Becoming successful in some other areas of the music industry seems to have been his destiny. He comes by his musical gifts naturally, coming from admirable musical and songwriting stock. He had three uncles who composed movie scores in Hollywood. One, Alfred Newman, won nine Academy Awards. He was awarded Oscars for *Alexander's Ragtime Band* (1938), *Tin Pan Alley* (1940), *The Song*

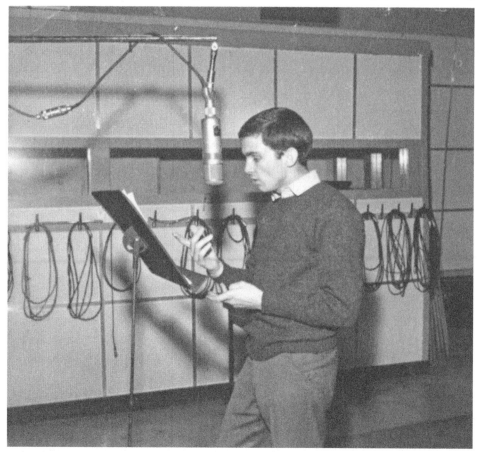

Early 1960s recording session.

of Bernadette (1943), *Mother Wore Tights* (1947), *With a Song in My Heart* (1952), *Call Me Madam* (1953), *Love Is a Many Splendored Thing* (1955), *The King and I* (1956), and *Camelot* (1967).

Randy's uncle Lionel Newman picked up eleven Oscar nominations during his career and won the Oscar for "Best Score of a Musical Picture" with co-writer Lennie Hayton for *Hello Dolly!* in 1969.

And, Randy's uncle Emil Newman was nominated for an Oscar for his musical direction for 1941's *Sun Valley Serenade* starring Glenn Miller.

Randy Newman eventually graduated from pop music to what seemed almost like the family business, which is, writing music for TV shows and films, garnering umpteen Oscar, Grammy, Emmy, and Golden Globe nominations and awards. He won his first Academy Award in 2001 for "Best Original Song" for "If I Didn't Have You" from *Monsters, Inc.* It was sung over the closing credits by John Goodman and Billy Crystal.

Newman got a star on the Hollywood Walk of Fame in 2010. He was inducted into the Songwriters Hall of Fame in 2002, the Rock & Roll Hall of Fame in 2013, and the Grammy Hall of Fame in 2015. At this time (2021) he is still alive, working, and relevant. He lives in Los Angeles.

Randy Newman is now universally regarded as a superstar in film music composition, but it should be remembered that his incomparable songwriting career began in earnest with a couple of pop songs that Gene Pitney recorded and turned into major hits in England in 1966.

Randy Newman's website is www.randynewman.com.

Favorite Lyric ("Just One Smile"): *"How I wish I could say all the things that I want to say…if some way you could see what's in my heart…"* Geez! Does this not sum up the dismay of every tongue-tied teenage boy in love with his teen queen? There is no worse feeling than not being able to truthfully tell her what she wants/needs to hear to keep her from losing interest or, worse yet, walking into someone else's open arms.

Favorite Lyric ("Nobody Needs Your Love"): *"I've tried so hard to make you see… that I'd be what you want me to be. But no matter what I do…I just can't get through to you. You don't want to love me…or are you tired of me?"* Randy Newman summed up romantic despair with a capital D here!

Factoid: While "Just One Smile" was a certified smash in the UK, it was what the music industry calls a "stiff" in the US. It topped out at #64 in 1967.

Factoid: No producer is listed for "Just One Smile" on either the Musicor (USA) or Stateside (UK) 45. On the Musicor album *Just One Smile*, Pitney is listed as the co-producer with Stan Kahan. As Pitney mentioned above, Kahan didn't care for the song. Garry Sherman is the arranger who wasn't fond of the song either. Sherman was also the arranger for "Nobody Needs Your Love." Pitney once said that Kahan told him that he should "give the song to PJ Proby and let him sort this mess out." Listen to the Blood, Sweat & Tears 1967 version of the song, and you'll see what he meant.

Factoid: The first recording of "Just One Smile" was done by The Tokens in 1965 as the flipside to their single "The Bells of St. Mary." Dusty Springfield, Sheena Easton, Scott Walker, and Blood, Sweat & Tears are some of the artists who have also covered this song.

Factoid: As of this writing (2021) Randy Newman has won a total of seven Grammy Awards and two Oscars.

Factoid: Randy Newman had his own hit record as a singer in 1977 with a song he says he wrote as a joke, "Short People." It hit #2 on the *Billboard Hot 100*. He also wrote Three Dog Night's 1970 smash "Mama Told Me Not To Come" and the British Top 10 hit "Simon Smith and the Amazing Dancing Bear" for The Alan Price Set.

And, the last word goes to…Lynne Pitney: "Wasn't Gene great? 'Just One Smile' is a great, great song. This is my brother Scott's favorite song that Gene ever did. I listen to this, and I fall in love with Gene all over again. No one can listen to this record and not be in awe of how Gene could interpret a song. He knew who his audience was. He always knew what they wanted to hear and how to sing it to them. It is so hard for me to pick a favorite song of his, but this would certainly be in my Top 5. I also like 'Nobody Needs Your Love' a lot. I love the Randy Newman songs that Gene recorded. This one just sounds like it came so naturally to Gene. I remember this period of his career, and I remember thinking, 'I can't believe how good he is, and he just keeps getting better.' He was really enjoying his career at this point, and you can tell on both of these songs."

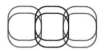

CHAPTER 16:
LAST CHANCE TO TURN AROUND

Lyrics and Music by Bob Elgin, Vic Millrose, and Tony Bruno

Fun Fact: Stan Kahan, who co-produced this record and co-wrote this song, and Garry Sherman, who arranged the music, also co-owned a production company that did commercial jingles for everything from laundry detergent to soda.

Gene Pitney said: "It wasn't challenging in its structure or in its notes, so I didn't have to concentrate on that aspect of it. I could just sell the hell out of the story." This was a song Gene loved to sing in concert because it was one of the few upbeat songs that was a hit for him, and it provided balance for all the ballads he had to sing in his show. "While all those weepy ballads made my career, I have to break them up just to keep myself awake as much as the audience," he once joked.

The song was co-written by Pitney's longtime friend, producer-songwriter Stanley Kahan. He used "Bob Elgin" as a songwriting alias. Kahan and Pitney produced this record. Garry Sherman, Kahan's partner in Sherman & Kahan Associates, a record production company, also did a lot of arranging on Pitney songs, and his name is all over albums like *Just One Smile, Blue Gene, Backstage (I'm Lonely)*, and *Looking Through The Eyes of Love*. On some of the 45 rpm versions of this song Sherman is credited with "Arrangement & Conception." While that does sound like an R-rated movie title, Pitney explained that Sherman came up with the idea, the concept if you will, of making the backing musical track give the impression of wheels turning and burning.

"Garry's track gave the song this sense of urgency and tension," Pitney pointed out. "It sounds like the music you'd hear behind a chase scene in an action movie. I loved the track right away, and it made me rise to the occasion with my vocal. I really loved this record."

To brilliant effect, Pitney and Kahan double-tracked Pitney's vocals at just the right time on this song. The double-tracking plays out on what might be considered secondary choruses:

I'm getting' out of town (I'm getting' out of town)
I won't back down (I won't back down)
I won't back down (I won't back down)

I saw her with that guy (I saw her with that guy)
That's the reason why (that's the reason why)
I'll be passin' by (I'll be passin' by)

He then explodes in a combination of bravado and bluster on the main chorus:

Last exit to Brooklyn, last chance to turn around
Last exit to Brooklyn, gonna keep these wheels of mine coverin' ground

"Last Chance To Turn Around" comes off as "It Hurts To Be In Love" on steroids. It was the type of song Pitney could perform without breaking a sweat. As so often is the case, Pitney's vocal on this record is unrivaled, and it becomes perfectly clear why so many of his contemporaries were in awe of him then – and to this day.

Pitney liked the touch that Stanley Kahan brought to his records. "We were simpatico," Gene said with a smile. "Stan always knew what was needed on each record; he knew how to explain it to me; and he pushed me to get it just right. He was in a class with Burt Bacharach but never sought the limelight like Burt did."

Kahan also produced all but one of the songs on Pitney's *Just One Smile* album, including the powerful and memorable title track, as well as many songs on the *Backstage (I'm Lonely)* album.

As a songwriter, Elgin/Kahan also co-wrote hits like the Gene McDaniels' smash "A Hundred Of Pounds of Clay," "Killer Joe" for The Rocky Fellers, and "The Girl With The Golden Braids" for Perry Como.

FLYING MUSIC PRESENTS

GENE PITNEY
IN CONCERT

with special guest
BOBBY CRUSH

TWENTY FOUR HOURS FROM TULSA
I'M GONNA BE STRONG
BACKSTAGE
SOMETHINGS GOTTEN HOLD OF MY HEART
TOWN WITHOUT PITY
NOBODY NEEDS YOUR LOVE

See reverse for details

Vic Millrose co-wrote "This Girl Is A Woman Now" for Gary Puckett. He was also a songwriting partner with Mark Barkan, who wrote a number of album tracks for Pitney as well as the international smash for Manfred Mann, "Pretty Flamingo." The pair also penned "I'll Try Anything" for Dusty Springfield and "I'm Indestructible" for Jack Jones.

In a 2021 phone interview, his son, Peter Millrose, said his dad was "a songwriter who didn't sing," and when The Beatles introduced the concept of the singer/songwriter, "guys like him, well, their days were numbered." Even though Millrose had a couple of sizeable hits, Peter said, "They did not pay his way into old age." Vic Millrose died in 2020.

"Last Chance To Turn Around" was Tony Bruno's biggest hit. In 1963, he scored a Top 20 R&B hit with Chuck Jackson's version of "Tell Him I'm Not Home," a song he co-wrote with his wife, Brenda Bruno. The couple also wrote the very underappreciated "Yesterday's Kisses," recorded by Maxine Brown. Bruno was a producer for a period of time at Scepter Records and recorded for Capitol Records in the late 1960s.

Over the years, Pitney fans wondered if there was a connection between this song and the 1964 novel *Last Exit To Brooklyn* by American writer Hubert Selby, Jr., because of the song's chorus: *"Last exit to Brooklyn, last chance to turn around…Last exit to Brooklyn…gonna keep these wheels of mine coverin' ground."*

Pitney always said, "Don't know. I didn't know about the book at that time so, obviously, I never asked."

The book came out a year before his record, and it dealt with the hard life in lower class Brooklyn where drugs and violence ran rampant in the 1950s, but nothing like that is alluded to in the song. "I think the guys probably just liked the sound of that phrase," Pitney said. "They were all New York and New Jersey guys, and the word "Brooklyn" seemed to set a scene for them. It created a realistic picture in the mind's eye of the listener. I was just glad it wasn't 'last exit to Schenectady.' I can't imagine singing that for thirty or forty years."

The story told in "Last Chance To Turn Around" is the type of song that was his bread and butter; i.e., the woman he loved did him wrong, and now she has to pay for it. Pitney once pointed out casually that "if you change the chorus from 'last exit to Brooklyn' to 'last exit to Nashville' or 'last exit to Georgia' you'd have the perfect country song. I can hear George Jones or Willie singing it."

Favorite Lyric: *"Last night I caught that girl lyin', tryin' to deceive me...and now all of these tears she's cryin' I'm not buyin' you better believe me."* Lyin', tryin', cryin', buyin'. Elgin, Millrose, and Bruno nailed it: simple but spirited words in a tenacious statement. And, without a doubt, they are so true in so many romances and relationships from high school to college to real life.

Factoid: Garry Sherman, credited with "Arrangement & Conception" on this song, played keyboards and arranged Van Morrison's iconic 1967 hit "Brown Eyed Girl." On some Musicor albums Sherman's name is spelled Gary.

Factoid: Garry Sherman retired from the music business to become a full-time podiatrist in Cedar Knolls, NJ.

And, the last word goes to...Lynne Pitney: "I didn't like this record for the most part. I liked the beginning of it; I didn't like the chorus. This sounded, to me, more like a song that Bobby Vee should have recorded. It was more his style. I think Gene was too good for it. It doesn't appeal to me. I don't know why, but it just doesn't."

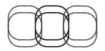

CHAPTER 17:
LET THE HEARTACHES BEGIN

Lyrics and Music by Tony Macaulay and John McLeod

Fun Fact: Gene Pitney got it right…Long John Baldry got the #1!

Gene Pitney said: "I wasn't sure I should do it. Long John did the definitive version." This song is included only because the author of this book, Dave McGrath, asked Gene Pitney to record it. This chapter is written in first person by Dave.

Gene's hit-making career waned in the late 1960s. Then, with a boost from a longtime fan of his, singer Marc Almond (from Soft Cell), Gene soared to the top of the British charts in January 1989, duetting with Almond on "Something's Gotten Hold of My Heart." The duet was a cover of Gene's solo version of this song that went into the British Top 10 in late 1967.

Hoping to capitalize on that sudden rush of renewed chart success for Gene, his UK tour promoters, Flying Music, arranged a deal with Polydor Records in 1990 to put out a Gene Pitney greatest hits repackage. Ironically, the deal included Gene also recording cover versions of eight other songs to appear on the album, which was to be titled *Gene Pitney: Backstage, The Greatest Hits and More.*

In a phone discussion with Gene as to what songs he should cover, I suggested one of my all-time favorite records, the Long John Baldry song "Let The Heartaches Begin."

"Let The Heartaches Begin" was not a hit in the US, but, it was a #1 for Baldry in the UK in 1967. The UK was the target market for this new Pitney album, so I figured, why not give them a song they already knew and loved. Gene asked me to send him the lyrics, so I did.

"This was such a big hit for Long John, and I was more than a bit apprehensive to record it," Pitney recalled. "When I had the discussions about the album with David Courtney, who produced it, I told him flat out I didn't want to do it the same way that Baldry did it. So we did a little more upbeat version."

I had always thought Gene should record this song. It was the perfect Gene Pitney song. Gorgeous melody; lyrics that encapsulated the heartache and grief of letting love go; actually throwing that love away before coming to the wistfully bitter realization that *"I was a fool to let my baby go."*

Let me back up a bit here. In 1985, when I went to work for Gene reorganizing and operating his International Fan Club and developing, producing, and selling tour merchandise for him, he completely managed every aspect of his career. Gene rarely sought or took advice from anyone about his career choices. The only exceptions to that rule in the years I worked with him were: Neil Warnock, his longtime agent in London; Derek Nichol, his UK tour promoter for about twenty years with Flying Music; Mark Howes, his tour promoter at the time of his death; and his New York-based financial advisor.

So, I was shocked and pleasantly surprised about a week after that phone discussion when he called to tell me he was going to record "Let The Heartaches Begin." We had been working together for about six years at the time, but he had never asked me to get involved in this aspect of his career.

It took Gene every day of those six years to come to trust me, trust my musical judgement, and trust my radio ears and to believe I always had his best interest at heart. He did not come to those decisions easily with anyone in his life, and I felt this was the moment I really became a part of his inner circle. It was the beginning of the shift of our relationship from star-and-employee to star-and-friend. While I did become a very close confidant of Gene's, I was never an advisor.

I knew of "Let The Heartaches Begin" because British Invasion music has always been near and dear to me. During my formative teen years I was consumed by music and radio. And, in a perfect storm, the British Invasion took place just as I was beginning to form my own tastes in music. By seventh grade I knew I wanted to be on the radio, and I dreamed of somehow getting involved with the music that I loved and the singer whom I admired. My radio career began in 1970; Gene made my other dream come true when he asked me to work with him in 1985.

When he was asked to cover eight songs for the Polydor album I thought lightning could strike twice in the UK with this magnificent song. After all, Gene was coming off a huge #1 with "Something's Gotten Hold of My Heart," and this song was the perfect follow up. On top of that, I speculated that America could embrace what I told Gene could be "both his comeback hit AND the biggest hit of his career?" I firmly believed the recipe for chart success was there.

David Courtney, who had worked with Flying Music on a number of other projects, was recruited to produce this album. The well-liked Courtney had previously produced Roger Daltrey, Eric Clapton, Jimmy Page, David Gilmour (Pink Floyd), and Leo Sayer.

In a 2021 phone interview, Courtney said he was excited when the offer to produce Gene Pitney came to him. "Look, I was a fan. Here was an iconic voice and somebody I grew up listening to. My thought was, 'How do I create something special around this?' It had to be the right material using his voice as the vehicle to re-create those songs, some of which, by the way, took Gene out of his comfort zone."

Courtney said Gene Pitney fit the bill for the kind of singer he admired and loved to work with. "Gene was always highly regarded as a first-class vocalist because he had such fantastic range and he had such great theatrics in his voice. That's what set him apart from the rest. That's what I like in the artists I work with."

He explained that he and Gene worked together on selecting all the songs for this album. That process went smoothly, and then they moved into the studio, Do Not Erase Productions in Fulham, to record. Gene had a well-earned reputation of getting deeply involved in producing his records. Courtney divulged that Gene never interfered with him on this

project at all. "He left it entirely up to me. We really got on famously. It went very smoothly without really any problems at all. He was a highly professional performer. Best of all, we got every song in one or two takes."

Without telling Courtney about my involvement in getting "Let The Heartaches Begin" on the album and indicating that I thought it was the perfect pop song, I asked him what he thought of the song. He admitted, right out of the box, it is not a song he would have chosen for Gene to cover. "Not because it's not a good song. It is. You're right, it is pretty much the perfect pop song. I wouldn't have picked it because I wouldn't have thought it would have been much of a challenge for him. It was a great song, and when Gene put his stamp on it, it became a whole different song."

As usual, Gene's vocal, unusually enhanced with computerized double tracking, was incomparable. David Courtney is right. Gene Pitney singing "Let The Heartaches Begin" makes it a vastly different song than the Long John Baldry version.

Baldry's mesmerizing version of this tale of lost love is glum and sorrowful. A blues singer by trade, Baldry used a rugged-but-affable crooner voice to sell this broken-hearted pop song. And sell it he did. He's unquestionably dejected as he sings this song, and you buy every single word of it: *I see the couples dancing through the night… they hold each other tight…as they dance on and on 'til the morning light. The soft embraces that they seem to share…just make me feel aware of the loneliness I find so hard to bear.*

The gorgeous strings on the Baldry record only serve to heighten his sense of despair. John McLeod, who co-wrote this song, also did the dazzling arrangement on it. His co-writer Tony Macaulay, in a 2021 phone interview, said, "I'm pretty upfront about my songs, and this one is one that I wrote and then sort of put away in a drawer. I didn't think it was anything special. John McLeod's arrangement was spectacular. It changed my whole perspective on this song."

Spectacular indeed. John McLeod created an opulent-yet-uncomplicated and unlayered backdrop for Long John Baldry's tormented vocal. This is a graceful and majestic record.

Gene's version comes across as a bit less martyrized. Less tragic; less forlorn; actually, less heartbreaking. I don't think for a moment that Gene intended it to sound as cavalierly as it did. It just did. Some, maybe a lot, of that coloring was brought about by the synthesizer-heavy production – budget restraints according to Gene. His version seems more like a pep talk for himself rather than him hanging himself on the lover's cross for turning his love away.

Also, Baldry was twenty-six years old when he took this song to #1 in the UK in 1967. Long John likely had one "heartache" after another out on the rock 'n roll road during the Swinging '60s. Gene was fifty when he recorded it in 1990 – a superstar and a family man. Those completely different stages in life certainly would add to the different interpretations of this song by the two artists.

After the album with this song was recorded and released, it became clearly evident that Polydor Records only wanted to market the album on TV as a greatest hits package. Pitney knew going in that Polydor was going to market the album that way in a big ad campaign, but he was hoping for more. "In the back of my mind I always felt they wouldn't have gone to the expense of a recording session for the new songs if they weren't going to actively release, promote, and market a single to radio," Pitney insisted. He was wrong.

Contact proof sheet from a British photo shoot from the 1980s.

Producer Courtney was also disappointed with how Polydor handled this album. "With an artist like Gene Pitney and a package like this, putting some of his greatest hits with covers of other great songs, you have an album with a different slant. I thought they would have celebrated that and run with it because it was not just another compilation of hits. They didn't."

When "Let The Heartaches Begin" was released as a single off the Pitney album I felt relieved and vindicated for all of the lobbying I did to get Gene to record it. I had no conversations with anyone else involved in this project, so it was clearly apparent to someone else that this was a strong song choice for Gene and a marketable single. The single was released in the UK and The Netherlands, but, as we now know, Gene worked with his tour promoters, Flying Music, to promote the single, but Polydor put in little if any effort in marketing and promoting it. So, with no aggressive record company buy-in to make it a hit, "Let The Heartaches Begin" died on the vine.

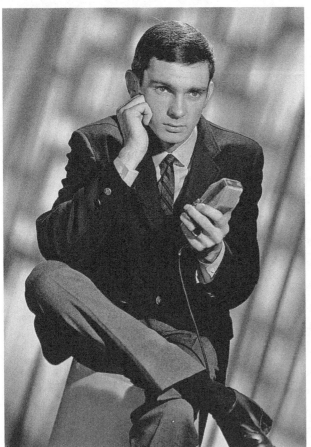

1960s promotional photo.

Favorite Lyric: *"I can see the couples dancing through the night…they hold each other tight…as they dance on and on 'til the morning light. The soft embraces that they seem to share… just make me feel aware…of the loneliness I find so hard to bear."* Some of the most heartbroken and arresting lyrics ever written. The picture these words conjure up in the mind's eye is so vivid that you can see the tears in his eyes and feel the devastation in his heart as he realizes that *"I've lost that girl for sure…and tears* *won't help anymore."* And then the realization of the finality of his loss: *"And now that she's gone…I can't hold back the tears anymore."* Let the heartaches begin…indeed!

Factoid: I played Gene's version of "Let The Heartaches Begin" over the phone for Tony Macaulay during our interview because he hadn't heard it before. "Gene got it! That's how I wrote it," he said. "I wrote it in The Drifters style like 'Save The Last Dance For Me.' A little more up-tempo than Long John's record. Nice job, Gene."

Factoid: Long John Baldry is credited with giving both Rod Stewart and Elton John their starts in the music business. In 1963, after hearing Rod Stewart busking on a train station platform in Twickenham, England, Baldry invited him to join his band Long John Baldry and his Hoochie Coochie Men. In 1966 Baldry formed a band known as Bluesology, and he hired a young Reginald Dwight to play keyboards. Reginald Dwight, of course, changed his name to Elton John and set out on his own. Long John Baldry had a long career but fell far short of his potential stardom. He died in 2005 at the age of 64 in Canada.

Factoid: Tony Macaulay is one of the most prolific songwriters of all time. He wrote or co-wrote many, many songs, including "Build Me Up Buttercup" and "Baby Now That I Found You" for The Foundations, "Don't Give Up On Us" for David Soul, "Last Night I Didn't Get To Sleep At All" for The 5th Dimension, as well as "Love Grows Where My Rosemary Goes," "Smile A Little Smile For Me," Sorry Suzanne," and "Home Lovin' Man." And this, from his website: *Tony Macaulay's songs have sold more than fifty-two million records/CDs worldwide. Thirty-eight of his songs have made the Top Twenty in the UK – eight made Number One. Sixteen of his songs have been hits in the USA – three making the Number One spot in the single charts there.*

And, the last word goes to…Lynne Pitney: "I really like this song. It's a gorgeous song. Truth be told, I like all the strings and the slower tempo of Long John Baldry's record, but Gene was asked to do a different version than that. This is the kind of song that could be recorded now and become a hit. I could see it as a great country song. It has a lot of heart; it's about lost love and broken hearts, and there seems to be whiskey involved!"

LOOKING THROUGH THE EYES OF LOVE

Words and Music by BARRY MANN
and CYNTHIA WEIL

Recorded by GENE PITNEY
on MUSICOR RECORDS

SCREEN GEMS—COLUMBIA MUSIC, INC.

75¢

04407

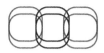

CHAPTER 18:
LOOKING THROUGH THE EYES OF LOVE

Lyrics and Music by Barry Mann and Cynthia Weil

Fun Fact: This is best known as a Gene Pitney hit, but The Partridge Family had a bigger hit with it…in the UK!

Gene Pitney said: "You look at who the writers are, and you know you're getting a great song. My record on this one was pretty darn good. It was well-produced and arranged." Just for context on his quote, it should be pointed out that Pitney and his friend and favorite producer, Stan Kahan, produced his 1965 version of the song.

This song was brought to Gene by Art Talmadge, then the head of Musicor Records. "Art had a pile of demos on his desk ready for me to listen to," Pitney recalled. "The first one was Barry Mann singing 'Looking Through The Eyes of Love.' Barry had a great voice, but I think he was forever tainted because of that silly 'Who Put The Bomp' record he had. He couldn't get another hit as a singer after that. When I heard his demo on this song I told Art right away, 'I want that one.'"

In the studio for the recording session, Pitney and his co-producer were not on the same page. "Stan and I had differing views on producing this one," Pitney explained. "Stan loved cymbal crashes and a lot of percussion. He wanted a lot of flourish on the chorus *'That she's looking through the eyes of love…looking through the eyes of love… looking through the eyes of love when she looks at me…'* I told him this song didn't need that. I probably got a little cocky when I told him 'Drums and cymbals won't sell this record; Gene Pitney will.' Sometimes I was wrong on a song. I was right on this one. I think it's a great record that stands the test of time."

Surprisingly, the first version of this song was recorded by The Drifters in early 1965. No one did them any favors on their record. It sounds like a garage band recorded it… in a garage. Also in 1965, the British Invasion band The Fortunes recorded the song for their first album.

In 1965, Pitney's version went to #3 in both Canada and the UK but stalled at #28 on the *Billboard Hot 100*. Stephen Thomas Erlewine, a reviewer/critic for the on-line site www.allmusic.com, correctly defined this song as "an underheard and undervalued '60s pop gem."

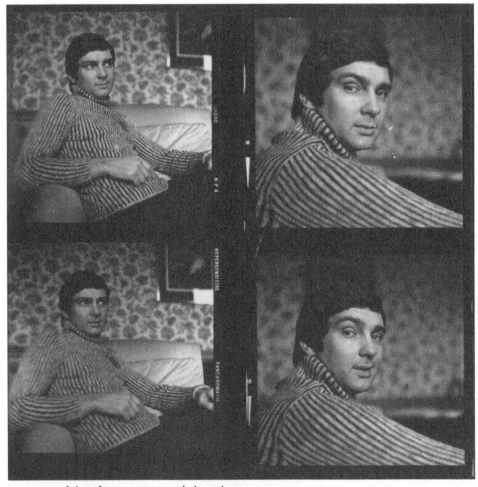

Contact proof sheet from a promotional photo shoot.

Just seven years later, in 1972, The Partridge Family's cover version hit #39 on the *Billboard Hot 100* chart and #9 in the UK. Legendary songwriter-turned-producer Wes Farrell produced The Partridge Family's version of the song using the vaunted LA session musicians known as The Wrecking Crew.

Who did the better version? While Pitney's voice was reedy, it was also resonant and unique. David Cassidy's voice was fuller than Pitney's, but he had a pretty common-place sound. Lynne Pitney alludes to this in her comment at the end of this chapter. The "smooth" factor of Cassidy's voice is what likely makes the Pitney version far more memorable than The Partridge Family's record. It turned out to be the group's final Top 40 hit.

Favorite Lyric: *"But in the eyes of my woman I stand…like a hero, a giant, a man who's as tall as can be"* and *"But in the eyes of my woman they're wrong…I'm a king and a lover as strong and as brave as can be."* In these simple, simple words, Barry Mann and Cynthia Weil summed up that awe-inspiring payoff that comes from the enduring bond formed when young lovers evolve into soul mates.

Factoid: On the Stateside label 45 release in the UK, the song title was printed as "Looking Thru The Eyes Of Love."

Factoid: Pitney also recorded the Mann-Weil song "Angelique" for his 1966 Musicor album *Backstage (I'm Lonely)*. He adored this song and pushed to have it released as a single but was rebuffed by Art Talmadge. On some releases around the world the title is spelled "Angelica." Of course, Pitney had a huge hit with another Mann-Weil song, "I'm Gonna Be Strong."

And, the last word goes to…Lynne Pitney: "I like this one a lot. It's a singable song. Gene had so much texture to his voice where so many other singers were good but they were just smooth…nothing special. A lot of people could sing this song, but it took a guy like Gene to interpret it. Again on this song Gene did harmony with himself, and it really stands out. He was really so good at that."

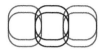

CHAPTER 19:
MECCA

Lyrics and Music by Neval Nader and John Gluck, Jr.

Fun Fact: Gene Pitney had a love/hate relationship with "Mecca."

Gene Pitney said: "I wasn't fond of it, but I was never able to say why. Maybe it's because nothing really happens in the song – you know, the story in the song. This guy stands outside this girl's window and does what?"

While this song was never a personal favorite of his, Pitney loved to sing it in concert because he could use all the power of his magnificent tenor voice and let it bounce around concert halls worldwide. But, in his later years, when he was no longer a fresh-faced twenty-three-year-old teen idol, he hated having to sing the phrase *"Oh she's my teen goddess…"* as he strode across all those world stages with his snow white hair. He found it to be a tad awkward, to say the least.

"Mecca" was likely the most curious and mysterious song that Pitney ever recorded. In lyrical concept and design, the 1963 hit seems to be a combination of Hank Williams' "Lovesick Blues" (without the yodeling), "Maria" from West Side Story, and Pitney's earlier hit "Town Without Pity."

Legendary songwriter/producer/arranger Jerry Ragavoy was responsible for creating the ethereal and exquisite flute-led Middle Eastern-inspired track (with the strange exception of that guitar break in the middle) over which Pitney soared for the entire two minutes and eighteen seconds of this record.

These two lines from the song say it all: *"Each morning I face her window, and pray that our love can be…"* and the aforementioned *"Oh she's my teen goddess…"* What teenage boy hasn't pined for the beautiful-but-out-of-reach girl-next-door or across-the-street and dreamed of what could be if she just noticed him? Just once! Pitney delivered those lines of devotion with understated fervor. So much so that it sounds as if he's walked that walk.

"Mecca" was one of those records that you knew was a Gene Pitney gem right at the opening line of *"I live on the west side, she lives on the east side of the street."* Unmistakable. "Mecca" is also one of so many songs that only Pitney could record and give credence to. All other singers would be ill-advised to try to tackle a song like "Mecca." Don't believe it? Punch in "Mecca" by The Cheetahs on YouTube. This was a British band that recorded this song for Philips Records in 1964. They botched the lyrics and bungled their way through the entire song. It sounds embarrassingly like Alvin and the Chipmunks on helium. You will cringe, cry and/or laugh.

The songwriting team that crafted the somewhat kitschy "Mecca" was an interesting coupling. Not much is known about Neval Nader. His full name was Neval Abounader, and he was born in 1917. Singer/songwriter/musician Al Kooper, who co-wrote the big hit "I Must Be Seeing Things" for Pitney, ran in the same musical circles as Nader for a while. He said, "I didn't know him well. I bumped into him all the time, and he was a funny guy. He was an older guy…definitely older. He was like Aaron Schroeder's age. (Nader was actually nine years older than Schroeder, who was Pitney's manager.) I got along with him very well, and I thought he was hilarious. Neval loved Gene Pitney's voice and wanted to write songs for it."

Kooper thought "Mecca" was a great song and a great record. "I loved it," he said. "I thought it was a great arrangement. But I didn't like the *'she's my teen goddess'* lyric."

John Gluck was a very prolific writer throughout the 1950s and early 1960s. He churned out countless forgettable songs recorded by stars like The Mills Brothers, Brenda Lee, Something Smith and the Redheads, Steve Lawrence, Rusty Draper, The Flamingos, The Poni-Tails, Frankie Lymon, Hugo & Luigi, Bobby Vinton, Cathy Carr, The Tokens, Connie Francis, and Steve Alaimo.

For a short while, in 1961, Gluck was paired up at Hill and Range Songs with the soon-to-be legendary Cynthia Weil, but they produced nothing memorable. Gluck couldn't get a hit until he was paired with Nader at Aaron Schroeder's January Music.

Nader and Gluck wrote their first hit together in 1962. At that point Nader was already forty five years old. Gluck was thirty seven. That hit was Bobby Vee's "Punish Her," which the affable Vee took to #20 on *Billboard's Hot 100*.

"Punish Her" borrows a lot in melody, structure, arrangement, and production from Vee's 1961 #1 "Take Good Care of My Baby," which was written by Gerry Goffin and Carole King. OK – it's pretty much the same record! It's kinda like the knock off, generic drug of the expensive original. Both songs were produced by the peerless pop producer Snuff Garrett and featured The Johnny Mann Singers on background vocals.

In spite of its rough and tumble title, "Punish Her" has nothing to do with domestic abuse. It is a sweet and touching song and is one minute and fifty-two seconds of highly melodic deception. *"If she has wronged you...found someone new...but you feel it's not over...here's what you must do...PUNISH HER...kill her with kindness...buy her red roses every day...PUNISH HER with so much affection...that she will cry for the love she threw away..."*

That same year, 1962, Gluck co-wrote with the prolific Ben Raleigh a bouncy, Bobby Vee-ish song titled "Cry Your Eyes Out." The song landed on Pitney's *Only Love Can Break A Heart* album. Raleigh's other credits included Eddie Fisher's "Dungaree Doll," Johnny Mathis's "Wonderful! Wonderful!," Lesley Gore's "She's a Fool," Lou Rawls' "Love is a Hurtin' Thing," and Ray Peterson's "Tell Laura I Love Her."

The next year, 1963, would be a great year for Nader and Gluck individually and as a team. In March, Pitney released "Mecca," and it became another international hit for the small town kid from Rockville, Connecticut. "Mecca" went to #12 in the US on the *Billboard Hot 100*; it hit #7 in Australia; and it went to #2 in Canada. It was released – but did not chart – in the UK.

Shortly after that, in April, 1963, Lesley Gore released her career-starting smash "It's My Party," co-written by Gluck with Wally Gold, Herb Weiner, and Seymour Gottlieb, who were all contract writers for Aaron Schroeder's January Music.

Nader and Gluck also landed two Pitney album tracks in 1963. Pitney put a sweet country tinge to "Don't Let The Neighbors Know," a song that sounds like it could have been written for Ernest Tubb. It could have been The Texas Troubadour's masterpiece. And, Pitney sang his tonsils out on "Lonely Night Dreams (Of Far Away Arms)." The lonely-soldier-far-away-from-home-missing-his-girlfriend theme of this song followed Bobby Vinton's hit with the same theme, "Mr. Lonely," by one year. This was a better written song with a higher caliber performance from Pitney than Vinton gave on "Mr. Lonely."

Neval Nader also co-wrote the bouncy "The Ship True Love Goodbye" with Mark Barkan for Pitney's 1963 *Just For You* album. Barkan would later go on to write "Pretty Flamingo," a massive hit for Manfred Mann, and co-write Lesley Gore's "She's A Fool" with the aforementioned Ben Raleigh.

It's clear that the Nader-Gluck team could produce hit material. "Mecca" is obvious proof of that. But, oftentimes it seemed like they were a bit lackadaisical in coming up with original ideas. Nonetheless, the Nader-Gluck team deserved more success. Their songs were melodically robust and lyrically solid.

Aaron Schroeder's wife, Abby, has fond memories of both writers. "John Gluck," she recalled "was very quiet, very conservative. A nice man. On the other hand, Neval Nader was full of the devil; different; never had any money; an unusual guy. Aaron and I liked them individually and as a team, and we tried to help them be successful."

When the songwriters were signed to Schroeder's January Music she said they would write and write and write. Finally, they hit paydirt when they came up with "Mecca."

"It must have been Neval's idea," Schroeder recalled, "because of his ethnic background. He was Middle Eastern. Just the melodic hook they created for that one word 'Mecca' was enough to convince Aaron and Wally Gold that they had something with this one."

(L-R) Maurice Merry, Gene, and longtime UK tour manager John Seyforth with some of the show girls from The Golden Garter in Manchester, England.

Abby Schroeder said that Pitney didn't like "Mecca" at first. "Gene rarely liked anything when he first heard it," she said with a sigh. "But, he did trust that Aaron and Wally were not going to steer him into something crazy."

While the singer never liked the song itself, Abby Schroeder agreed that he did like singing it. "He liked 'Mecca' because it was lively, and it really got your attention when he sang that word 'Mecca-a-a-a.' Gene could show off this vocal prowess."

Neval Nader died in 2009 at the age of 92. John Gluck died in 2000 at the age of 75.

Favorite Lyric: *"And though her folks say we're too young to know of love I worship at her shrine."* Yup. What do those old farts know?

Factoid: Jerry Ragavoy, who did the arrangement and conducted the orchestra on "Mecca," was the owner of the internationally-famous New York recording studio The Hit Factory.

Factoid: "It's My Party," co-written by John Gluck, was sampled on Robin Thicke's 2009 Blurred Lines song "Sex Therapy." Gluck, who died in 2000, wasn't around to cash in on the success.

Factoid: John Gluck, Jr., also has a small spot in Beatle history! He co-wrote a song in 1958 titled "Nothin' Shakin' (But The Leaves on the Trees)" that The Beatles recorded on July 23, 1963, for the BBC Radio program *Pop Go The Beatles*. The song showed up on their 1994 compilation album/CD *Live at the BBC*.

Factoid: The Mecca Leisure Group was a British company that owned and operated nightclubs, hotels, and bingo parlors. During the 1960s, Mecca was an entertainment powerhouse with numerous nightclubs throughout major United Kingdom towns and cities. Gene said they put up the money behind one of his earliest UK tours because they wanted the tie-in with his song "Mecca."

And, the last word goes to…Lynne Pitney: "I know a lot of people love it, but to me it's just a song that Gene recorded. It wasn't my favorite. If I'm listening to one of Gene's CDs and 'Mecca' comes on, I just wait for it to be over so I can hear the next song. I know that sounds bad, but that's just how I feel. You know, sometimes a song just doesn't suit you. And, I'm pretty sure Gene was not overly fond of it either. He sang it at shows because he felt he had to."

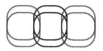

CHAPTER 20:
OCEANS AWAY

Lyrics and Music and Phillip Goodhand-Tait

Fun Fact: Roger Daltrey from The Who actually recorded this song before Gene Pitney did.

Gene Pitney said: "This is absolutely one of the best songs I ever recorded and one of my favorite songs to sing." "Oceans Away" was the first of two singles extracted from the *Pitney '75* album issued by Bronze Records in the UK. It was never a chart hit anywhere, but it was/is a fan favorite for the ages. This meticulously crafted song, written by the under-appreciated English singer/songwriter Phillip Goodhand-Tait, was a song Pitney loved to sing in concerts, in spite of the fact that it wasn't a hit.

"The melody is haunting, and it has great lyrics with a very memorable chorus. Over time it took on a special meaning to my fans in the UK and Australia because our relationship was 'oceans away' when I wasn't performing on tour. It is just a touching song to sing from that perspective.

"On top of that, it's a great song to sing. I've never seen the sheet music for the song, but I'm pretty sure it's all in one octave. That means I can sing my heart out without distracting myself by thinking 'Uh oh, those BIG notes are coming up.' I like to believe I interpret songs, not just sing them. And when you interpret songs you get to add your coloring, your personality, your emotions. And, Phillip's lyrics add more than a bit of romance and mystery to the song as well."

While this song wasn't written specifically for Pitney, it certainly met all of his requirements: a sublime melody, tear-jerking lyrics, and the melodramatic chorus – *"Oceans away, go where you may, love will be with you, oceans away"* – where Pitney can be theatrical without being schmaltzy.

The opening verse to this record is pure Pitney magic. Over a tender piano played by acclaimed English classical pianist John Barham, Pitney sets the stage for this love song with this transcendent lyric *"Don't wake me up if I should be dreaming, I don't want to miss one minute of this dream."* He then delivers a wistful and flawless performance that captivates the listener from beginning to end.

This song is three minutes and nine seconds of pure genius. Romantic and enduring lyrics by Goodhand-Tait; a Gene Pitney vocal beyond compare; a quintessential arrangement by the above-mentioned John Barham, who also arranged and orchestrated George Harrison's albums including *All Things Must Pass*, which included "My Sweet Lord"; and, a first-rate production by Gerry Bron.

In a 2021 email interview, Phillip Goodhand-Tait revealed why he loved Gene's version of his song: "When I first heard Gene had recorded it, I assumed it was an album-filler. It was many years later before I gave much thought to his interpretation. I believe the key to understanding his relationship with the song lies in his lifelong dedication to performing 'live' for his fans. He is the only person to have taken the words of the chorus, *'Oceans away, go where you may, (my) love will be with you, oceans away'* as a leaving card to his audience, sometimes thousands of miles from his next stop, and what a beautiful message to give any fan.

"Of course I have no way of knowing if this was what attracted him, but he did feature the song on his live performances, and, of course, as he was forever known for 'Twenty Four Hours From Tulsa,' I surmise that he was always conscious of distances between lovers. More than anyone, he could sing *'love will be with you, oceans away'* and make it true."

Discovering how certain songs make their way to certain artists is always intriguing. Today, most artists write their own songs, but that was not the case during much of Pitney's recording career. "Oceans Away" came to Gene Pitney's attention in a very typical show business fashion: it's who you know. In this case, Phillip Goodhand-Tait knew Neil Warnock, Gene Pitney's agent.

Goodhand-Tait explained how it happened: "I was leaving publisher Dick James Music (publisher of The Beatles) and, thanks to pop fashion's progression to the internet on which songwriters could release albums, I had a new chance. There was enough interest in my songs and singing to provide me with a new recording contract. Neil Warnock was already my agent for gigs, and he was bloody good. Tough but astute and honest. He was easily the best-qualified contender to be my

new manager, and I wanted him to represent me. I cannot be sure, but I think Neil was proving to me that he was much more than an agent by presenting my songs to Gene."

For the record, it should be noted that Roger Daltrey, from The Who, recorded "Oceans Away" first, for his *Ride A Rock Horse* solo album. Daltrey is a much different type of singer than Gene Pitney. Pitney is a gifted pop singer who sang every note and squeezed out every bit of melody from a song. Daltrey is a rock singer. A great rock singer, but a rock singer without the three-octave range and attention to the structural detail of a song that Pitney had.

In the interview for this book, Goodhand-Tait wrote about Daltrey's recording of his song: "Roger was the first to cotton on to the song. The circumstances were quite bizarre. My friend Gordon Coxhill, a freelance writer for *The Sun* newspaper, took me to Ramport Studios in south London where he was to interview Roger, who was about to record his first solo album produced by Russ Ballard.

"Gordon was astonished to find Roger and Russ hadn't decided which songs to record, and he told me that. As a songwriter newly-freed from publishing constraints, anxious to get covers, and full of self-confidence, I went back into the studio, sat at the piano, and played 'Oceans Away' for Roger and Russ. They must have liked it. They kept my piano and replaced my vocals with Roger's. Then other instruments were overdubbed, so that's how I played piano for Roger and never worked with any of the other musicians on Roger's *Ride A Rock Horse* album!"

The affable songwriter also divulged the most surprising tidbit about this now time-honored Pitney fan favorite: he wrote it as a duet! He explained, "Like all songwriters, I am often asked, 'Which comes first, the music or the words?' Someone famous once replied, 'First comes the phone call – I need a song!'

"I have always conceived words and music together, but, most often, as with 'Oceans Away,' I began by singing a thought. However, here is something I find odd about 'Oceans Away': no one but me seems to recognize that the song is a duet! Aside from the chorus, two lines of each verse is answered by two lines from the person being sung to. They would join together for the chorus: *'Oceans away, go where you may, love will be with you, oceans away,'* and that's how I thought the song would be sung.

"However, successive singers seem to have no problem 'un-dueting' the lyric, and I'm comfortable with that now. The chorus idea being that no distance can part true love may have been subliminal. I certainly knew oceans to part romance. I'd used that idea before, notably on the hit song 'A Day Without Love' that I wrote in 1968 for the UK teeny-bopper group Love Affair.

Goodhand-Tait also pointed out this unusual tidbit: "'Oceans Away' has no middle. I felt an instrumental 'break' should portray waves and the sea, and I listened to Si-

Gene signing autographs at his hotel in Leeds, England. His friends Howard and Barbara Matthews are in the upper right-hand corner.

belius for inspiration. My own recording of 'Oceans Away' makes the most of that orchestral intro and middle."

Read all about Phillip Goodhand-Tait; buy his music, including his version of "Oceans Away"; or send him a thank you note for writing this showpiece for Gene Pitney through his website: pg-t.com

Favorite Lyric: *"Don't wake me up if I should be dreaming, I don't want to miss one minute of this dream."* Poignant with a capital P! Whether it's about a first love, a lost love, a parent, a child, a best friend, or even a hometown, we've all had one of these dreams. Phillip Goodhand-Tait's everlastingly sweet words and Gene Pitney's tender delivery of them will have you weeping as you look back on that much-loved person or place.

Factoid: Gerry Bron, who produced "Oceans Away," was an English record producer and band manager. He was also the founder of Bronze Records, the independent label that issued the *Pitney '75* album that included "Oceans Away." Bron and Pitney were friends and business partners. Gerry Bron also produced Gene's records that were recorded in London in the late 1960s and early 1970s, including "Maria Elena," "A Street Called Hope," and "24 Sycamore." Bron was also responsible for the success of the band Uriah Heep. He died in 2012 at the age of 79.

Factoid: Gene said this record only took two takes in the studio. Both of them are available on YouTube. Also, Tony Lee, a British singer who does a Gene Pitney Tribute show, spliced together a video duet with Gene on this song, and it's also on YouTube.

And the last word goes to...Lynne Pitney: "This is gorgeous. One of the loveliest songs Gene ever recorded. This has to be my favorite. He sounds like an angel on this song. That's how I liked his voice the most. Soft and sweet and, again, with that texture to it. I could listen to this song all day. I would like it if it were longer so I could listen to it longer. Gene did a beautiful job on this song. He recorded it in London, and he was so excited because it was recorded at George Martin's studio. Gene just knew instinctively how to sing a song like this. He had that special touch. He was always very proud of this song, even though it wasn't a hit. It stops you in your tracks because it is just that good."

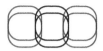

CHAPTER 21:
ONLY LOVE CAN BREAK A HEART

Lyrics by Hal David and Music by Burt Bacharach

Fun Fact: "Only Love Can Break A Heart" was the biggest American hit Gene Pitney ever had. Surprisingly, it was a song he did NOT want to record. Nonetheless, he did! Then, he tried to get radio stations NOT to play it. Nonetheless, they did!

Gene Pitney said: "When this song was submitted to me, I didn't really like it." Would Burt Bacharach and Hal David, who wrote "Only Love Can Break A Heart" specifically for Gene, have pitched it to someone else had they realized how he really felt about it? We'll never know.

"Only Love Can Break A Heart" hit #2 on the *Billboard Hot 100* in November 1962. Pitney had grave doubts about recording the Bacharach-David song. "I always thought the song had too few lyrics," Gene conceded with some chagrin. The song has a total of 116 words. "But," he added, "that's the brilliance of Hal David and Burt Bacharach, being able to get it done like that."

After he recorded it, Gene was still so unsure of the song that when he went out to promote it, he tried to kill it. "That song really worried me. Up to that point I hadn't really done anything that slow. When I went to promote it at radio stations, I tried to get the DJs to play the other side, 'If I Didn't Have A Dime.'"

Conversely, co-writer Burt Bacharach, in a 1987 *Gene Pitney International Fan Club Newsletter*, said, "That's my favorite. I knew right away when we left the studio it was a hit. Everything came together on that song. It was one of my best melodies; Hal David came up with a very poignant lyric; and Gene performed it magnificently. That's my favorite of the songs we wrote for Gene."

In his 2013 memoir, *Anyone Who Had A Heart*, Bacharach echoed much of the above. Pointing out that Gene always arrived at the studio prepared to go, he said, "The song didn't take long to do, and I walked out of the studio feeling good, thinking, 'Wow, this sounds like a hit.'"

Hal David, the lyricist, didn't remember Gene's trepidation about the song. Agreeing with Bacharach, he said, "Gene was magnificent on that song. He sold the heartbreak; he sold the reproach; he sold the pleading. Gene Pitney was a master song salesman. I think that song took only three to four takes. Burt and I felt the magic."

All that notwithstanding, Pitney had a lot of angst in the studio while recording the song that he thought was too short on lyrical content, so much so that he came up with a stratagem he thought would bolster the record and pump it up a bit.

"That's how my whistling came about on the record," he explained. "I was born a natural whistler. And, I was in there recording that thing in the studio, and I thought, 'My God! I gotta give this thing all the help I can! So, on my own, while they were listening in the booth, I started answering the horn figures with the whistling. Finally, someone said, 'Hey, let's leave that in!'"

A number of other singers recorded this song, but none of them could sell it like Pitney did. His singing dripped with agony as he implored and pleaded with his girl-friend to accept his apology, let him atone for whatever offense he committed, and let him back into her life.

But, at the same time, Pitney imbues the song with so much sweetness that it really doesn't come off as annoyingly whiny. Instead, this record displays masterful execution and an exquisite performance from the man who was known as "The Prince of Pain." It is likely one of the ten best records Gene Pitney ever made.

In retrospect, Pitney's uneasiness over the shortfall of lyrics in "Only Love Can Break A Heart" might have been a real, not an imagined, concern. The gifted Oscar- and Grammy Award-winning songwriter Paul Williams agreed with Pitney about Hal David's lyric output, but Williams perceived its results exactly the opposite of how Pitney did.

Following Hal David's death in 2012, Williams wrote in tribute, "As a lyric writer, Hal was simple, concise and poetic – conveying volumes of meaning in the fewest possible words and always in service to the music."

In her book *Hal David: His Magic Moments*, Eunice David, the songwriter's widow, wrote, "Hal always strove for simplicity in his lyrics. He thought that Cole Porter was very sophisticated and described Irving Berlin as being earthy; he deemed Oscar Hammerstein poetic and found Lorenz Hart witty. But, he pointed out that the one thing they all had in common was that their lyrics were the epitome of simplicity, in the best sense of the word. Of his favorite lyricist, Johnny Mercer, he said, 'Whether he is being poetic or humorous, he is never complicated.' About his own lyrics Hal said that he liked to use everyday words and tried to paint a picture that conveyed what he felt."

Hal David assessed his approach to writing lyrics best when he told *Daily Variety* in 1998: "I always looked for an emotional impact and I always looked to tell stories. I like a narrative quality. I look for simplicity as opposed to being simplistic."

The last line of his quote certainly sums up "Only Love Can Break A Heart."

Bacharach explained in his memoir that he and Hal David had written this song specifically for Gene. And, he recalled, it was one of those songs where the lyrics came first. "The melody doesn't sound like something I would have written without having first seen the lyrics, and the song has a very odd structure. Hal must have given me the line, *'Last night I hurt you…but darling remember this,'* because the hook, which is almost like the chorus, comes in four bars after the song starts. It's an unusual form but that never bothered me so long as it made sense."

Hal David died of a stroke at the age of 91. As of this writing in 2021 Burt Bacharach is still alive.

Gene talked at length about "Only Love Can Break A Heart" in a 1994 *Gene Pitney International Fan Club Newsletter*.

Question: How did this song get to you?
Gene: It's hazy, but I think Burt Bacharach played it on the piano for me. It's very

hard to have someone play a song and have to pretend you like it! I know that this was one of the first times I realized that another person's viewpoint of what could be a successful song for me might be better than my own. I respect Burt's, Hal David's and Aaron Schroeder's intuition, for lack of a better word, as to what would fit my vocal ability. I just didn't see it as a great song right away. And, sometimes I don't realize how well a song came out until years later.

Question: You have said that you were reluctant to record this song. Could you please expand on that? To the casual listener it is a very singable song with a sweet lyric.

Gene: I think the main reason was when you look at the lyrics there are so few words to fit the melody that I wondered if there was any substance to it. I think that tells you something about the ability of Hal David to say it all very simply and eloquently. The melody was just not the type of song I was interested in at the time. I was wrong!

Question: Did this – either consciously or subconsciously – become the prototype for a "Gene Pitney song," i.e., big ballad, sad song?

Gene: No. This was a one-off type of song that I don't think fits the category of "big ballad." It has a very low range and is not difficult to sing. I think that may have been, in the end, one of its selling points. The "big ballads" began with "Backstage," "I'm Gonna Be Strong," and "Looking Through The Eyes of Love."

Question: In your large body of work, on a scale of 1-10 with 10 being high, where do you rate this song and why?

Gene: I would rate "Only Love Can Break A Heart" an 8 now! I can feel its power when I perform it on stage. The chorus simply sweeps the audience into the song in

a majestic manner, but its simplicity makes it acceptable to everyone.

Question: It was a huge hit in the United States but not in the UK. Do you have any idea why – and – did that disappoint you?

Gene: I believe that this release started the double plateau recording sessions that became part of my career. One was for the US market, one for outside the US. Somehow, I was

looked at as two separate recording artists.
The success of my appearances on all the TV
shows, in the UK in particular, created an image that continues to this day. I would say the
lack of TV [appearances] in the US deprived
me of any particular image, but I'm not sure
that was a bad thing. This was a hit in the US
because my career was just starting to build
here. It would really be another year before I
conquered the UK.

Question: How did the whistling come about
on the record? When did you discover that you could whistle?

Gene: I have whistled all my life. As a kid I whistled all the time and found out that I
was really good at it, and so I worked at it to become even better. A lot of people don't
know this, but my mother was an incredible whistler, and possibly there is something
genetic – or – a bone and mouth construction that makes it work. It ended up on the
record because Burt heard me doing it, liked it, and thought it would sound great. I
would whistle all during rehearsals at all my sessions. This time it just struck him that
it might work. And, when I perform it live, I always whistle on "If I Didn't Have A
Dime," too. Something just compels me to do it even though it's not recorded that
way.

Question: Did Bacharach and David have a certain pre-conceived way they wanted
this song done – or – did they leave it open to your interpretation?

Gene: The flow of the song is definitely Burt. If you know him you can just see him
bobbing and weaving at the piano playing the song. We had worked together before
so I knew what I was capable of delivering for him. There was implicit trust there.

Question: What can you tell us about the session?

Gene: The session was done live with an orchestra at Bell Sound in New York City.
Burt was at the baton and controlled and ran the whole show. I believe Bucky Pizzarelli was responsible for that great guitar sound.

Question: "Only Love Can Break A Heart" stalled at #2 in the US charts because a song
you wrote, "He's A Rebel," was at #1. A truly amazing feat. What was that feeling like?

Gene: It was great being at #1 and #2, but I'm afraid that I was so busy that I didn't have time to savor the wonder of it all at the time. Most things sink in after the fact for me.

Question: You recorded this song in Spanish ("Solo El Amor") on your *Gene Pitney Espanol* album. But it came out a little odd. There were hardly any lyrics. You seemed to whistle through most of the song. What happened?

Gene: We needed one more song to complete the Spanish album, so we dug out the music track and found a guy at Bell Sound who spoke Spanish! We had him dash off the simplest possible lyrics at the last minute. They ended up being stuff like "If I love you will you love me?" Thank God for the whistle! It filled the rest of the song.

Favorite Lyric: *"Please let me hold you and love you for always and always."* What a simple but effusively affectionate way to say "I love you!" Kudos to Hal David.

Factoid: Burt Bacharach wrote in his book, *Anyone Who Had A Heart*, that there was never a demo of this song. "Hal (David) and I went over to 1650 Broadway, the home of Musicor Records, so I could play the song for Gene on the piano."

Factoid: As mentioned in the newsletter interview, this record peaked at #2 on the *Billboard Hot 100*. Although every singer wants a #1, in this case Pitney really didn't mind. In a very ironic twist, "Only Love Can Break A Heart" was kept out of the #1 spot by a song Pitney wrote, "He's A Rebel," recorded by The Crystals. Pitney was becoming a double threat as a singer and songwriter, and in November of 1962 those two careers collided at the top of the music charts. Prior to "He's A Rebel," Pitney had written "Hello Mary Lou" for Rick Nelson and "Rubber Ball" for Bobby Vee (in the US) and Marty Wilde (in England).

Factoid: "Only Love Can Break A Heart" was never released as a single in the UK. It hit #2 in New Zealand and #11 in Canada (CHUM Radio Chart).

Factoid: Gene always said this was one of his favorite songs to sing in concert because he loved the audience reaction. "This was the one that always got to the audience," he

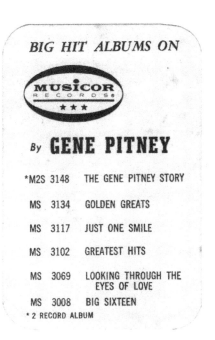

GENE PITNEY

BIG HIT ALBUMS ON

MUSICOR
R E C O R D S®
★ ★ ★

By **GENE PITNEY**

*M2S	3148	THE GENE PITNEY STORY
MS	3134	GOLDEN GREATS
MS	3117	JUST ONE SMILE
MS	3102	GREATEST HITS
MS	3069	LOOKING THROUGH THE EYES OF LOVE
MS	3008	BIG SIXTEEN

* 2 RECORD ALBUM

said. "I could watch the entire front row melt into tears." He also enjoyed it because he could show off his whistling prowess.

Factoid: Burt Bacharach said, "I've worked with many, many talented singers over the years, but there is only one Gene Pitney."

And, the last word goes to…Lynne Pitney: "'Only Love Can Break A Heart' is so identified with Gene. This is one of the songs that really broke his career open. The other was 'Town Without Pity.' 'Only Love Can Break A Heart' is a song where his voice just sounds so beautiful. It's actually stunning. I was more into rock 'n' roll at that time, and I wasn't a big fan of the crooners. When Gene played this for me, I almost couldn't believe my ears. I thought to myself, this isn't just some silly little teenage record. This is a big-time record. We weren't married when this record was released. I was so proud of him. This song just brings back so many wonderful memories for me. Those were great days for us!"

Gene with fan in Leeds, England. She looks like a princess!

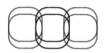

CHAPTER 22:
PRINCESS IN RAGS

Lyrics by Roger Atkins and Music by Helen Miller

Fun Fact: This was a Gene Pitney hit that almost didn't get recorded.

Gene Pitney said: "My reason for doing it was that I like it as a song and thought it could be a successful single, which I needed at the time!" The lyrics to this song, sung confidently by Pitney, about keeping the faith that *"the only girl for me"* would some day be his came from Roger Atkins, the same man who wrote the lyrics for "It's My Life" by The Animals, "Make Me Your Baby" by Barbara Lewis, and "Workin' On A Groovy Thing" for The 5th Dimension.

The simple but provocative melody was written by Helen Miller, who also wrote the melodies for "Foolish Little Girl" by The Shirelles, "Charms" by Bobby Vee, "Make Me Your Baby" by Barbara Lewis, and Gene Pitney's earlier hit, "It Hurts To Be In Love."

Roger Atkins recalled, in a lengthy 2019 phone interview, exactly where and how this song was written and how it got to Pitney. "We wrote the song when Helen and I were both under contract to Screen Gems/Columbia Music in New York, and we wrote the song in their offices in the Columbia Pictures Building in Manhattan.

"Every week or so we'd get the list of artists and upcoming recording sessions. We'd look through it to see if there was someone we wanted to try to write a song for or see if we had something already written that might fit that artist. We both were very big Gene Pitney fans, and we said 'Let's try to write something for Gene to do.'

"I came up with the idea for 'Princess In Rags,' and Helen loved it. I started writing some words because she always loved to have words first. I wrote the first verse and then a little bit of the second verse and showed them to her. She started playing at the piano and started coming up with the tune."

While he and Miller were putting "Princess In Rags" together, Atkins said he could imagine Gene singing it. "Absolutely! I could hear his voice in my head. And, when Helen wrote the first bit of music that went with the words, *There's a girl…who lives down the track…*' I said to myself 'If Gene doesn't sing this, he's crazy.'"

After the song was tweaked and finished, they had to get it in front of Pitney and his record label, Musicor Records. "Because of her previous connection to Gene when he recorded her song 'It Hurts To Be In Love,' [Helen] already knew the people at Musicor," Atkins recalled.

But, Atkins admitted there was some nagging doubt as they headed over to Musicor to try to place it with Pitney. "To be perfectly honest, we didn't know if it would catch Gene's ear or if he would like it. When you write songs for specific artists, in your mind you convince yourself that what you're writing is perfect for them. You sorta have to deal with the fact that you could be wrong, but, at the moment you don't think you're wrong. You know completely that this song is perfect for them, and they're insane if they don't record it. Otherwise, why are you spending your energy and time and the emotional attachment to write the song for them if you don't think it's good for them?"

However, Atkins' apprehension was quickly dispatched. "I think we actually played the song for Gene at the Musicor office. They loved the song; and Gene loved the song right away."

Atkins said the song was very loosely based on a real-life romance of his. "Well, at the time, I was going out with a girl who did eventually become my now ex-wife. We weren't in a rich-boy poor-girl situation, but my family, at the time, was better off than her family was. So that did enter into my thinking when I wrote the song, but it wasn't specifically about that. It did, however, influence me."

And, the title? "I was just looking for something that would be good for Gene Pitney, and it was just one of those things that just popped into my head. What better way to describe somebody you worship so much who happens to be at the lower end of the spectrum – society-wise. It just hit me: 'Princess.'"

Atkins loved the title, but even moreso he loved the fact that he used the word "timber-wood" in the lyrics. "To me, that just set up this amazing little picture...of a poor home."

As usual, Pitney sang his heart out. He started the record at a leisurely pace and let Atkins' tender story slowly build through all of its romantic angst. At the end of this song, however, Pitney didn't take his fans on the thrill ride he did on most of his hits. He reined in that towering voice, rising above but not overwhelming Miller's seductive melody, and ended the song on a wishful and wistful note, *"she's the only girl for me and some day it's gonna be...just me and my princess in rags..."* "Princess In Rags" was nicely and gently done.

The real story about "Princess In Rags" is that the song ever got recorded in the first place. According to Roger Atkins it was a bit of a miracle. While Atkins was NOT at the studio for the "Princess In Rags" session, he recounted a story told to him about it by the song's producer Stanley Kahan. Kahan was producing the record with Gene. Garry Sherman was the arranger.

"Stanley invited me to the session where they were going to master the finished product," Atkins explained. "That's where they make the master from which all the 45s would be pressed. When I got there, Stanley tells me what I was about to hear is an exercise in 'leaking.' It kinda floored me, and I wasn't particularly happy or excited because I wanted so badly for this record to be a hit. He comes out and tells me that when they went to the studio to record the song, Gene was only going to be in town for that one day. He was on a USO tour and came back to record, and he was leaving the next morning to finish out the USO tour. He could be gone for another couple of months, so this was the only time they had to record.

"Stanley said when they got to the studio, Mirror Sound, a very famous, very successful, very good recording studio in New York City, there was an ambulance parked in front. They always used the same engineer there, Brooks Arthur. He was a very famous, very well-known engineer, one of the best of the decade by far.

"Well, he was being wheeled out on a stretcher to the ambulance. Apparently he

had had an inner ear infection that completely messed up his equilibrium, and he couldn't stand. Now, I don't know how true it is, but Stanley tells me when they went into the studio to record, Bob Liston, one of the owners of the studio, said he was going to work the control board. According to Stanley, Bob hadn't worked a control console in about twenty-five years. At one point Stanley asks Bob to bring up the volume on Everett Barksdale, a highly-respected New York jazz guitar player who was playing rhythm guitar. So, Bob proceeded to systematically turn off all the individual faders for all the instruments and then turned them back up one at a time to find out what input Everett Barksdale's guitar was on!

Gene with some unidentified friends "working out."

"At that point Stanley said he knew we were in trouble since Brooks Arthur wasn't going to be engineering, and he knew we were in monumental trouble when Bob Liston didn't even know what faders the musicians were on to control the volume levels and everything. Everything was just leaking into one another and – when you listen to the record – you can hear the leakage. It's not a clean production. It's not a clean-sounding record. You can hear the leakage of instruments that's going on in there. I think that hurt us a lot when the record came out."

To the average radio listener, though, there was likely absolutely nothing wrong with Pitney's "Princess In Rags" record. It was melodic and dramatic. It was the tender story about infatuation, young love, and overcoming life's obstacles. It was pure Gene Pitney. You could fall in love with it at the first listen. Atkins, it turns out, wrote a perfect Gene Pitney song

At this writing, Roger Atkins lives in Ventura, California, and is still writing songs.

Helen Miller died in 2006 at the age of 81. Roger Atkins remembered her fondly. "Helen was a tough, wonderfully talented, no holds barred, mouth like a drunken sailor, very easy to work with collaborator who became a close friend even though she was about eighteen years older than I was. She loved to have words in front of her to write to or at least a title to inspire her. I always thought she could write an opera from the names in the phone book, if she liked the names. She definitely leaned towards R&B whenever possible, but she could do pop with the best of them. The first song we wrote together was 'Make Me Your Baby' for Barbara Lewis, but the first song that hit the Top 40 charts for us was 'I Can't Let You Out Of My Sight' by Chuck Jackson and Maxine Brown.

"She told me how much she enjoyed Gene when she worked with him on 'It Hurts To Be In Love.' So she and I were both very excited when we found out he was recording 'Princess In Rags.'"

———————————————

The following is a reprint of an interview with Gene about "Princess In Rags" originally published in a 1993 *Gene Pitney International Fan Club Newsletter.*

Musicor Records released "Princess In Rags" in the US at the tail end of 1965 on the heels of Gene's chartbusting and heartbreaking "Looking Through The Eyes of Love." It was his nineteenth Musicor single and the fourteenth to go into the Top 40. "Princess in Rags" spent eight weeks on the American charts, peaking at #37.

As usual, during the height of his hit-making career, the single was a much bigger hit in England than at home. Released in England on November 4, 1965, it debuted at #46 and rose to #9 by early December before falling off the charts in January 1966. The year-end success of this record kept Gene in the highest echelon of recording stars. He was the #12 best-selling artist in the UK for the year and the best-selling US artist. Overall, he outperformed Elvis, Tom Jones, and Jim Reeves. Quite a feat!

"Princess In Rags" is a very simple melody (the opening bar is similar to that of the Jay & The Americans 1964 hit "Come A Little Bit Closer") with a simple boy-meets-poor-girl-and-wants-to-rescue-her-because-of-his-undying-love-for-her lyric. His pledge of love is sincere and pragmatic: *"I'll work and slave, scrimp and save, to change her rags to silk and lace."*

Gene's performance on the record is dramatically subdued, underlying the basic and simple message: love conquers all. The sob in his throat is evident but not over-wrought. Once again, he took a very simple melody, much as he did with "That Girl Belongs To Yesterday," brought it to life, and made it jump off the record into our ears and memories.

I go back to something that lyricist Hal David told me in an interview two years ago: "You always knew you were going to get a great read out of Gene anytime he was in the studio. And he always got it the first or second time. He had an innate ability to get inside a song, no matter how simple it was, and wring out every note, every emotion, and every nuance. That's something most singers work for years trying to do. Gene could do it at the drop of a hat. He constantly amazed me and Burt and everyone involved with him."

We took Gene back to the winter of 1965 to remember "Princess In Rags."

Question: How and where did you find "Princess In Rags"?

Gene: I don't think I found "Princess In Rags." I know I came back from an Australian tour to do the recording session and all the songs were there, including "Princess." Somebody else had to have picked them out.

Question: Is that you singing high harmony on the record?

Gene: Yes! If there's harmony on one of my records, it's usually me. I even think in harmony! I very seldom sing the melody when I am singing along with a song at home or on the radio. It must sound weird to anyone around.

Question: On the record you sing the lyrics as written: *"There's a girl who lives down the tracks in a little shack made of timberwood..."* In concert, you have changed that from *"timberwood"* to *"earth and wood."* How come?

Gene: No idea! Why do you ask me these infernal questions? Some build with timber; some use earth and wood...

Question: What drew you to this song?

Gene: The need, at the time, for a new single and the hope that this one might be the one that would be the winner from this session.

Question: The songwriters are listed as H. Miller-R. Atkins. Who are they? Did they write other hits, or was this the beginning and end of their chart career?

Gene: To be honest with you, I always wondered who wrote this song! I never realized it was Helen Miller. I guess I was somewhat in the dark because it was one of the few times I flew in to do a session with the pre-recording work already done by others. I didn't know the writers.

Question: This song is almost thirty years old. When you hear it on the radio, what goes through your mind?

Gene: I NEVER hear this song on the radio!

Question: If, in your body of work, someone asked you to rate your songs from 1 to 10, with 1 being a great song and 10 being an average song, what would "Princess" rate?

Gene: It's hard to judge "Princess" because it was a nightmare session where the engineer went to the hospital right in the middle of the session with an inner ear infection. The engineer they called in to replace him didn't know very much about the studio so a lot of the parts of the song that were being played by musicians were never recorded

Gene boating on Crystal Lake (Connecticut) in the summer of 1964.

because the microphones weren't all turned on. Hence, I'm not sure how much of the arrangement ever got on the record! The way it eventually came out I would rate it a "5." My reason for doing it was that I like it as a song and thought it could be a successful single, which I needed at the time!

Question: Is it the kind of song you would record today, taking into consideration the state of music and your personal tastes now in 1993?

Gene: No, this song would not be a success in today's market. The musical structure and the innocence of the lyrics are now outmoded. There is also very little timber and earth and wood construction!!!

Question: Did you consider the song a radical departure from the other type of material you had been doing up to that point, i.e., "I'm Gonna Be Strong," "Only Love Can Break A Heart," "True Love Never Runs Smooth," et cetera?

Early 1960s promotional photo.

Gene: No. I think this was in the mold of the verse-chorus-verse-chorus type of song musically, and it had the same Cinderella-type innocent lyrics.

Question: Do you remember when and where you recorded it? Easy or tough to record?

Gene: As I said before, it was a nightmare to record. The studio was Mirror Sound in New York, and the engineer should have been the legendary Brooks Arthur. He came down with a bad inner ear infection and had to be replaced by an engineer from Columbia Studios who did the best he could under the circumstances. You see, the studio was designed and built by Arthur and ONLY he knew where all the wires went!!! We only got a small part of the sound we were looking for.

Question: If someone could persuade you to re-record your songs, what would you do differently with "Princess In Rags"?

Gene: I've never thought about re-recording "Princess." And I doubt that I would even if someone came up with an offer. It was fitting for its time, and now I believe that time has passed. However, I never have a problem singing the song in concert, which means it is a very strong song the way it is written. There are new pastures out there on which I would like to build a titanium and epoxy house and let the timber and earth and wood be a fond memory!

Question: Tell me something about the record that would surprise your fans.

Gene: When the words were being written for the British release of "Princess" the producers were trying to get "shilling" to rhyme instead of "dime," i.e., "...though she hasn't got a shilling I sure hope she will be willing..." Hey, I like it!

Favorite Lyric: *"I know some day I'll find a way...to take her out of this old place...I'll work and slave, scrimp and save...to change her rags to silk and lace."* Bravo Roger Atkins! He adapted the "American Dream" for this short and sweet ode to love, faithfulness and devotion – and he made it rhyme!

And, the last word goes to...Lynne Pitney: "Another song that I just love. Gene has such a touching quality to his voice on this song. You believe every word he sings. I know it sounds like a simple song, but I think these are the ones he did the best. He never ceased to amaze me. From the beginning of this record you hope that poor guy gets the girl of his dreams, don't you?"

Gene with the "co-writer" of "Rubber Ball": his mother Anna (Anne) Orlowski Pitney.

Gene's mother Anna (Anne) decorating the Pitney Christmas tree circa 1976.

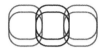

CHAPTER 23:
RUBBER BALL

Lyrics and Music by Gene Pitney (Ann Orlowski) and Aaron Schroeder

Fun Fact: Gene Pitney did NOT have the hit on this record. He did, however, co-write this oh, so engaging smash.

Gene Pitney said: "I knew that Bobby hadn't had his biggest records yet. 'Devil Or Angel' preceded 'Rubber Ball.' I think the matchup came at a great time for all."

It was in 1961 when "Rubber Ball" bounced into the Top 10 in the USA, UK, and around the world and, in the process, launched an eighteen-year-old kid from Fargo, North Dakota, into international stardom. His name was Robert Thomas Velline, and he became known around the world as Bobby Vee.

Most music fans know that Bobby Vee's star was launched when he and his band stepped in to perform on the ill-fated *Winter Dance Party* tour following the plane crash that killed Buddy Holly, Ritchie Valens, and The Big Bopper. "Rubber Ball" took him to the dizzying heights of pop superstardom.

In a dual interview, first published in the October-November-December 1996 *Gene Pitney International Fan Club Newsletter,* Gene and Bobby sat down to explore the creation of this pop masterpiece that became a legendary hit song.

Question: Gene, can you recall when and where you wrote "Rubber Ball"?

Gene: I wrote "Rubber Ball" at the old player piano at my home in Rockville, Connecticut. It was "Rubber Band" in the beginning, but that didn't have enough bounce in it!

Question: How long did it take to write it?

Gene: It was a relatively short time in the writing. The idea was to create a Buddy Holly-ish type of song, so the musical concept was already there. Sort of *"an' like a (hiccup) rubber band…*

Question: Why did you change the title?

Gene: That was where the influence of my manager Aaron Schroeder came in. He was a great song doctor. He could look at a song in the rough and know where to strengthen it.

Question: Was it written specifically for Bobby Vee?

Gene: I don't think so because when I first heard the acetate of Bobby's version in Aaron's office in New York it was unexpected. Perfect fit AFTER I heard it!

Question: Bobby, can you recall when, where, and how you first heard this song? Was it a demo that Gene sang? Did you know it was originally titled "Rubber Band"? Was it written specifically for you?

Bobby: August of 1960 my producer, Snuff Garrett, made a visit to New York looking for songs for me. Aaron Schroeder presented Gene's demo of "Rubber Ball" to him, adding that it had been written – and turned down – as a follow-up to "Handy Man" by Jimmy Jones. We both loved the "bouncy bouncy" fun spirit of the song, and it turned out to be a perfect follow-up to my first hit "Devil or Angel." We recorded it in October of 1960 (take #6) at United Studio B on Sunset Boulevard in Hollywood. It was released November 7th and hit the *Billboard* charts on November 28th. By early January 1961 it peaked at #6 on the *Billboard Hot 100*. It was the first time that I recorded harmony parts for my label, Liberty Records, and it set a path that I continued to follow throughout my career. The most frequently asked question I get about "Rubber Ball" has been: "What are the words to the opening of the third verse?" So-o-o, here goes: *"I'm like a rubber band when on my shoulder you do tap."* Maybe that's where the original title came from?

Question: Was the "bouncy bouncy" chorus on the demo, or did you and/or Snuff Garrett come up with that?

Bobby: I don't recall. I do remember that the female answers "*You don't even put her down*" were done on the demo by a solo voice in falsetto. We gave the lines to the female backup singers for two reasons: first, they added the listeners' perspective ("why do you let her get away with that, you schmuck") and second, they sang it better than I did!

Gene: The Bobby Vee record is a direct copy of the demo we made, which included the *"bouncy bouncys."*

Question: The opening riff is very ear-catching. Do you know where the opening riff came from?

Gene: It's hard to remember perfectly, but I think that riff was the product of the arranger and Snuff Garrett, Bobby's producer. We did the same notes, but our demo only consisted of piano, bass, guitar, and drums. Snuff fluffed it up with the strings.

Bobby: Ernie Freeman arranged the song. Ernie was a genius at coming up with catchy intros and string line hooks. I loved working with Ernie. He arranged nearly everything I recorded 'til about 1969.

Question: Who played on this song? What else can you tell us about this session?

Bobby: What's interesting to me about this session is when people get into stereotypes about white- and Black-sounding music, I am reminded of the fact that the majority of the rhythm section on "Rubber Ball" and most of my records was Black. Earl Palmer on drums, Red Callender on bass, Evelyn Freeman, Ernie's sister, on piano. The guitar solo was played by Barney Kessel, and the rhythm guitar was Tommy Allsup, Buddy Holly's guitar player on the *Winter Dance Party* tour. They were the recording family, and they made up the nucleus of all of my Liberty Records recordings.

Question: Did you seek out Gene to play your record of "Rubber Ball" for him before it was released?

Bobby: I didn't have time! It was a very exciting record. The radio airplay was immediate. All the major markets hit it at the same time, and it moved very quickly up the charts. I ran into Gene a short time later, and he told me the story of putting his mother's name on the record, as a writer, for contractual reasons. He joked about how he taught her to play the song in case someone from ASCAP came around for proof that she was, in fact, the writer. For years I had an image of this sweet little ol' gal in a flowered dress, head tossed back, sweat rolling off her nose, left foot pounding on the floor, tea cups rattlin', and piano bench flyin'! Man, the stuff we put our moms through!

Question: Gene, would you explain why your name does NOT appear in the "Rubber Ball" writing credits?

Gene: There are two major performance rights organizations: BMI and ASCAP. These are the companies that police how many times a song is played on radio, TV, jukeboxes, background music, etc. If you belong to one you agree not to belong to the other. Most music publishers belong to both for business purposes. They wanted to divide the income between their companies that were affiliated with one or the other. Seeing as we had songs already recorded that were in the BMI companies (January Music and Sea Lark Music), my manager/publisher, Aaron Schroeder, decided to put this song into his ASCAP company (Arch Music). I had to become someone else under a nom de plume. When asked who I wanted to be I said, "Ann Orlowski." It's my mother's maiden name. I thought she would get a kick out of having her name on a hit song!

Question: How long was it after the record came out that you finally met Bobby?

Gene: I don't remember. I'm sure it was on tour. He's a great guy, and he has kept his life on a very high plane. No, not a 747! I mean he lives in Minnesota, still has the same wife, and his sons are on the road having a ball with him. How good can it get? I just saw him on a TV show in Sydney, Australia, and he looked great! I remember thinking to myself about the immense difference in the way Bobby smiled and how he looked really happy to be there performing as opposed to what the performers of today have to display when on video or TV! It must be a reflection of the times, but Lord, it must be hard to be miserable all the time. The snarls and nastiness of most groups create a mood that typifies the genre as it exists today. Give me the sex and lighthearted sneer of rock and roll any day in comparison to the instant depression and anger of most of today's pop musical message. At least Alanis Morissette has a great sense of humor and goes to the movies a lot!

Question: Bobby had a hit with "Rubber Ball" just a month or two before you charted with your first hit "(I Wanna) Love My Life Away." Was there any thought of keeping "Rubber Ball" for yourself, or did you not think of it as a Gene Pitney-type record?

Gene: I never had any plan as to what to hold. I was quite happy just to have a hit – mine or anyone else with one of my songs. Aaron Schroeder was very aggressive in exploiting the songs in his publishing firms. He's the only man I know who would give several people exclusives on the SAME song!

Question: Bobby, after "Rubber Ball" was such a big a hit, did you get any other Gene Pitney-written songs offered to you?

Bobby: I don't remember getting any other songs from Gene after "Rubber Ball." My sense is that he was focusing on his own career and keeping the good stuff for himself! I would have recorded "(I Wanna) Love My Life Away" in a heartbeat. It's a great rockin' record, and it would have been a terrific follow-up to "Rubber Ball." In line with your question, I had a great working relationship with Carole King and Gerry Goffin thanks to "Take Good Care of My Baby," and I went on to record a couple dozen of their songs.

Question: You shared the hit on "Rubber Ball" in the UK with Marty Wilde. Did you like his version?

Bobby: There were actually three versions of "Rubber Ball" in the UK Top 20 at the same time! Mine reached #4 (thank you very much!). Marty Wilde's record and a version by The Avons also did very well. I went to England (the first of many visits) to promote my record, and I think that made all the difference in my chart position. And…I think I had the BEST record.

Question: Gene, did you like Bobby's or Marty's version better?

Gene: I thought Bobby's version was more real and fit his style to a T. Marty was a different kind of rocker, and I'm not sure this was his best type of material – not that he didn't do the song justice. I just think Bobby Vee was meant for this song.

Question: Bobby, in your sizable body of work, where do you place "Rubber Ball"?

Bobby: I thought of it as sort of a novelty record. I expected when it made its chart exit that no one would ever want to hear it again. That was NEVER the case. In reality I think the song captured the spirit of the '60s and the "age of innocence" and all that. In a light and very simple way it represents an honesty of young emotion that is universal. Today, I actually think it is a better song than I did when I first recorded it. It's impossible to listen to it and not smile!

Question: Gene, how did you get the idea for the lyrically-clever song?

Gene: No idea. I always tried to start a song with a picture in my mind – by that I mean a colorful concept, usually the title. In this case it was lucky that most of the words from "Rubber Band" fit "Rubber Ball".

Question: What came first: melody or lyrics?

Gene: Always both at the same time. I find that playing the music lends itself to the rhythm of the syllables in the lyric. The master of all times at this is Chuck Berry. I am always amazed when I hear "I'm gonna write a little letter, gonna mail it to my local DJ. Got a rockin' little record that I want my jockey to play." Phew!

Question: Did you write "Rubber Ball" on guitar or piano?

Gene: This was a piano song. I go in totally different directions when I write with piano as opposed to guitar. I hear different harmonies and musical patterns with one or the other!!

Question: This was the first hit you wrote for someone else. Do you recall where and when you first heard Bobby's record of "Rubber Ball"?

Gene: It was sent to Aaron Schroeder's office, and when I heard it I told him that this would be our first big record. He looked at me and said, "How can you say that?" I still had what I call "listener ears" at that time, and I knew it was a hit on first hearing. "Listeners ears" are ears that don't think in terms of highs and lows, mixes, balances of instruments, etc. when hearing a song. You just like it or you don't.

Question: Was this song your first real show business paycheck?

Gene: Yes. My first money came in from this song. I would see $1,000 here, $800 there. The returns were much less then than they are now. The pay now is on a higher scale as it's been negotiated over the years. The coverage has increased, and the dollar is worth a lot more than in the 1960s. My payment statements on the same songs are twenty times more now than what they were in the beginning. Just shows how powerful the 1960s music has remained after all these years!

Question: After "Rubber Ball" you wrote "He's A Rebel." At that point, did you think, A: I'm gonna be a songwriter. B: Now I'm stuck being a songwriter. C: I'm gonna be a singer/songwriter. D: I'd prefer being a singer, making my own records.

Gene Pitney: "Most of the people I have met who had anything to do with one of my songs have been most gracious."

Gene: Again, I didn't plan anything. I was getting a taste of being successful at everything, and I loved it. It was becoming increasingly difficult to keep up with the demands of all the areas of success. When you have a hit record, everyone immediately starts thinking of the next one. When you have a hit album then you start looking for songs for the next one. Do a tour in one country and wonder if you've left it too long in some other country. It got even more difficult when a certain type of material was successful in only certain countries. This meant the same songs would not be sufficient for the whole world. Twenty-four hours were not enough for each day! I wanted to be a singer who writes hit songs and recorded hit records as well!

Question: When a songwriter gives a singer a great song like "Rubber Ball" does that singer ever say "Thank you"?

Gene: Most of the people I have met who had anything to do with one of my songs have been most gracious.

Bobby Vee died on October 24, 2016, at the age of 73 from complications of Alzheimer's disease.

Favorite Lyric: *"If you stretch my love till it's thin enough to tear…I'll just stretch my arms to reach you anywhere…"* Pangs of romantic regret "bounce" straight into a pledge of undying love. Did Alfred Lord *"tis better to have loved and lost than never to have loved at all"* Tennyson have something to do with this song?

Factoid: In a 2004 email, Marty Wilde wrote what "Rubber Ball" meant to him. "The appeal of the song was immediate and had an invincible commercial quality that is still there to this day. A certain smash! My version of 'Rubber Ball' is similar to Bobby Vee's version, apart from a sax solo in the middle of the song instead of the string solo on Bobby's. My record has that typical 'Brit Sound,' which musicians in our country used to get, until The Beatles got them back on track a few years later! Johnny Franz produced the record, and my record made our Top 10. The song is performed at most of my concerts and still hits the spot. I have never spoken to Gene about this song, but if I did I would compliment him on having great ears for a dead certain smash. The song played a big part in keeping my career up at the higher end of the public's commercial tastes. As I said at the beginning, the song sounded like such a high grade

Getting ready to record.

hit that I would have bet my house, wife, and career on it reaching the top, and it did! Gene is a very talented man, and my house, my wife and career are still intact!"

Factoid: George Sylvester "Red" Callender, who played bass on "Rubber Ball," was a member of the vaunted "Wrecking Crew." This was the group of Los Angeles studio musicians who played on thousands of records, including several hundred Top 40 smashes. Both Glen Campbell and Leon Russell were members of the Wrecking Crew before launching their solo careers. They were the group of musicians who Phil Spector used to create his "Wall of Sound." They are known worldwide as the most successful and prolific group of recording session musicians in the history of pop music. You've heard them on hits by Jan and Dean, Sonny and Cher, The Mamas and Papas, The Fifth Dimension, Frank Sinatra, Nancy Sinatra, The Byrds, The Monkees, and The Beach Boys, to name just a few.

Factoid: Johnny Franz, who produced the Marty Wilde version of "Rubber Ball," also produced "You Don't Have To Say You Love Me" for Dusty Springfield and "Make It Easy On Yourself" and "The Sun Ain't Gonna Shine Anymore" for The Walker Brothers.

And, the last word goes to…Lynne Pitney: "It was different, wasn't it? Gene never felt it was the right song for him to record. I agree. It may have been too fluffy for him. I got the biggest kick out of it because it was written under his mother's maiden name…Ann Orlowski. Knowing his mother, it just made me laugh. Gene used to coach his mother, 'Now Mom, if anybody comes and asks if you wrote that song…say YES!' I think he even tried to teach her how to play a bar or two of it on the piano, just in case. I can still picture this little Polish lady telling her friends, 'I wrote that song!' And, wasn't Bobby Vee so cute?"

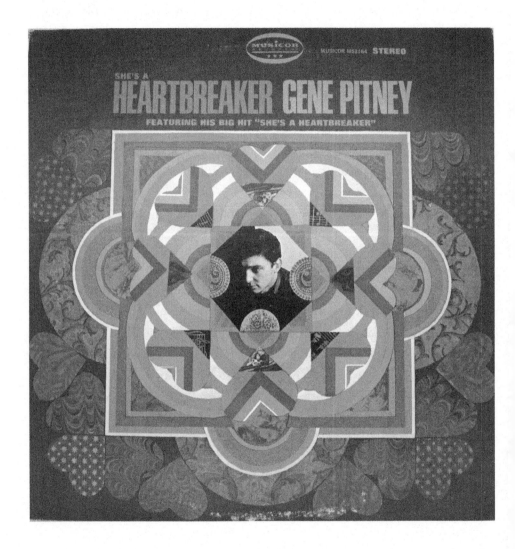

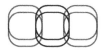

CHAPTER 24:
SHE'S A HEARTBREAKER

Lyrics and Music by Charlie Foxx and Jerry Williams, Jr.

Fun fact: Worst Gene Pitney hit ever!

Gene Pitney said: "A lot of people didn't want me to record this song. A lot." It's not the worst song he ever recorded. Oh no. That accolade most certainly goes to "Animal Crackers (In Cellophane Boxes)," which was released one year earlier, in 1967.

But, back to "She's A Heartbreaker." This was Pitney's last chart hit in the US. His last hurrah. Somehow, it snuck into the Top 20 on both the *Billboard* and *Record World* charts. That likely means not all Gene Pitney fans agree on the merits of this third-rate song.

How much was Pitney out of his element on this song? Think Tony Bennett recording "Twist and Shout" or Petula Clark knocking out a version of "Wild Thing." Or, maybe Vera Lynn having a run at "Under My Thumb."

It's painful to write this entry because Gene Pitney usually had impeccable taste in his song selection. But, some things just don't go together: like mashed potatoes and chocolate syrup; like orange juice and toothpaste; like alcohol and good decisions; like Gene Pitney and "She's A Heartbreaker."

While it became a Top 20 hit, its fate is reminiscent of the Titanic vs iceberg disaster. It likely sunk his recording career because the collision of Gene Pitney the crooner with this screecher was a titanic mess.

Pitney, who heard the criticisms of the record from the moment it was released, remembered that Art Talmadge hated it so much he initially refused to put Pitney's name on it. "On the initial pressing of my record," Pitney recalled with a laugh, "the artist was listed as 'P.G.' In Art's defense, he thought it would damage my career if people knew or thought it was me. So he didn't put my name on the record. It took a pretty good shouting match to get him to put my name on it. Eventually he gave in. To his surprise, it became a hit. I always liked the song and the record. I liked to climb out of the Gene Pitney box every now and then. We didn't have many disagreements, but this was one of the biggest. By the way, most of my records aren't considered collector's items. I've been told that one, with the P.G. is."

Pitney just sounds like he's straining his voice to come up with some sort of R&B sound that he thought was compelling. Rather than compelling, though, it ended up being shrill and earsplitting. He can't be blamed for the now outdated lyrics like

Gene with his favorite arranger Garry Sherman in the early 1960s. Sherman was also the Best Man at Gene's wedding.

"You're dynamite, you've got me uptight, the way you sock it to me girl, you're out of sight..." He can, however, be blamed for thinking this was a good fit for him when he heard the song's writers working on the song in their office at Musicor Records.

The song was written and produced by Charlie Foxx and Jerry "Swamp Dogg" Williams, Jr., who were under contract to Art Talmadge at Musicor Records in 1967. Like all songwriters, they were looking to get their songs recorded by major recording stars. By 1968, Gene Pitney was at the tail end of his hit-making years, but he was still considered a major star. Surprisingly, Foxx and Williams never intended to pitch this song to Pitney. He came to them and asked for it.

In a 2019 phone interview, Jerry Williams said he and Foxx would frequently see Pitney around the Musicor offices. But, Williams explained, they were told by Art Talmadge, co-owner of Musicor Records, that the young star was off limits to them.

"We were told in no uncertain terms by Talmadge that we were not to ever approach Gene," Williams said. "'Do NOT talk to Gene Pitney' is what he said to us every fucking day. We were R&B writers, and he didn't think what we were writing fit Pitney's style. Gene was this good-looking, white teen idol, and Art Talmadge didn't want him doing R&B. Period."

It's not that Talmadge didn't like R&B; he did. As a co-founder of Mercury Records he had his share of R&B hits there. But, as an astute record executive, Talmadge realized that anything the Foxx-Williams team wrote would not be in Pitney's wheelhouse.

Williams then offered another reason why Talmadge didn't want Pitney listening to their musical output and venturing into R&B. "Gene Pitney was really Musicor's only star. And, he was a pop star. That's where Art wanted to keep him. If there was any more money to be made with Gene Pitney, Art felt it would be on the pop charts."

In early 1968, Williams recalled that Pitney was spending a lot of time at Musicor, looking for songs for his next album and single. Williams didn't want to jeopardize his job and the steady income it provided, so he followed Talmadge's advice and steered clear of Pitney. But, Pitney wasn't under any similar restraints from Talmadge and kept walking past the Foxx-Williams office because he liked what he heard them working on. He had already dabbled in country and western and foreign language records. Now he seemed intent on flirting with some R&B.

Williams said, "I specifically remember him coming in the day we were putting the finishing touches on 'Heartbreaker,' and he asked 'Who are you writing that for?' We both froze. Then I think I mumbled something like 'Do you think you can do it?' Gene said he would record it but only if we worked on it with him. Talmadge blew his top, but he was stuck. Gene wanted us, and he got us. We did 'Heartbreaker' and three other songs with him. That felt good to get one up on Talmadge."

Williams explained there was also something bigger at play at Musicor. There was some personal animosity between him and Talmadge. "The son of a bitch fired me

Gene trying out a song on an unidentified friend.

once," Williams said with a chuckle. "Then he re-hired me the next day. We just rubbed each other the wrong way. Look, he hired me to do A&R and write songs and then kept giving me shit. You tell me."

Apparently, Art Talmadge was not the only one Williams didn't see eye-to-eye with. There was some animosity, as well, between Williams and his writing partner, Charlie Foxx. Williams, who shoots from the hip, was clear in his animosity for Foxx. "Charlie thought he was big shit because he and Inez had that hit record with 'Mockingbird' and another hit with something in 1967 just before Art teamed us up. I didn't have the commercial success that Charlie had, and he felt it was real fucking important to remind me of that any chance he got."

While Foxx and Williams are credited as co-writers on "She's A Heartbreaker," Williams insists he wrote the bulk of the song. And, in a 2013 interview about "She's A Heartbreaker" with the independent music magazine *L.A. Record*, Williams upped the ante and the dissatisfaction over how he was treated by his late partner, Foxx, and former employer, Musicor Records. "I produced the m*****fuck out of it, and Charlie Foxx put me down on the label as 'vocal arranger.' What the fuck is that? When they took out the full page ads in *Billboard* and *Cashbox*, there was a picture of Charlie on one side and a picture of Gene Pitney on the other and no mention of me. This record is Gene Pitney possessed by the spirit of Swamp Dogg."

Williams stood by those statements in his phone interview for this book. He said the aftermath of working on the *She's A Heartbreaker* album was the dissolution of his partnership with Foxx and his exit from Musicor. "Talmadge was losing no time in trying to get rid of me," he recalled. "But, Jerry Wexler and Phil Walden over at Atlantic Records liked what they heard and hired me to produce and engineer for them. Hot damn. I jumped at that. That was a great job. Screw Art Talmadge and Charlie Foxx."

Williams also ended up in a lawsuit with Talmadge over royalties for the songs he wrote while under contract, though he did not disclose the outcome of the lawsuit. His wife, Yvonne, died in 2003, and at this writing he lives in Canoga Park, California.

Favorite Lyric: You're kidding, right?

Factoid: Charlie Foxx, who also wrote the duet "'Mockingbird,'" which was a hit in the 1960s and again a decade later, died from leukemia in 1998 in Mobile, Alabama, at the age of 64, despite what you may see otherwise. It seems that some sources shaved a few years from Foxx's life. The same can be said for Gene himself. When Gene died in 2006, many fans believed him to be 65; he, in fact, was 66, having been born in 1940, not 1941 as had typically been reported.

Photo shoot from the *Pitney '75* album.

Factoid: Foxx and his sister, Inez, had the original hit with "Mockingbird" in 1963. It was based on the lullaby "Hush Little Baby." James Taylor and Carly Simon's version was a hit in 1974. The Foxx duo later had a Top 20 R&B hit with the song "(1-2-3-4-5-6-7) Count the Days," which Foxx co-wrote and Gene Pitney also recorded for his 1968 *She's A Heartbreaker* album. (That album was titled *Pitney Today* in the UK.) Coincidentally, Jerry Williams' wife, Yvonne, was another co-writer of that song.

Factoid: Foxx's obituary mentions that at one point their backup band was a group of Alabama youths who later found fame as The Commodores.

Factoid: The other songs Williams and Foxx worked on with Pitney were: "Hate," which they co-wrote with Bill Coley and Larry Harrison; the aforementioned "(1-2-3-4-5-6-7) Count The Days" and "Run, Run, Roadrunner," written solely by Williams.

Factoid: Gene LOVED this song and LOVED singing it in concert. "It adds some balance to my show," he would always say. "You know, after this ballad and that sad song you need something up-tempo. 'Heartbreaker' fills the bill."

And the last word goes to…Lynne Pitney: "To me, this isn't who Gene was. I wanted to hear him sing the big ballads. I loved the songs he chose because he had an ear for a melody. This one surprised me. It was out-of-character. I wouldn't list it as one of my favorites."

SOMETHING'S GOTTEN HOLD OF MY HEART

Words & Music by ROGER COOK & ROGER GREENAWAY

Recorded by GENE PITNEY on STATESIDE

MARIBUS MUSIC LIMITED

3/-

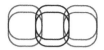

CHAPTER 25:
SOMETHING'S GOTTEN
HOLD OF MY HEART

Lyrics and Music by Roger Greenaway and Roger Cook

Fun Fact: This is the tale of two hits – with one song!

Gene Pitney said: "What's weird about this song is that both versions almost never got recorded." Lightning struck twice for Gene Pitney with this song. What Neil Sedaka had accomplished with "Breaking Up Is Hard To Do" Gene Pitney did with "Something's Gotten Hold Of My Heart." In two different versions, this song was a huge hit twice in the UK for Gene Pitney.

The Pitney solo single was first released in November 1967 and peaked at #5 in the second week of December 1967. It finished its chart run the third week in February 1968. By 1967, Pitney had a good seven years of hits under his belt. In the US, he had scored nineteen legitimate hits, four that went into the Top 10; the other fifteen made it into the Top 30. But, by 1967 it was becoming clear that his popularity was fading at home.

On the other hand, across the ocean in the UK, he had attained superstar status. He reaped all the rewards that went with that, including being offered the best quality songs from the best songwriters in the world. Pitney was on top of the British music world. He had scored nine Top 10 UK hits by this point. He had the Midas touch.

And then when he needed another UK hit, what should fall into his lap but a remark-ably melodic song written by "the Rogers," as they are called in the music business, Roger Cook and Roger Greenaway. The lyrics told the story of all the magic and all the mystery of love. In this case, a man overwhelmed and overcome by the love of a magical woman. *"And a feeling unknown shook my heart, made me want you to stay. All of my nights and all of my days."*

Giving "Something's Gotten Hold Of My Heart" to Gene Pitney at the top of his game in 1967 was like pitching underhand to Babe Ruth. He belted it out and ca-ressed it in the same stanza. He oversold and undersold it at just the right times. It was another wondrous Pitney performance that easily climbed into the UK Top 10 within three weeks of its release and stayed there for six weeks. That surprised nobody. What happened next is what surprised everyone.

There is absolutely no way Pitney – or anyone – could know that this song would be the end of his Top 10 run in the UK. His next release, "Somewhere In The Country," snuck into the Top 20, but all the subsequent Pitney releases inexplicably stalled in the lower reaches of the charts.

The high caliber and popularity of his body of work would keep him returning to the UK year after year for concert tours, now in smaller and less prestigious venues, but his recording career was heading into hibernation.

The untold story of the 1967 version of "Something's Gotten Hold Of My Heart" is that it almost never got recorded. In a 2011 phone interview, Gerry Bron, a longtime Pitney friend and producer, explained that Gene had heard the original version of the song by David and Jonathan (the recording alias of the song's writers Roger Cook and Roger Greenaway) while on a UK tour. "He loved it and wanted to record it right away since the original had flopped," Bron recalled. "Cook and Greenaway were OK with it, too. If Gene Pitney could get a hit with their song they would be over the moon. Gene's plan was to record it back home in the States after a few weeks' rest from his tour."

Bron remembered a late-night phone call from an exasperated Pitney: "He told me they couldn't get it right. 'It's not working out. I need your help.'" According to Bron, that phone call put Gene in a professional pickle. The version being recorded in the States was being produced by Gene's friend and favorite producer at the time, Stan Kahan. But, Gene said it wasn't the sound he wanted. Bron said Gene then asked for the original track that David and Jonathan had produced.

Bron, a record producer himself, warned Pitney that might be a bad professional move. "I told him it could ruin his relationship, both personally and professionally, with Stan. I suggested to Gene he release two different versions of the song, one for the US market and one for England."

And that's what he ended up doing. Pitney's UK version is sung over the top of the original track and is pitched in a higher key in order to match Roger Cook's original range. Pitney's US version is less highly-produced and in a slightly different key. The UK version went into the Top 10; the US version flopped.

Roger Greenaway's recollection is very similar to Gerry Bron's. In an email he wrote: "We recorded the demo at Regent Sound in London. We knew Gerry, and once our demos were mixed and put on acetate it was my job to play our songs to producers in the hope of getting a recording. Gerry loved the song and played it for Gene. I was told that Gene made two attempts at laying tracks in New York but wasn't happy with the results. He asked Gerry if we could let him have our demo track, which included six rhythm section musicians plus Roger Cook on lead vocal and some backing voices. I believe Gene overdubbed our demo track with strings and girl backing singers. He obviously stripped out our vocals. 'Something's Gotten Hold of My Heart' was Roger Cook's song although we always worked together on the demos and productions. We had a kind of Lennon-McCartney relationship where we wrote some songs together and some separately but shared everything we did. I love both versions of this song!"

Needless to say, no one could have predicted that this song – in a radically different form – would give Pitney's career a huge boost more than two decades later. Through an unusual chain of events, Gene was invited in January 1989 to do a "duet" on a remake of the song with British glam star Marc Almond. No one had any idea how fruitful the coupling of the two stars from two different words, literally and figuratively, would be.

The "duet" story begins in 1988. Thirty-one-year-old Marc Almond, who grew up loving Gene Pitney, had already recorded his cover version of "Something's Gotten Hold Of My Heart" for his first album for EMI, *The Stars We Are*. Off-handedly, one day, he wondered out loud to EMI's Clive Black, the head of A&R, about the possibility of getting Gene Pitney to somehow duet with him on the record.

"I knew the song, and I loved the song and I just thought it worked for Marc," Black recalled in a 2021 phone interview. "I always thought that Marc was a great interpreter of songs as was Gene. Cook and Greenaway are two of my favorite writers to come out of the pop culture of this country. I thought it was worth a shot."

Black gets a lot of credit for getting the Almond-Pitney duet done, but he maintains that it was Andy Pryor, then Managing Director of EMI and Neil Warnock, Gene's UK agent, who really made it all happen. "I went to see Andy and told him I had this great idea about a Marc Almond-Gene Pitney duet on 'Something's Gotten Hold Of My Heart.' He looked at me and said, 'My best mate is Neil Warnock. He is Gene Pitney's agent.' I said it would be great if I could get Gene on this record. Andy gave me Neil's phone number, and we spoke and it went down well. We had it worked out in just a couple of days. Andy Pryor and Neil Warnock should get most of the credit."

Pitney recorded his part of the "duet" during a day off on his UK tour in early 1989. Ironically, like with the original version of this song, Pitney almost didn't get it recorded. At first it wasn't something he wanted to do. "The last thing I wanted to do on my day off," he said, "was work. Neil called, pitched me the idea, and I wasn't keen on it. Nothing against Marc, I just didn't want to do it. Neil worked on me and changed my mind."

Pitney and Marc Almond were never in the studio together. Clive Black, much to his chagrin, ended up producing Pitney's portion of the record. "Bob Kraushar, the real producer, was delayed at an airport," Black recalled with a laugh in a 2021 phone interview. "There was no engineer in the building for some reason. Marc was supposed to be there, but this was a bad time in his life as far as his health and his addictions were concerned. He never showed up. So, I took Gene into the studio. I was in a bit of panic because it was just me, a tape recorder, and Gene Pitney. I knew if we lost him on this day then we wouldn't get him back."

According to the affable Black, Gene was the ultimate professional: on time and prepared. Pitney wanted to sing the song through completely once. He wanted to whistle through it once. Then he wanted to sing through it once again. "After the first sing through," Black recalled with some bewilderment, "Gene yelled out, 'Do you mind if I sing topless?' I said, 'Knock yourself out, Mate. Whatever it takes.' So he rips his shirt off and sang it through again, half naked, brilliantly! He listened to the playback and realized he had fluffed something, and he said, 'Let's do it once more from the top.' He did it once more from the top, and we had it. He was in the studio less than thirty minutes. I was bowled over."

Neil Warnock, who accompanied Pitney to the recording session, said in an email, "I was in the studio with Gene when he recorded it, and the only reason he fluffed the take is because Marc had changed the lyric a little bit."

Over the course of his career, Pitney had proved he could sing anything from wide-eyed and joyful examples of early rock 'n' roll like "(I Wanna) Love My Life Away" to the formulaic teen angst of "Mecca" to sophisticated jewels like "Half Heaven-Half Heartache" to classy Hollywood movie themes like "Town Without Pity." He had swagger when he needed it; he had charisma when he needed it; he also knew when melancholy and sadness were the name of the game. But what about a duet with a gay, British glam star? Could it work?

The record was released on January 14, 1989. To everyone's shock, two weeks later it was #1. It stayed atop the British charts for four weeks. Then, it took off around Europe and hit #1 in a number of other countries.

Marc Almond told the story of his second #1 hit in the 1980s in his 444-page autobiography *Tainted Life* (a take-off on the title of his first #1 with Soft Cell, "Tainted Love"). That book was published by Pan Macmillan in 2000. Marc has given us permission to use this full excerpt from his book.

"The song that really made *The Stars We Are* a huge success was 'Something's Gotten Hold Of My Heart,' a cover of the '60s Gene Pitney classic. It was during a live performance at the London Astoria for a Japanese TV special that I first performed the song, and as soon as Clive Black heard it he knew it was possibly a hit, and insisted I record it for the album. If Clive was excited, so was I. I rearranged the song to add an Elvis Vegas-style 'you, you, you' section, and Billy arranged a stunning string section. We wanted to get it absolutely right, so Bob Kraushar was brought in to produce the track as he had already done such a fine job with the rest of the album. Bob pushed me, making me sing again and again until I hit the right notes.

"I can't clearly remember how the idea for the song to be a duet came about. I think I dropped a flippant remark about it to Clive Black, who took it seriously. At that time Gene Pitney was touring Britain. Perhaps I'd said he might come in and sing a few bars with me. But I'd never thought Clive would take me seriously. After all, I thought, why would Gene Pitney want to sing with me on a record that he had made famous? I was concerned that he might be offended. But Clive had the chutzpah to ask him.

Gene was delighted to oblige. As it turned out, his son was a fan of mine, and Gene himself liked 'Tainted Love.' It's surprising what you can get just by asking.

"A week later I went to see Gene in concert at Bow Town Hall in the East End of London. He looked great, the consummate performer – cool, professional, and sounding like he always did. 'Why isn't he performing at a major London venue?' I asked myself. People needed to be reminded of him. We all need a bit of that from time to time.

"I was still on tour when Gene went into the studio to record his parts. He graciously acknowledged that it was my version, my record, and was happy to let me lead. Apparently he removed his shirt and sang bare-chested. When I was presented with the finished track I was thrilled. I had always been a huge fan of his, ever since, as a child, I had watched him on television singing 'Twenty Four Hours from Tulsa' on *Ready Steady Go!* And, he was on my record! He has such an instantly recognizable voice, and a career that spans so many impeccable songs. I could have quite happily recorded a Marc Almond tribute album to Gene covering them all.

"I was first told of the song charting while I was doing a showcase for a record company conference in Germany. Clive Black knocked on my hotel door and broke the good news that the single was a new entry at #20 in the chart and getting massive radio play. It looked like it might be on the way up. After he left, I tried to locate some feelings of joy or excitement, but just felt numb. Everyone seemed to be a lot more excited than I was. The following week the record moved up to #10. Then, the next week, bad news: the midweek position (which record companies loved to find out) indicated a drop to #11. Still, I had some TV appearances…and everyone was optimistic these would prevent it falling any faster. Surely Saturday' sales would make a difference.

"On Sunday, when the chart was revealed, no one called me. It was nearly seven, so the record must have gone down. Then Stevo (Almond's manager Steve Pearce) called and told me for the second time in my career that my record was #1. It seemed to be not real, to be happening to someone else and I was just looking on. I acted the part of being overwhelmed and excited, but the truth was more to do with shock, and then bewilderment and finally anxiety. I knew that all the mainstream glory would bring unwanted attention. Then came the doubt that the record was untypical and unrepresentative of me as an artist, and finally that it had taken another cover version to get me a #1. All of these things nagged away at me.

190

"The first time I met Gene in person was when we filmed the video together in Las Vegas in November 1988. We went out there for a week to film. It was freezing in Las Vegas that night we filmed – a bitter wind cutting through you, burning your face and penetrating your clothing. I was taken to meet him in his Winnebago. It was a strange meeting between two artists from different worlds – he was a clean-cut family man, and me with greasy hair, a rockabilly quaff and dubious reputation. I was clutching a bundle of records of his for him to sign, like a star-struck fan. He was friendly and polite – always the professional. I couldn't believe he was here for me, on my record. I said to a journalist who had accompanied us to cover the story, 'Who would have thought that Marc Almond from Southport would watch a singer on *Ready Steady Go!* in his youth and years later would be in Las Vegas with that singer who was guesting on his record?' My mind was boggled.

"Gene was brilliant, though one sensed that he expected utmost professionalism or else. I respect people who do. I was informed by his manager that he was not entirely comfortable with the white tuxedo and red cummerbund that he had been dressed in. I naturally sided with Gene, but he relented and agreed to wear it. I was in a black tuxedo and he in a white one – contrasting and conflicting. Our climaxing verse was filmed in what was a neon graveyard in the desert – a haunted place where half the neons of yesteryear's glamorous locations ended up, half still working, headily symbolic of the changing Las Vegas. It was blowing a storm with dust everywhere, and we were freezing as we were led from our trailers, like boxers about to fight, to sing the final verse. Three takes only and then we were out of there. It was pure magic.

"Gene came over to Europe for the rounds of promotion, a *Top of the Pops* appearance, and various other TV shows, including the *Wogan* show. Terry Wogan wanted to interview Gene and me together about the record, but I was having none of it and gave the stage to Gene, allowing him to do the interview alone. But such graciousness had an ulterior motive. Obviously I felt uncomfortable about television interviews anyway, but I also wanted to remain mysterious and aloof. And my presence might have inhibited Gene in his flattery of me. So it was that Gene did the interview and said all the things I had hoped he would say and more, reminding everyone of what a star I was. A living legend flattering me – I ask you!

"The TV appearance and the constant radio play ensured the record stayed at #1 for four weeks, until I became completely blasé about the whole thing – even bored. So there it was. Another #1. I'd begun the '80s with one and I'd closed the '80s with another. Not bad going.

"'Something's Gotten Hold Of My Heart' went to #1 all over Europe. Gene benefited from the hit record. His greatest hits were reissued, and on his next tour he was playing at West End theatres. I went to see him and took a bow from the box. A couple of years later, when I was performing a retrospective show at the Albert Hall, I was sorry when Gene didn't join me on stage to sing 'Something's Gotten Hold Of My Heart.' He was in London at the time, but he said he had a bad back. I felt a little let down in one way, because I know he would have brought the house down."

———————————

The hit record breathed new life into Pitney's touring, career allowing him to move into bigger and more prestigious venues. However, it did nothing to revitalize his recording career. First of all, Capitol/EMI refused to issue the record in the US. Pitney said they didn't think "a duet by an older, silver-haired singer singing a love song with a younger, gay singer would work. I tried and tried and tried to convince them it was a hit, but no one would listen." So, the biggest worldwide hit of his career was never heard by his still large group of American fans. He was disappointed.

Also, even after the rousing success of the duet, his phone never rang with a record deal from the UK and/or Europe. Pitney said, "They all thought it was a one off, and it really didn't make me relevant. Nothing to be done about that."

In a bit of a panic, he decided to put out a follow-up record on his own label, Pitfield Records. The A-side was a gorgeous Allan Leckie ballad "You're The Reason." But, without major label promotion money or distribution behind it, the record fizzled. It is, however, a record that any Gene Pitney fan would want to own. It is a classic. Pitney produced it; Maurice Merry, his longtime musical director, arranged it. (For information on how to buy a copy contact us at Pitneyfan@genepitneybook.com.)

This kind of undertaking was a burden for him. It was uncomfortable for him. He called it "drama." He turned down a lot of intriguing opportunities with the likes of Bruce Springsteen, David Letterman, and others because "it was too much drama."

Nonetheless, he loved the way this record turned out. "Marc has this nice, sweet voice very similar to what I used on my original version back in '67," Pitney said. "So, to give some contrast to his voice I decided to growl a little bit. It was a vocal I really sank my teeth into. I really liked the arrangement they came up with for this version. This was Marc's record, but I wanted my signature on it, too."

Favorite Lyric: *"And a feeling unknown shook my heart, made me want you to stay…all of my nights and all of my days."* Is it luck or is it fate to meet THAT person who does THIS to you? You are one of the lucky ones if you have had that kind of kismet. As Marc Anthony sang, we don't fall into this kind of love, we crash into it!

Factoid: Gene was compensated for his vocal prowess and performance on this record. Clive Black said, "Yes, he was paid a fee and points on the record, and all his costs were paid. He was treated like royalty!" Clive Black also recalled a very nice gesture on Gene's part. "He sent me a note from The Skyline Hotel at Heathrow Airport that read, 'Dear Clive, I'm leaving today, but thanks for making me feel like a star again. Best, Gene Pitney.' It was the nicest note I ever got in my whole life from anyone."

Factoid: Neil Warnock, one of the key matchmakers for this record, said, "Marc never met Gene until I introduced them to each other in Vegas for the video shoot of the song. Marc was so nervous to meet Gene I thought he would pass out!!"

Factoid: Neil Warnock was appointed a Member of the British Empire (MBE) in 2019. At this writing he is the global head of touring at United Talent Agency in London. As part of this executive role, he oversees a robust roster of UK agents and artists, advising on both regional and international touring business strategy. He is one of the most experienced music agents in the world and a key architect of the modern live music business.

Factoid: Roger Cook said he was inspired to write "Something's Gotten Hold of My Heart" by The Righteous Brothers' record "You've Lost That Lovin' Feeling." "There were three separate parts to that brilliant song, and they all came together at the end," he said. "I wanted to write a song more or less like that, and that's how this song came about. It took me three to four weeks to get it finalized. I really like Gene's original record on this song. It was inspired."

And, the last word goes to…Lynne Pitney: "This is such a great song…both versions. This is another one of those songs where Gene took a softer approach – on the original version – than he did on some of his other records. It's like he was singing a fairytale. This is his voice that I loved. But, I loved Gene with Marc Almond, too. I loved their voices together. If you made me pick one version over the other I would say it was Gene's solo hit only because it was just Gene."

One of the earliest Musicor promotional photos.

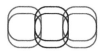

CHAPTER 26:
THAT GIRL BELONGS TO YESTERDAY

Lyrics and Music by Mick Jagger and Keith Richards

Fun Fact: You read that right. The Glimmer Twins, Mick Jagger and Keith Richards, wrote this pop gem for Gene Pitney. Then, he turned down the chance to represent them in the US.

Gene Pitney said: "It was completely wrong for me at the time so I changed the entire melodic structure of the song. They loved it because they hadn't had any success yet." That's what Pitney told "Wild" Wayne Jones on his oldies show on WWUH Radio in Hartford, Connecticut, while discussing the genesis of this record.

Unless you are an expert at 1960s music trivia, you would likely never mention Gene Pitney and The Rolling Stones in the same sentence when discussing music. Their musical styles, physical presence, and vocal abilities are light years apart. Yet their lives and careers came together for a brief, shining, odd, and remarkable moment in time in early 1964.

Bill Wyman, the longtime bass player for The Rolling Stones, explained the basis for their friendship with Pitney in his book, *Stone Alone*. "The Everly Brothers' tour had changed us perceptibly; their music was a million miles from ours, but we admired their sound, the quality of their songs and their professionalism. We had the same views about an American singer who was to become a firm friend."

That singer, of course, was Gene Pitney.

Pitney became the very first artist to score a Top 10 hit in the UK with a Mick Jagger-Keith Richards song. And, while the triumph was not as towering, he was also the first artist to ever get a Jagger-Richards song into the *Billboard Hot 100*. It hit #49 on that chart. These were two huge accomplishments for a small town boy from Connecticut in the big time world of pop music.

In both cases that song was the strikingly sublime "That Girl Belongs To Yesterday." This is one giant rollercoaster ride showing off the vocal genius of Gene Pitney telling the very down-in-the-dumps story about the girl who broke his heart. *"Last night I needed you so bad…I was alone and feeling sad. But now that I recall…you left me after all…the only girl I've ever had."* The record hit #7 in the UK on March 25, 1964. In the US, the record peaked at #49, one month earlier, on February 22, 1964.

There are a number of stories about how Gene got this song. They are all variations on a theme: The Stones and Pitney were both appearing on a popular British music TV show when they first met. Again, Bill Wyman described that fateful meeting in his book, *Stone Alone*: "We were at Birmingham and after miming to 'I Wanna Be Your Man' on *Thank Your Lucky Stars* we returned to our dressing room to mess around with some songs. Later, Andrew (Loog Oldham) took Mick and Keith to Pitney's room, and Gene told them he was disappointed by his lack of success in Britain. This was at a time when Mick and Keith were being encouraged by Andrew to write songs together. Mick and Keith began loosely playing and singing one of their songs called 'My Only Girl.' Pitney asked Andrew (who was soon to become his publicity officer) to arrange a recording session; he could not wait to cut the song.

"Only three days after we'd first met we were in the studio with Pitney to cut a demo version of the song. Gene converted it into more of a ballad for his style, re-wrote the chorus with Mick and Keith, and re-titled it 'That Girl Belongs To Yesterday.' Everyone was having such a ball that we ended up recording demos for kicks."

"That Girl Belongs To Yesterday"/"My Only Girl" was written at the beginning of The Stones' recording/songwriting career and was certainly not the type of song that they wanted to write, sing, record, or perform. But, you gotta start somewhere.

And, while Mick and Keith likely never envisioned themselves competing against giants like Barry Mason and Les Reed who were writing fabulous pop hits for British Invasion bands like The Fortunes ("Here It Comes Again") and The Dave Clark 5 ("Everybody Knows") and stars like Tom Jones ("Delilah) and Engelbert Humperdinck ("The Last Waltz," "Lonely Is A Man Without Love," and "Les Bicyclettes de Belsize"), the Glimmer Twins turned out a couple of pretty respectable pop ballads themselves during that period, including their own hit "Tell Me (You're Coming Back)" and Marianne Faithfull's "As Tears Go By."

The aforementioned Andrew Loog Oldham, a twenty-one-year-old jack-of-all-trades publicist, manager, and record producer, was not only the link between The Rolling Stones and Gene Pitney, he is also credited with getting Jagger and Richards started on their extraordinarily remarkable songwriting careers.

Memories fade over the years, and people remember stories the way they want to. In Ian McPherson's book *Jagger/Richards: Songwriters Part 1*, Keith Richards remembers that their meteoric songwriting partnership started, this way:

"So what Andrew Oldham did was lock us up in the kitchen for a night and say, 'Don't come out without a song.' We sat around and came up with 'As Tears Go By.' It was unlike most Rolling Stones material, but that's what happens when you write songs, you immediately fly to some other realm. The weird thing is that Andrew found Marianne Faithfull at the same time, bunged it to her, and it was a fuckin' hit for her – we were songwriters already! But it took the rest of that year to dare to write anything for the Stones."

And, Richards also pointed out bluntly and colorfully, this was NOT the direction the band wanted to go in. "That's why I take my hat off to Andrew. He had no idea, but it was worth a try, and it worked. In that little kitchen Mick and I got hung up about writing songs, and it still took us another six months before we had another hit with Gene Pitney, 'That Girl Belongs to Yesterday.' We were writing these terrible pop songs that were becoming Top 10 hits. I thought, 'What are we doing here playing the fucking blues and writing these horrible pop songs and getting very successful?' They had nothing to do with us, except we wrote 'em."

In the book *According to the Rolling Stones*, Mick Jagger waved off Keith's recollection as a somewhat whimsical view.

"Keith likes to tell the story about the kitchen, God bless him. I think Andrew may have said something at some point along the lines of 'I should lock you in a room until you've written a song' and in that way he did mentally lock us in a room, but he didn't literally lock us in. One of the first songs we came out with was that tune for George Bean, the very memorable 'It Should Be You.'"

Pitney, the guy who recognized that "That Girl Belongs To Yesterday" could be a hit with some melodic massaging, doesn't remember it originally being titled "My Only Girl." But, his memory of meeting The Stones coincides pretty much with Bill Wyman's: "I don't think I was complaining about my lack of success in the UK," he explained. "I was coming off a Top 5 hit there with 'Tulsa.' I was simply trying to point out to them that I needed British-type songs written by British guys in British bands if I was going to stay successful. That's when they gave me 'That Girl Belongs To Yesterday.' They were still songwriting novices at the time and didn't realize how strong a hook they had in (starts singing) 'that girl belongs to yesterday…' I just punched it up and made the backing track far more dramatic."

After 1964 he rarely sang the song in his UK concerts and never sang it in his US concerts. The reason for not doing it in the US? "It wasn't a hit for me at home so I never bothered to have charts put together for it," he admitted one night after a show in Pigeon Forge, Tennessee, in the 1990s. "Back in the day in 1964 the tour bands I used in the UK just played by ear. Later on, when I put together my own shows with a full orchestra with strings and horns, they wanted charts. I didn't have charts for them so I never sang the song in concerts."

He added that he made a mistake and should have paid the money for the charts because "it would have been fun to tell the story about the song, me and The Stones, and then sing it. A lot of casual fans don't know my early connection with them."

––––––––––––––––

Here is a full interview with Gene about "That Girl Belongs To Yesterday" that was published in the *Gene Pitney International Fan Club Newsletter* in 1993.

Question: Do you know who wrote the lyrics and who wrote the music?

Gene: I don't know who wrote what on "That Girl Belongs To Yesterday." I never asked.

Question: How and where did you first hear the song? Did you know you wanted it right away?

Gene: I first heard the song at Olympia Studios in London where Andrew Loog Oldham had the master tapes. Andrew was my publicist as well as the publicist, producer, and manager of The Rolling Stones. The track had already been recorded when I first heard it, and the vocalist on the original recording was a guy named George Bean. Andrew and The Stones were not happy with the tape so they offered it to me. I loved the sound of the musical track, but I wasn't thrilled with the melody. I asked if I could change the melody to fit the musical track, and they said OK.

Question: You and Andrew Oldham are listed as the producers. Who did what on the session? Who else was at the session?

Gene: Remember that the musical track had already been recorded, so when I went in to make my record it was just little ol' me and the master tape. No musicians, no band, nothing. Mick, Keith, and Andrew were at the studio controls. I was at the microphone. Seeing as the concept was mine, I got a production credit. Seeing as Andrew did produce it in the original form – the master tape – he, too, got a production credit. Andrew was very good at putting all the pieces of a project together to get an end result. We worked very well together. The Stones were just starting out at the time and, as irreverent as they were even then, they still listened to Andrew.

Question: Did you like the finished product? Were you happy with the record?

Gene: I thought the record was good, but I realized the melody had its shortcomings. When you are locked into an existing track it really limits where you can go with the melody. It was also a hurry-up job in the studio because I was in London only for a short time for concert promotion. It could have been an awful lot better!

Question: The song went Top 10 in England but only got to #49 in the States. Were you disappointed – or – surprised by the lack of chart success at home?

Gene: I think I learned an early lesson with those chart results in the US. The record-buying public had a certain idea of what I was supposed to sound like from the hits I had before "That Girl Belongs To Yesterday," and I broke the stereotype and the rules by putting out a very British-sounding record. This was to become more and more apparent in the future with the eventual situation unfolding where we would release one song for the British and world market and a different one for the USA.

Question: It has been written that the original title of the song was "My Only Girl." Did you change the title and/or any lyrics?

Gene discussing a song at a recording session. The background singer in the photo is unidentified.

Gene: Nope. The original title was "That Girl Belongs To Yesterday," and the lyric was always the same. That was another reason why creating a new melody was difficult. The notes had to fit the syllables of the original lyric.

Question: As you mentioned, The Stones were just starting out then. This had to be a big deal in their career. Did they ever thank you for recording the song and getting it charted both in the UK and the USA?

Gene: The Stones were very excited about getting the song on the US charts. And, I'm sure they were disappointed it wasn't a bigger hit! The friend of mine who was travelling with me at the time, by the way, never let me forget that Andrew offered to let me represent The Stones in the US market for the price of six round trip airfares from London to New York. Oops!

Question: How long did it take to record the song? How many takes? Was it a hard song to sing?

Gene: I don't think the recording took that long. If anything, the harmonies were probably the most difficult. By the way, if you take away the harmony you'll see just how weak the actual melody is. It really doesn't stand on its own.

Question: If you could change anything about the record, what would it be?

Gene: I would change the whole melody. As you can tell by now, I'm not too fond of it. Maybe that is why I haven't sung it in a concert that I can recall.

Question: If you knew then what you know now about royalties, would you have asked for a writing credit on the song?

Gene: No. I don't believe in taking away writer's credits – or accepting them – just because it is politically possible to do so. I know that a song is like your own baby, and it is so hard to let other people hack away at it. Today it is a common practice for very popular artists to lend their name to the writing credits because they are in a position of power. It's "Either you put my name on it, or I don't record it." Colonel Tom Parker used to do that for Elvis all the time. I am a songwriter, and I wouldn't want that done to me, so I never did it to anyone else.

Gene added this interesting anecdote on "That Girl Belongs To Yesterday." It really highlights how different – almost naïve – the recording industry was in 1964. "Seeing as I would record the song and have it released worldwide," Pitney explained, "Andrew Loog Oldham naturally said he would supply the already-recorded track to me at no cost.

"Well, I found out about three months after the record charted that I was being sued by Pakkamak Music, the company that owned and published the track, for illegal use of a track not owned by me. Surprise! It seems that Andrew never did own the track. He just arranged to have someone else put up the money for the original recording session. I ended up paying many thousands of dollars to clear up the mess. It was another lesson I learned the hard way."

In both the US and the UK, "That Girl Belongs To Yesterday" was released on the heels of "Twenty Four Hours From Tulsa." In the UK it followed "Tulsa,' which had peaked at #5, straight into the Top 10. In the USA "Tulsa" had become a Top 20 hit, peaking at #17, while "That Girl Belongs To Yesterday" only made it to #49.

As Gene surmised, the song may have flopped in the US because it didn't sound like "a Gene Pitney record." His previous hits were "(I Wanna) Love My Life Away," "Town Without Pity," "(The Man Who Shot) Liberty Valance," "Only Love Can Break A Heart," "Half Heaven-Half Heartache," "Mecca," "True Love Never Runs Smooth," and "Twenty Four Hours From Tulsa."

"That Girl Belongs To Yesterday" was a darker melody with pretty scrawny production values, compared to his previous hits. The music business is, at best, a crapshoot. An artist puts out a record and hopes radio will play it and the public will like it. There is no predicting what will be a hit and what won't. Every artist from Frank Sinatra to Elvis Presley to Elton John to

Another picture from the photo shoot for the *Pitney '75* album.

Bruce Springsteen have put out records that failed to capture the public's ears.

Perhaps, had this song been released a year later, after The Stones broke big in the US, it would have been a different story. Having Mick and Keith as the writers likely would have been the cachet needed to make it a big hit. Pitney put it out almost six months before anyone in the US had a clue who The Rolling Stones were, and it was a full year before The Stones became major players in the US charts with their first Top 10 hit, "Time Is On My Side," in late 1964.

Imagine how the record might have been received in the US had it come out in late 1965, right after The Stones had scored their back-to-back #1 classics, "(I Can't Get No) Satisfaction" and "Get Off My Cloud." Think of the prestige that would have then been attached to the Pitney record. Timing is everything.

Favorite Lyric: *"I never ever made you cry…No, no I didn't even try…You promised you'd be true…You said you loved me too…My only girl told me a lie."* Jagger and Richards wrote those lyrics as neophyte songwriters in 1963. It's fascinating what a difference three years and massive wealth, fame, and power can do to the lyrics produced by songwriters. Here's Jagger-Richards in 1966: *"Under my thumb…the girl who once had me down…Under my thumb…the girl who once pushed me around…"*

Factoid: You can hear The Rolling Stones demo of the song, recorded at Regent Sounds Studio in London in November of 1963, on YouTube. Compared to what Gene Pitney did with the song, their version – admittedly a demo – is surprisingly sophomoric and unsophisticated. Mick Jagger just seemed to dash through it with an uncaring and un-emotional detachment. This demo shows what a really average singer The Stones' front man was/is. And, as bombastic as some critics think Pitney's version is, in its essence, it really is a highly-orchestrated but unpretentious blues song about the girl who wasn't there when it counted. And, let's face it, Gene sang the hell out of that song. In the Fan Club interview, Pitney said he extensively reworked and enhanced the melody line for his version. Mick and Keith never contradicted that. The piano work on The Stones demo, however, is a nice touch, sweet in its daintiness and simplicity.

Factoid: In his book, *Life*, Keith Richards wrote this about this song, "[Pitney] improved on the words and our original title, which was 'My Only Girl.'"

Factoid: It's also been written in many accounts of The Rolling Stones-Gene Pitney encounter that the English folk/rock singer George Bean, mentioned in Mick Jagger's previous quote, also recorded "That Girl Belongs To Yesterday." No version of his recording has yet to surface. Other songs of his, including another Jagger-Richards composition, are up on YouTube. He died of a brain aneurysm in 1970.

And, the last word goes to…Lynne Pitney: "The thing that always stood out for me on this record was the harmonies that Gene did on it. I've always liked this song a lot. And the fact that it was written by Mick and Keith makes it so cool. I never knew why Gene didn't do it in concert. I never asked. Now I know!"

Contact proofs from a promotional photo shoot in 1975.

(THE MAN WHO SHOT) LIBERTY VALANCE

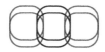

CHAPTER 27:
(THE MAN WHO SHOT)
LIBERTY VALANCE

Lyrics by Hal David and Music by Burt Bacharach

Fun Fact: This song did NOT appear in the movie of the same name. Why not? Well…it depends on who you believe! And, that's not to say any of the versions of the story is wrong; it's more like there's a little bit of truth in each one.

Gene Pitney said: "The movie's director, Hollywood legend John Ford, didn't want some crummy pop song in his movie that starred John Wayne, Jimmy Stewart, and Lee Marvin."

Over the years, Pitney shared a number of versions of what happened. He is absolutely certain that Paramount Pictures, the company that produced the movie, also paid for his recording session for this song. "I knew this song came to me because I had just had a hit with another movie theme, 'Town Without Pity.' Paramount wanted to piggyback on that. They paid me quite a bundle to do this song."

Pitney explained that at some point the left hand at Paramount apparently didn't always know what the right hand was doing. "While I was recording the song at Bell Sound in New York, Paramount in Hollywood released the movie. It was a big oops.

"Like 'Town Without Pity' before it, 'Liberty Valance' was not the kind of song I would have chosen to record. I wondered why they didn't get Marty Robbins to do it. I think I told an interviewer once I thought the song was 'hokey.' I didn't mean corny or old-fashioned. I meant it kinda sounded like a square dance song (*laughter*). You know, with that violin and those wedding band drums."

At other times, likely when he had been asked the question for the millionth time, he would wave it off with "It was some sort of business thing. I think it was a fight over money between the film company and maybe Burt and Hal or maybe my manager, Aaron Schroeder. I was still a kid, a rookie in the business."

In his 2005 book *Always Magic In The Air*, published by Penguin Books, Ken Emerson opined that "either the 74-year-old (John) Ford failed to appreciate the song's humor, or he didn't cotton to greenhorns." The "greenhorn" would have been the newcomer Pitney. The humor? Emerson wrote that Hal David's lyrics "pay homage to the Hollywood-on-the-range ballads sung by the likes of Frankie Laine in the 1950s while it gently pokes fun at them with a wheezy country fiddle and gunplay on the snare drum."

In a 1997 interview with Terry Gross for the NPR program *Fresh Air*, lyricist Hal David explained the song's absence from the movie this way: "We were asked to write it for Paramount. They were called exploitation songs in those days. The film companies had you do those songs to have a song come out and perhaps become a hit and exploit the film. Every time the title song was played (on the radio), people would hear the title and think of the film.

"The song turned out to be a rather good song, and we and the Paramount Publishing Company made every effort to try to get the song into the film. John Ford resisted it because he didn't conceive of a song being in the film at that point. As much as Paramount pressed him to put it in, they were not successful, and we were not successful.

"So, the song came out, Gene Pitney had recorded it, did a very good record, and it became a big hit. And I suspect Mr. Ford might have been a little regretful that he didn't have it in the film."

Gross pointed out that the lyrics in "(The Man Who Shot) Liberty Valance" were markedly different from the more sophisticated prose that Hal David composed for his love songs. For example, "*'cause the point of a gun was the only law that Liberty un-derstood. When it came to shootin' straight and fast, he was mighty good.*"

David told her, "I don't know. I seem to hear those things. I find it kind of natural for me to do. I've never had a problem writing western songs, country songs. You know, most of the work we do as songwriters or any kind of creative person is really done in the imagination. And I guess I imagine things like '(The Man Who Shot) Liberty Valance.'"

His writing partner, Burt Bacharach, always thought the world of Gene Pitney. Gene's recording of this song certainly justified his opinion of Pitney. "Love that record," said Bacharach in a 1987 Fan Club newsletter interview. "Gene's splendid on it. I was not at all surprised it became a hit. There are maybe only two or three other singers who could have recorded that song and done as good a job as Gene. That song proved to me that he was a star. We gave him a good song, and he gave us back a great record. I've worked with many, many talented singers over the years, but there is only one Gene Pitney."

Abby Schroeder, wife and business partner of Aaron Schroeder, concurred with Hal David. In a 2021 phone interview, she said, "It was plain and simple. John Ford did not want a pop song in his movie. There is no more to the story than that. We all liked

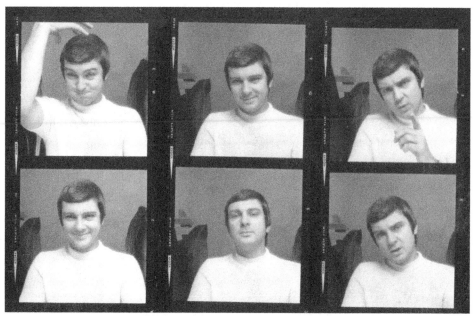

Contact proofs of Gene letting his personality shine through on a photo shoot.

the record, and we lobbied hard to get it in the movie, but, in the end, Ford gave it the thumbs down. And, he likely never even listened to Gene's record."

For Pitney to tackle this song at all was more than admirable. His vocal on the song is nothing but sterling. He certainly could have played it tongue-in-cheek, as the opening violin strains seemed to forewarn the listener to what was coming. But, he was bound and determined to tell this no-nonsense story in the most definitive way he could. Also, because his diction was always impeccable, the listener was never left guessing about what transpired in this song.

As he mentioned in an earlier quote, this was not the type of song he wanted to do. He was only twenty-two years old when he recorded "Liberty Valance." This song was really tailor-made for artists like Frankie Laine or Marty Robbins, who had very successful track records in this genre. Pitney was being marketed as a pop star and a "teen idol," and this song did not fill that bill at all. He was worried "Liberty Valance" could sidetrack his career.

Soaring to #4 in the US charts in 1962, "(The Man Who Shot) Liberty Valance" certainly didn't hurt his burgeoning career. It served him quite well. It showed off his vocal strengths and versatility. It gave him his second hit and set the table for his third straight hit, "Only Love Can Break A Heart," the biggest US hit he ever had. Ironically, "Only Love Can Break A Heart" was another song he didn't want to record!

"Liberty Valance" also travelled well internationally and helped open more doors around the world for Pitney. It became a big hit for him in Australia, in particular.

For Details Of

THE GENE PITNEY FAN CLUB OF AUSTRALIA

WRITE TO

ANNETTE WARD

21 Seaview Street,
Balgowlah Heights,
N.S.W.

Looking back on this record while sitting backstage at The Foxwoods Resort Casino in Connecticut in 2001, preparing to tape a TV show, Pitney admitted he was angry for a number of years about the song not getting into the movie.

"I felt that whatever happened could have been rectified," he said. "We had all the components in place to get 'Liberty Valance' nominated for an Academy Award as 'Town Without Pity' had been. I would have loved a second shot at an Oscar. I know Burt and Hal would have gotten it, but, remember, everyone knows that Andy Williams sang 'Moon River.' Few people really know who wrote it.

"Someone should have or could have done something about it. This business is as much about the money as it is about the art. I was too young, too green to get involved. This song was a big league deal, but I was still a rookie. There were some pretty big players who could have figured it out. I lost a big opportunity with that song. I'm over it now, but I held a grudge for a while."

Favorite Lyric: *"When Liberty Valance rode to town...the women folk would hide, they'd hide. When Liberty Valance walked around...the men would step aside."* Nine years later, in 1971, Isaac Hayes wrote this: "You see this cat Shaft is a bad mother (Shut your mouth.)" Did Liberty Valance change his name? Asking for a friend!

Factoid: There were a number of cover versions of this song, most notably James Taylor in 1985. Other well-known artists who took it on were Jimmie Rodgers (1962), The Royal Guardsmen (1967), The Greg Kihn Band (1980), and Rex Allen, Jr. (son of the great western movie star) (2007).

And, the last word goes to...Lynne Pitney: "Everything was all so new and exciting when this song came out. This wouldn't have been the kind of song that I would have liked, but it is a great record, and it would have been a great song for that movie. They missed the boat by not using it. Gene sold every word of every line of that song. I always loved that line, *'alone and afraid she prayed that he'd return that fateful night...'* It's so dramatic, and it paints such a vivid picture in your mind's eye. Another song no one else but Gene could pull off."

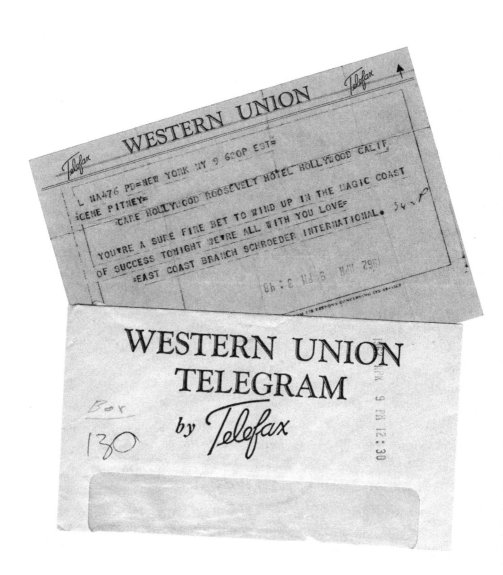

WESTERN UNION

Telefax

L NA476 PD=NEW YORK NY 9 620P EST=
=GENE PITNEY=
=CARE HOLLYWOOD ROOSEVELT HOTEL HOLLYWOOD CALIF=

YOU'RE A SURE FIRE BET TO WIND UP IN THE MAGIC COAST
OF SUCCESS TONIGHT WE'RE ALL WITH YOU LOVE=
=EAST COAST BRANCH SCHROEDER INTERNATIONAL.

WESTERN UNION
TELEGRAM
by Telefax

Box
130

Telegram sent from Aaron and Abby Schroeder to Gene on the night of the Oscar ceremony in 1962.

210

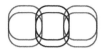

CHAPTER 28:
TOWN WITHOUT PITY

Lyrics by Ned Washington and Music by Dimitri Tiomkin

Fun Fact: This song was "born" to be a hit! The parents – if you will – of this song were two writers with a total of thirty three Oscar nominations – one of which was this song –and seven Oscar wins for their music. What a pedigree! This song was featured in the 1961 movie of the same name starring Kirk Douglas.

Gene Pitney said: "It is simply a winner of a song to walk off to. It has those singing, swinging horns, and it just pulses. I get pumped up when I hear that walk off chorus, and I head to the front of the stage to shake hands. It is just an electric moment every night."

Pitney sang "Town Without Pity" live at the *34th Academy Awards Show* (honoring the best in film for 1961) held on April 9, 1962, at the Santa Monica Civic Auditorium in Santa Monica, California. Here's how he was introduced by the legendary Bob Hope: "There are five nominees for the 'Best Song,' and the first one that is going to be played this evening has music by Dimitri Tiomkin and lyrics by Ned Washington. It was to have been sung originally by one of the big screen's outstanding personalities…but the producer didn't want me to sing it (*crowd laughter*). He said he'd rather have a town without pity than an audience full of it (*more crowd laughter*). So, here's the young man who sang it behind the titles of the movie and inside jukeboxes everywhere… Mr. Gene Pitney."

Pitney's performance of "Town Without Pity" that night was as stellar as the song it-self. He was blessed to have recorded this song at this point in his career. Later in life, looking back on that performance of a then fresh-faced and scared-to-death twenty-two-year-old-soon-to-be-teen idol, Pitney recalled how petrified he was that magical night. "People don't realize that I was the first pop singer to ever perform at the Oscars. That held me up to a lot of scrutiny. You gotta remember…this was live! And, there I was, this skinny kid from Rockville, Connecticut, rubbing elbows with stars like Burt Lancaster, Judy Garland, Marilyn Monroe, and, of course, Kirk Douglas. They were all there; every name that I had ever heard of in the film industry. It was a very scary moment for me. To this day I am amazed that anything came out of my throat at all and that it didn't sound like a squeaky door."

To be surrounded by all those stars and then have to perform for them was just one fear that Pitney had to deal with that night. To make things worse and ratchet up the tension for the young, green kid from Rockville, at the rehearsal, the producer presented him with the plan for his performance of the song and his stage directions.

Pitney recalled that plan with a laugh. "The producer told me, 'Now, Mr. Pitney, what we want you to do is to start singing your song up on top of the staircase on this set we built for you, then when you get to the instrumental break of the song, we want you to walk down those seven steps, down to the level where Mr. Hope is. Now, Mr. Pitney, we don't want you to look down when you're walking down the stairs. Look at the crowd; acknowledge the crowd.'

"That's when my life flashed before me. Right then and there. I wasn't really thinking about the whole world watching me on television, you know the millions of people out there, I was thinking about the people at home. I knew that my family and friends were going to be watching, and I thought to myself, 'You're going to fall down the damn stairs.' I really thought this was the end of my career.

"Dave McGrath, a great friend and the President of my International Fan Club, was able to wrangle a tape of that show, which was hard because the Academy hoards those things. I watched it, and I still shake my head in amazement. On the show I looked like a pro…like I did this every day of my life. I looked as calm as could be. I don't know how I did that. My stomach was churning from the opening strains of that song. That night at the Oscars was at the same time a nerve-wracking and ecstatic experience for someone as young and naïve as I was in 1962. I knew when I got through that performance that I could do anything."

Pitney's "Town Without Pity" was also nominated for a less prestigious Golden Globe Award that year. Those are the awards given out by the Hollywood Foreign Press Association. Talking on the air about that show with his friend "Wild" Wayne Jones on WWUH Radio in Hartford, Connecticut, Pitney said the same Hollywood stars were there. "Fred MacMurray stepped on my foot while I was waiting to go on to sing (*laughter*). We did win that one for Best Song in a Motion Picture for the world. I didn't know I was the only one singing that night. They did it at the Beverly Hills Hotel, I think, in the old Hollywood way with a big giant spotlight aimed at the back of the room. I had to walk all the way down the aisle, like a gangplank, then up some steps, then walk up to the middle of the stage. And I looked down and everybody was there. To this day I don't know what I sounded like. There was rather limited applause at the end. I'm not sure I did it that swift, but it gave me guts."

Lyricist Ned Washington was one of the all-time greats. His other credits include Frankie Laine's hits "Rawhide" and "High Noon (Do Not Forsake Me Oh My Darlin')," as well as "When You Wish Upon A Star" from the movie *Pinocchio*, "I'm Getting Sentimental Over You," big band leader Tommy Dorsey's theme song, and the Johnny Mathis hit "Wild Is The Wind."

Ned Washington had picked up eleven Academy Award nominations during his career and won two Best Song Oscars for "When You Wish Upon A Star" sung by Cliff Edwards in *Pinocchio* and "High Noon (Do Not Forsake Me Oh My Darlin')" sung in the movie by Tex Ritter. "When You Wish Upon A Star" was the first Disney song ever to win an Oscar.

Ned Washington died in Beverly Hills in 1976. He was 75 years old.

Russian-born, self-taught composer Dimitri Tiomkin wrote the music for "Town Without Pity." He also shared the writing credits with Ned Washington on those two aforementioned Frankie Laine hits and the Johnny Mathis song. He also wrote the scores for a slew of movies, including *Giant, Friendly Persuasion, The Alamo, You Can't Take It With You, Mr. Smith Goes To Washington, It's A Wonderful Life, Gunfight at the O.K. Corral, High Noon,* and *Dial M For Murder.*

Over the course of his storied Hollywood career, Tiomkin received twenty-two Academy Award nominations and won four Oscars, three for Best Original Score for *High Noon, The High and The Mighty,* and *The Old Man and the Sea.* He also won an Oscar for Best Song for "High Noon (Do Not Forsake Me Oh My Darlin')."

According to a 2002 story in *Soundtrack Magazine*, between 1948 and 1958, the prolific Tiomkin composed fifty seven film scores. He quickly became the highest-paid film composer in Hollywood and was writing music for an average of one movie per month.

Dimitri Tiomkin died in London in 1979. He was 85 years old.

So, it's no surprise that "Town Without Pity" would pick up an Oscar nomination for Best Song in 1961. It lost to the Henry Mancini-Johnny Mercer song "Moon River" from *Breakfast at Tiffany's*. As Gene always said, "Too bad that 'Moon River' was nominated, too. Can you imagine what a career I would have had if THAT song hadn't come along!"

That relatively laissez-faire perspective on losing an Oscar bothered his manager, Aaron Schroeder, and his wife and business partner, Abby Schroeder then and now. "We were disappointed; Gene was not. It became evident on this trip that Gene was not fond of Hollywood and didn't want to be in films. Aaron and I did...in a big way. We even arranged for Gene to get a screen test with Annette Funicello, that beautiful little Mickey Mouse Club star. She loved Gene. He didn't want to do it. He had his singing career and was getting some notoriety and getting noticed. So, that was it. No film career for Gene Pitney."

While Pitney's voice may be his greatest gift, this song was a big, big gift to his career as well. But, Pitney said he was never keen on recording the song. He told Bob Greene of *The Chicago Tribune* in a 1997 interview, "I was frightened of this song. I would never have written a song like this, and I would never have picked it to record. I saw this song and thought, 'How do I sing it? What do I do?' I decided to sing it as slowly as I possibly could."

Gene's vocal on "Town Without Pity" may be one-of-a-kind. It's a semi-growl, nothing he'd ever done on another of his original recordings. Pitney loved talking about the recording session and the "technique" he used on this record.

"We went into the studio, in Los Angeles, to record the song about 7:30 or 8 pm," he explained. "I don't know how many takes we did. I was singing great; hit all the notes. But no one except me seemed happy. Then, about 4 o'clock the next morning, we all decided to do 'one more take.' That's when it happened. I was exhausted and a little irritated. So, what started out as me singing in a Bing Crosby-like crooner style turned into me kinda growling because my pipes were worn out. When I was done with the take, they all stood up in the recording studio and said, 'That's it! That's what we're looking for.'"

Abby Schroeder explained that her husband, Aaron, may have surreptitiously rehearsed Gene for that vocal "technique" prior to the trip to Hollywood. "Gene would come into our office and sit down at the piano with Aaron, and they'd noodle around on some songs they were writing together. Gene had this beautifully pure voice, but on some of the songs Aaron told him to 'rough it up a little bit.' I think Gene was too young to know that he was being covertly coached by Aaron."

She was at the "Town Without Pity" recording session and doesn't completely debunk Pitney's recollection of how that record came together. She amplified that story by giving some of the credit to her husband in a direct and plausible way. "Aaron produced it, and he wanted it done with spunk and emotion. He didn't want Gene to use that pure voice of his. He didn't want a crooner on this record. He wanted some extra oomph. He probably kept having Gene do 'another take' and 'another take' to get him where he wanted him vocally. It was the start of the 'Pitney rasp.'"

If you want to hear what the song sounds like with Gene using his "pure voice," check out the video of his performance at the Academy Awards on You Tube. The difference is unquestionably clear.

While Gene always said he loved this record and was glad he was pushed to create the vocal sound he did on it, he later admitted that he never liked the way the song, as recorded, sounded in concert. He thought it sounded like a funeral dirge at that tempo when done live.

"It always sounded, to me, that singing it that slowly in concert made me sound like I was in a trance," he explained. "It worked on the record; it didn't work on stage. I think all the instrumentalization demanded something a little more brash from me."

So, much to the dismay of a number of concert-goers, Pitney had the charts re-done. "Yeah, I wanted more of a Bobby Darin quasi-swing sound to it," he said. "I love it the way we do it now. I'm not sure if Dimitri Tiomkin would agree with me (*laughter*)."

A number of fans didn't agree with him. His International Fan Club constantly received post-concert comments from people who were surprised at the more up tempo version of the song in concert. He closed every one of his American shows – and

most of his UK shows – with "Town Without Pity." He said it was fitting for two reasons. First, it was the first BIG hit he ever had. "I wanted it to be the last song people heard," he said. "That's the one they should walk away with in their heads because that is likely the first song of mine they ever heard. That's the one that got them hooked!"

Second, he pointed out, "It is simply a winner of a song to walk off to. It has those singing, swinging horns, and it just pulses. I get pumped up when I hear that walk off chorus and I head to the front of the stage to shake hands. It is just an electric moment every night."

"Town Without Pity" was the last song Gene sang at his last concert ever, at St. David's Hall, Cardiff, Wales, April 4, 2006. He died early the next morning – in his sleep – on April 5, 2006.

Gene commented, at length, in a 1994 *Gene Pitney International Fan Club Newsletter* interview about "Town Without Pity." It is reprinted here.

"Town Without Pity" was Gene's first Top 20 hit in the US…peaking at #13 on the *Billboard Hot 100*. It established him as both a compelling recording artist AND a new teen idol. They were two very divergent roles that would fight each other throughout his career.

After "Town Without Pity," a song of tremendous integrity, settled into the higher reaches of the US charts, Gene's career was off and running. The fact that it was written by two legendary composers, Dimitri Tiomkin and Ned Washington, and was the theme song to a major motion picture starring Kirk Douglas, gave it the legitimacy that none of Del Shannon's or Bobby Vee's songs, for instance, ever achieved. To the music world, "Town Without Pity" was a real song, not one of those little rock 'n' roll ditties. To confirm their own feelings, the music establishment added another layer of legitimacy on the song by nominating it for an Academy Award.

Gene was invited to the Oscar ceremony to sing the song live, and that truly cemented his reputation as a singer and not just a teen idol. As you know by now, Henry Mancini's "Moon River" took home the award, but Gene was now a household name. He appeared on the MOST famous TV show of them all, and, even though his song lost, he came out the big winner!

This is one of Gene's favorite songs, and it was with pleasure that he sat and thought about those heady days and answered our questions about "Town Without Pity."

Question: When and where did you first hear the song? Was it a demo record or was it played for you by the composers? If it was a demo do you know who sang on the demo? Were you asked to sing it a certain way?

Gene: The first time I ever heard "Town Without Pity" was on a demo record that the composers must have had made. It was simple, and the singer sang it straight. I don't know who he was. I don't think anyone had any special idea as to how the song should have been sung, but I wrestled with the different possibilities for a long time. I wasn't exactly thrilled with the song to begin with, so it's hard to know how to sing something that's alien to your own taste!

Question: Who finally decided that the take used on the record – the growling sound – was the "sound" they wanted for the song? You? The record company? The composers?

Gene: I was so damned tired by the time the powers-that-be in the recording booth were happy with a take that I didn't care what they considered the definitive take! My manager, Aaron Schroeder; one of the writers, Dimitri Tiomkin; and the producer, Jimmy Haskell, were the guys trying to figure out what the "sound" should be. I just sang the song over and over and over…

Question: Have you ever seen the movie?

Gene: I actually went to a theater in Hartford, Connecticut, with Lynne, before we were married, and two friends, to see the film when it came out. It was weird sitting there and listening to myself on a soundtrack with Kirk Douglas up on the screen!

Question: Can you recall some of the memories of the trip to Hollywood to record the song. Who went with you? Where did you stay? Did you go sightseeing? Did you meet anyone famous?

Gene: The trip to LA to record the song was truly exciting. It did start out a little strange, however. We had to wait in one cab while another cab was bringing us the arrangements for the recording session. The arrangements were done by Don Costa, who did a lot of work with Frank Sinatra, and he had just finished them the morning we were leaving New York for LA. I flew out with my manager, Aaron Schroeder, and we stayed at The Hollywood Roosevelt Hotel. My room was right on the pool side. I remember seeing The Dovells ("You Can't Sit Down" and "The Bristol Stomp") romping in the pool, but I was shy and didn't know them so I didn't go out. It wasn't until years later that I got to know Len Barry and the other guys. I had dinner at Chasen's, a famous Hollywood spot, with Mack David, Hal David's brother. Little did I know then how Hal would figure in my career! I did some press shoots while there, and I got to see a lot of LA because of them. One of the photo shoots was with an actress named Jana Taylor, who, at the time, was on the soap opera "General Hospital." We posed by all the LA landmarks, The Greek Theatre, Grauman's Chinese Theatre, etc. It was a lot of fun.

Question: It had to be a nerve-wracking session for you – the small town kid from Rockville, Connecticut, in a major Hollywood recording studio doing a movie theme. What were your feelings and thoughts going in? When did you get comfortable – if ever – in the session?

Gene: I was pretty comfortable at the session. I loved being in a studio and was always happy there no matter how hard or stressful the situation was. I am still that way today.

Question: Looking back at all the milestones in your career, was this, in fact, the biggest record of your career? Not in terms of sales or chart position, but in establishing Gene Pitney as a musical force to be reckoned with? Or, if this record never happened do you think you would still have had a big career?

Gene: I think I was destined to have a career as a singer, and I'm sure I would have had one with or without "Town Without Pity." On the other hand, the fact that I was the first pop singer legitimized by singing a movie theme song and then consolidating that position by singing on the Academy Awards Show, this song certainly was the one that made a major impression on the American public.

Question: In live concerts you pick up the pace of the song quite a bit. Why?

Gene: I tend to sing everything faster in concert. And, once you do that a few times, it's very hard to go back to the original tempo because then it seems like you're dragging the song along.

Question: With more than thirty years of singing this song behind you, do you still like the song?

Gene: Yes, I still like this song! It is still unique. The chord progression and the lyrics are not your everyday typical three chord pop song. It's also a great song to open a show with because of the opening sweep of the arrangement and the great voicing of the saxes and horns.

Question: If you were offered the chance to re-record it, what would you do differently?

Gene: I would never re-record this song. It's been too good to me in its original form and must stay the same!

Question: Where and when did you first hear that the song had been nominated for an Oscar? What was your reaction?

Gene: I don't remember where I was when I heard about the nomination. That's probably because I was also told at the same time that I was going to sing the song at The Golden Globe Awards in front of all the Hollywood "glitterati," and I was too busy being scared to death!!!

Question: How did you get invited to sing "Town Without Pity" at the Oscars? Who called you? How did all that take place?

Gene: Dimitri Tiomkin was a master at lobbying for his songs that were up for Oscars. The Academy is very political, and you have to aggressively go after the available votes as if you're running for office. From the time between the Golden Globes and the Academy Awards, I was hustled from one party to another, some at the famous Beverly Hills Hotel, that were attended by all of the people I had ever seen on the movie screen. Just to name a few: Marilyn Monroe, Rock Hudson, Burt Lancaster, Judy Garland, Mahalia Jackson, Bob Hope, Steve Allen, and on and on. In realistic terms I sang the song on the show because I was the one who had the record, and all the people at the film company, record label, writers, publishers, etc. had a lot to gain if the record was a success. It was a wonderful situation to be in. Absolutely a win/win situation for me.

Question: What was your parents' reaction to their son singing at the Oscars?

Gene: My parents were very proud and a little frightened by the whole thing. I know my mother still considered me her "little boy" and wasn't totally sure I was capable of pulling it off! I understand that much more now that I'm a parent. It's a difficult realization that your son or daughter is a capable individual and probably better at a lot of things than you are! You tend to keep thinking of them in diapers and needing you!

Question: What was that trip to Hollywood really like? Pretty heady stuff?

Gene: I saw a lot of cracks in the veneer of Hollywood right from the start. I'm a pretty independent cuss and was pretty sure about my priorities even then. It might be easy for some actors/actresses to believe a lot of their own press releases, but I think I would have deflated my own ego if no one had done it for me.

Question: Was this a situation where you went in thinking "Henry Mancini is Hollywood royalty and he probably has it all but locked up with 'Moon River' but this is great fun anyway, and I might just win?"

Gene: I wasn't even thinking of winning or losing. In rehearsal I heard the other songs by Johnny Mathis, Andy Williams, and Ann-Margret. "Moon River" was just one hell of a song. It was also from the most successful film, *Breakfast at Tiffany's*, so it WAS considered a shoo-in. I was simply thinking, "God, please let me remember the words! God, please don't let me trip and fall down the stairs in the instrumental break! God, please don't let my fly be open when I'm singing!

Question: How do you think your career may have been different IF "Town Without Pity" had won the Oscar?

Gene: I don't honestly think my career would have been different if "Town Without Pity" had won the Oscar. Now, ask me IF my career would have been different if I was singing "Moon River"!!!

––––––––––––––––––––

Favorite Lyric: This is such an impeccably written song that it's hard to choose one line, but, this line probably sums up the angst, anxiety, dread, and uneasiness teenagers feel in the throes of young love: *"The young have problems, many problems…we need an understanding heart…"* An eleven-word short story from Ned Washington!

Factoid: While "Town Without Pity" lost the Oscar for Best Song to "Moon River," it did win the Golden Globe Award that year for Best Song in a Motion Picture. The other Oscar-nominated songs were "Moon River," "A Pocketful of Miracles," "The Theme From El Cid," and "Bachelor in Paradise."

Factoid: In a 1999 interview for *The Gene Pitney International Fan Club Newsletter*, Kirk Douglas, the star of *Town Without Pity*, said, "I really think Gene Pitney is a great singer. You know that his recording of 'Town Without Pity' is what really made the movie a big hit. The movie did not do that much box office, initially, here in the United States. It was a bigger hit overseas. But, after Gene's recording hit the charts, it caused a greater interest in the film domestically. Gene Pitney made that movie a hit."

Factoid: Pitney also recorded versions of "Town Without Pity" in German titled "Bleibe Bei Mir" and Italian titled "Città Spietata."

Factoid: Country star Narvel Felts said in a 2000 *Gene Pitney International Fan Club Newsletter* interview, "I first realized Gene was a great singer when I heard 'Town Without Pity.' That one blew me away. I really liked his performance on that. I think that's the big difference between Gene and a lot of the other artists back then. He was a singer AND a performer on his records. And each record after 'Town Without Pity' proved that."

Factoid: Abby Schroeder lovingly described Dimitri Tiomkin as an "out-of-a-cartoon" Russian with a BIG VOICE!

And, the last word goes to…Lynne Pitney: "This is Gene Pitney the Crooner. But, I love that voice; the voice he used on this record. I loved that side of him…when he sang that way. That's what this song needed. I got used to it. I was very young when it came out and that wasn't the kind of music that I normally listened to. I liked the up tempo rock songs. This was just a very slow movie song. I loved it because it was Gene doing it. I did see the movie, and I heard Gene sing in it. That was very cool. I loved it. That was the first time that I ever heard anything like that. I was in awe, you know?"

GENE PITNEY

TOUR 1992

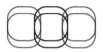

CHAPTER 29:
TRUE LOVE NEVER RUNS SMOOTH

Lyrics by Hal David and Music by Burt Bacharach

Fun Fact: In a "Midsummer Night's Dream" William Shakespeare wrote: "The course of true love never did run smooth."

Gene Pitney said: "This wasn't the biggest hit I ever had with a Bacharach-David song, but it's the one I'm most proud of." He had good reason for that sentiment: Everyone – Hal, Burt, and Gene – loved this song and his version of it.

As a matter of fact, even critics of Pitney had high praise for it. Author Serene Dominic, who is not a Gene Pitney fan in any way, shape, or form based on his caustic comments and tone about Pitney recordings in his book *Burt Bacharach Song By Song*, wrote this about "True Love Never Runs Smooth, "Pitney's majestic take on the song makes for one of his most stirring sides ever, with the singer alternating between boldly belting out la-la-la-las and commiserating about *'the heartaches and paaaaaain that we two may share."*

In unpublished comments for an interview for *The Gene Pitney International Fan Club Newsletter,* lyricist Hal David said somewhat jokingly, "I said it better than Shakespeare. I was certainly more pithy!" David did write an exceptional lyric about the angst that love, especially young love, can create. "I was already in my forties when I wrote that song," he explained, "and I had lost at love a few times in my youth, and that's what I was trying to conjure up. Love is teamwork; love is working together through the good times and the bad times. I just had to make all that rhyme in a way that hadn't been done before (*laughter*)."

FLYING MUSIC PROUDLY PRESENT

Gene Pitney
IN CONCERT
PLUS SUPPORT

1990 UK TOUR
SEE REVERSE FOR TOUR DATES

And in his lyric for this song he also swerved into the words of another great writer, Abraham Lincoln. In 1858 Lincoln said in a speech in the Illinois State Capitol in Springfield, *"A house divided against itself cannot stand."* Hal David wrote, *"Stand beside me all the while no matter what goes wrong...separately we're weak, together we'll be strong."* This time not as pithy as the original but certainly far more sweeping and vivid. And romantic!

Hal David said, time and time again, he liked to write short stories as often as he could in his lyrics. There is not a better short story ever written than the one captured in this line from this song: *"But true love is worth all the pain, the heartaches and tears... we have to face."*

Gene Pitney's relationship with the Bacharach-David songwriting team was with the younger Burt Bacharach, who was still in his thirties when they met. As was usually the case with a Bacharach-David song, Burt would play the song he was pitching to Gene on the piano. That is how Pitney first heard "True Love Never Runs Smooth." That process always intrigued him.

Speaking on the BBC documentary *Walk on By: The Story of Popular Song*, Pitney said, "There's one thing about Burt Bacharach that I've tried to explain to people and it's difficult. Burt is not really a trained singer; he doesn't have a great voice; and, I think, his instrument is actually trumpet moreso than piano. But when he sits down and plays a song for you, you're never going to do it as good as him. I don't know what it is about it, but he has this piece of him that he leaves in every one of his songs."

This song was a hit for Pitney in 1963, a year he was dominating the US charts. He started that year off with "Half Heaven-Half Heartache," followed by "Mecca," then "True Love Never Runs Smooth," and he capped the year with the smash "Twenty Four Hours From Tulsa," another Bacharach-David song. The first three of those records were not hits in the UK or the other world markets he would soon conquer. "Tulsa" was the door opener to the world for Gene Pitney.

Looking back on 1963, Pitney would always smile and say, "Like Frank Sinatra said, it was a very good year." It was nice to have four hits in a row, but Pitney found something else equally fulfilling. "Each of those hits was completely – and I mean completely – different from the other. That's what made me happy. I didn't want to get pigeon-holed like some of the other guys who were out there then. When I met with Aaron Schroeder and Wally Gold looking over songs, we wanted strong melodies and good lyrics. And that combination came in a lot of different forms. 'Mecca' is a million miles from 'Tulsa' as far as songs go. That's what I wanted. They had to sound good on the radio, but I didn't want them all to sound the same."

Pitney knew he had a great record right after the "True Love Never Runs Smooth" session. "Burt gave you these great melodies, but they always came with challenges like key changes and tempo changes, and I loved that. It's always been part of my personality to do better with a song that challenges me. This was the second or third song that we cut at that session, so by the time we got to it I was in top form.

"When I saw mandolins show up for the session I thought, 'What can this sound like?' Well, Aaron and Wally showed me what it would sound like, and I loved it.

Another shot of the powerhouse trio of Musicor Records. Gene with Aaron Schroeder (at the piano) and Art Talmadge.

They knew how to make my records sound different than everything else on the charts at the time. I got chills when I heard the final playback. This is one of my favorite records that I ever did. At that point, this was the third Bacharach-David song I had a hit with, and I told Burt this was the one I was most proud of. By the way, he didn't disagree!"

In a brief phone interview for a 1987 *Gene Pitney International Fan Club Newsletter,* Bacharach said, "I love this song. I wasn't sure it was hit material but again Gene sang his heart out on it. He was a guy who sang every note that I wrote for a song. Not every singer I have worked with was that precise. I appreciated that a lot. He always came to every session prepared. He was the ultimate professional. A great, great talent. It was always a joy to work with him. It's a very hummable song. I really like it. I'm glad I wrote it. It's a pretty compelling melody right from the start. I'm pretty sure that Hal brought the lyrics in first and I had to write the melody to fit his lyrics and his syllables."

Favorite Lyric: *"When the world outside my arms is pulling us apart…press your lips to mine and hold me with your heart."* Similar to the sense and feeling of "Town Without Pity," this spoke volumes to those teenagers in the throes of puppy love that their parents just wouldn't understand and/or appreciate even though they had been there themselves. Hal David nailed this song from that perspective.

Factoid: The first version of this song was recorded in 1962 by the doo-wop duo Don & Juan of "What's Your Name" fame. Petula Clark also did a version of "True Love Never Runs Smooth." It was the last UK single she had out before her international breakthrough with "Downtown" in 1964.

Factoid: Author Dave McGrath and the love of his life, Guida Brown, have lines from this song engraved inside their wedding rings: "True love never runs smooth" in hers; "That's what they say," in his.

And, the last word goes to…Lynne Pitney: "This was another one of Gene's songs that was simple and easy to sing along with. But, Gene had the knack of making those simple little songs sound so engaging and memorable. The sentiment of this song is sweet. We've all felt this way at one time or another in our lives and relationships. This is another one that I love a lot."

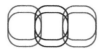

CHAPTER 30:
TWENTY FOUR HOURS FROM TULSA

Lyrics by Hal David and Music by Burt Bacharach

Fun Fact: Legendary songwriter Burt Bacharach, who co-wrote this with his longtime partner Hal David, didn't think it was good enough to be a hit.

Gene Pitney said: "I never thought my performance was that great! I felt I could have done it much better." "Twenty Four Hours From Tulsa" was Pitney's tenth single in the US for Musicor Records. Most fans would be surprised to discover it was NOT a Top 10 record for him. It snuck into the Top 20 on the *Billboard Hot 100*, peaking at #17 in December 1963. Yet, it is considered, by many, to be one of his biggest hits and perhaps the song that really made him famous. It is a Gene Pitney signature tune.

It was a completely different story on the other side of the Atlantic Ocean. "Twenty Four Hours From Tulsa" was not just an important record for Pitney in the UK; it was THE record that launched his career there and opened up the rest of the world to him. It made Gene Pitney an international star. It was a smash!

Released in England in December 1963, "Twenty Four Hours From Tulsa" broke into the Top 10 on Christmas Day, when it hit #9. By the second week in January 1964 it had inched up into the #5 spot. By the time he turned 24 on February 17, 1964, Gene Pitney was on a full-tilt run to becoming one of the top-selling American stars in England along with Elvis, Roy Orbison, and Jim Reeves.

In addition to being his first major hit in England, Pitney derived a secondary benefit from "Twenty Four Hours From Tulsa." During the British tour promoting the record, Gene met and befriended The Rolling Stones when both acts performed on the Birmingham-based TV show *Thank Your Lucky Stars*. He would, of course, go on to record the Mick Jagger-Keith Richards composition "That Girl Belongs To Yesterday" as the follow up to "Tulsa" and place it in the British Top 10. That song is also profiled in this book.

This was an era when few recording artists wrote their own songs. "Twenty Four Hours from Tulsa" is a prime example of a practice that was prevalent in the music business in the "Golden Age" of rock 'n' roll: collaborations and partnerships between prolific songwriters and popular singers to produce most of the big records in the 1950s and early 1960s. According to lyricist Hal David, "Twenty Four Hours From Tulsa" was written specifically for Pitney's voice and style. It was tailor-made to be a Gene Pitney hit. Pitney recalled, "After I had a few successes with Burt and Hal they started writing songs specifically for me. 'Tulsa' was one of them. They thought I was the guy who could do the best job on this song."

Hal David's lyric was, essentially, a two-minute and fifty-three second novella. On the surface it's a "Dear Jane" letter, a goodbye letter from a boy to a girl. But, it's more than that. Fleshed out, as only Hal David could do under pop music's rigorous three-minutes-or-less time constraints, it's really a great, sexy Harlequin romance novel. What a yarn! Boy meets girl. Love at first sight. They dance the night away. They fall in love. Boy has to dump girlfriend waiting back home for him in Tulsa.

"Twenty Four Hours From Tulsa" is "Strangers In The Night" and "Some Enchanted Evening" taken one step farther with that bittersweet "Dear Jane" twist. Hal David's potboiler was pure genius. Burt Bacharach set this story of love found/love lost to a stark, dark, and driving melody that grabs you from the opening horns to the plaintive closing piano notes. He was the Einstein of pop music for his era.

In his book, *Anyone Who Had A Heart*, Bacharach wrote, "'Twenty Four Hours From Tulsa' is a song I really liked because as it was getting born and coming together, it became a miniature movie. Hal and I didn't write a lot of songs together that told stories, but whenever we did, it was always an adventure. I loved orchestrating this song because the story was so dramatic and the orchestration propelled it forward."

Also in that book, Hal David is quoted explaining that he would write short stories

1995 UK Tour Book.

in one of those black-and-white high school composition notebooks. He would then write song lyrics based on the stories. "Doing this really helped me," he said, "because in the beginning I used to wander all over the place with my work, especially when I was telling a story, and doing this enabled me to keep myself on track."

And, Gene Pitney, as usual, rose to the challenge of telling and selling the fateful story without overshadowing it with his performance. He did an understated but nonetheless killer vocal on the song. And, at that point in his career, that was difficult for him. "I was young and still a bit green, and I had this big voice that I wanted to use all the time," Pitney explained. "Burt didn't produce this record, but he had a lot to say about how I recorded it. He was famous for beating up singers to do things his way. He didn't do that with me. I think it was after the first take he just came over and said, 'Look, just sing it as if you're sitting at a crummy desk in a crummy motel and writing the letter and reading it out loud.' I did that, and that's what you hear on that record."

Pitney did more than that. He actually makes it sound like he's nervously pacing the floor while singing/reading that apologetic opening line: *"Dearest...darling...I had to write to say that I won't be home anymore...'cause something happened...to me...while I was driving home and I'm not the same anymore..."*

But, when he launches into the next verse with *"I saw a welcoming light and stopped to rest for the night...and that is when I saw her...as I pulled in outside of a small motel... she was there...and so I walked up to her...asked where I could get something to eat and she showed me where"* there is a subtle metamorphosis in his voice that sounds less apologetic and more matter-of-fact.

He then effortlessly explains away his adultery simply, and again, matter-of-factly, *"She took me to a café...I asked her if she would stay...she said okay."*

And then he spells it all out in exultant ecstasy for the lady-in-waiting in Tulsa, *"The jukebox started to play...and night time turned into day as we were dancing closely...all of a sudden I lost control as I held her charms...and I caressed her, kissed her...told her I'd die before I would let her out of my arms."*

What a singer; what a story; what a song. Much later on, speaking in the BBC Documentary *Walk on By: The Story of Popular Song*, Pitney admitted he was trying to emulate Burt Bacharach's vocal style on this record. What's really intriguing about Pitney's vocal is the fact that, in real life, he was only twenty-three years old when he recorded

"Tulsa," yet he delivered this story with the swagger that Frank Sinatra only had when he got into his forties and fifties.

This whole record is wrapped in genius: Pitney's vocal, Hal David's sexy/sad Nora Roberts story line, and Burt Bacharach's driving, sweeping orchestration. No wonder Gene Pitney soared into international stardom with this towering performance.

In a 1993 *Gene Pitney International Fan Club Newsletter* Gene talked more about this song that was paramount to his career.

Question: When and where did you first hear this song? Did Burt Bacharach and Hal David perform it for you live or was there a demo record?

Gene: Burt played the song for me. It was written with my style in mind. Burt sang it to me in his unusual voice, and it sounded great! He ALWAYS put a part of himself into his songs, and, as a result, I never thought anyone could perform them as well as he did. I don't mean to leave Hal out of this. He is a brilliant lyricist. My association was with Burt, though.

Question: Did you like the finished product? Were you happy with your record?

Gene: I never thought my performance was that great! I felt I could have done it much better. When you do three or four songs in a three-hour session with everything being done live – from scratch – sometimes you just don't get the definitive performance. On the other hand, sometimes the pressure of necessity creates great performances.

Question: What appealed to you about the song?

Gene: The story. The melody. The way I could twist the words and notes. I think they wrote it knowing I would bend the notes where I felt the need to.

Question: Did you record it exactly as written?

Gene: Yes. Being a narrative story it has a beginning, a middle and an ending, albeit the whole story is left kind of open for interpretation by the listener.

Question: If you could change anything about the record what would you change?

Gene: NOTHING! This record was so important to me in opening up the world market that I wouldn't change a thing.

Question: Anything memorable about the recording session? Anyone famous, other than you, Burt, and Hal, on hand? Where was it recorded?

Gene: If memory serves me right it was done in Studio B at Bell Sound in New York. The "famous" people on hand, to me, were my favorite drummer, Gary Chester, and I think two great session guitarists, Al Gorgoni and Bucky Pizzarelli, were there. It was always a kick to watch Burt conduct an orchestra. The musicians all had such a great respect for him that they always excelled. I have also experienced the opposite, i.e., no respect and lousy playing!

Question: Do you think it was a bit risky NOT to put out a traditional love song or ballad on the heels of your three previous hits: "Only Love Can Break A Heart," "True Love Never Runs Smooth," and "Half Heaven-Half Heartache"?

Gene: No. You HAVE to change types of songs to have any longevity in the music business. The audience needs a surprise to keep them interested. In my case, even though my ventures into different areas of music – country, foreign language and R&B – didn't produce any advantage for me in chart positions, it satisfied my creative juices. I also find, years later, that I built a solid base of knowledgeable fans, as well.

Question: Do you think "Tulsa" stands the test of time and could it be a hit today?

Gene: The song was great for when it was written. I doubt very much it could be a hit today. Nonetheless, I am working on a rap version…

Question: How long did it take you to record the song? How many takes? Was it a hard record to make? Were there differing opinions on how it should be sung?

Gene: It was one of three or four songs on the session. I'm not sure if it was considered the strongest piece of material. Not many takes were necessary. I think three. The third take has the strange three guitar notes at the end which was either Al or Bucky stating musically that he had made a mistake!

Question: In concerts you change one word in the opening line. Why?

Gene: The opening lyric, as written by Hal, is "I HAD to write…" It was probably a mental lapse or a thought as to how I would have said it. So, I have switched the line to "I HATE to write…" "I HATE" makes a much stronger statement as to how the dude felt. It seems to show a much harder decision on the move the narrator was making.

Question: If and when you hear the song on the radio do you listen to it? If so, what do you hear?

Gene: Yes, I listen. I find myself analyzing the production, my vocal, the orchestra, etc. I am very critical of what I do.

Question: When did you start using "Twenty Four Hours From Tulsa" as the opening song of your concerts?

Gene: I have no idea! I think the

Gene Pitney

Gene Pitney International Fan Club
P.O. Box 326
Rockville, Conn. 06066

"live" shows were paced so that the strength of "Tulsa" kept it isolated from the other Bacharach-David songs I sing in that medley. Also, I like starting a show with a song that has tempo but isn't really upbeat. It allows me to go either up or down in tempo. That gives me many options as to which song follows "Tulsa."

Question: The song went Top 10 in the UK and Top 20 in the USA. Why do you think it was a bigger hit there than at home?

Gene: I was in love with the countries that were new to me, and I think it showed in my performances on radio and TV, especially in the UK. Remember, it was the early – and very exciting – 1960s, and I was very much caught up in it all. Britain was coming into its own musically with The Beatles and The Stones, etc., and, ironically, I had great success on a whole different plane with a totally different kind of music.

Question: This was your fourth and last hit with a Bacharach-David song. What happened?

Gene: Burt and Hal are very sharp people, and they saw their future as an association with their own productions as well as business ties with Dionne Warwick and others. It was nothing personal. Just good old show business!

––––––––––––

Hal David died of a stroke in 2012 at the age of 91. As of this writing (2021) Burt Bacharach lives on.

––––––––––––

"Twenty Four Hours From Tulsa" cannot be profiled without mentioning Billy Joe Royal and his Gene Pitney sound-alike 1965 hit, "Down In The Boondocks." In a 1999 *Gene Pitney International Fan Club Newsletter*, the Georgia-born star recalled how he came to record that song. Here is the text of that article:

"Joe South had written this song, 'Down In The Boondocks,' which he wanted Gene to record. It was a little odd because he called me knowing full well that I was trying to launch a career as a recording artist, and he asked me if I could do a demo of his song using my Gene Pitney voice. I had been mimicking Gene for years at that point. I said 'OK' and went to Atlanta and recorded it."

Fortunately that demo never made it to Gene. If it had it might have died on the vine. He would not have recorded it. He didn't think it was a song that would have worked for him. In that same interview, Gene said, "It would have been like recording 'Twenty Four Hours From Tulsa' upside down. I loved Billy Joe's record, but it's not something that I could have or would have recorded at the time."

That demo did, however, make its way to Columbia Records, and they quickly proceeded to sign Billy Joe to a six-year recording contract. The song became an instant hit, going all the way to #9 on the pop charts. It was Billy Joe's breakthrough record, and it catapulted him into teen idol status as well. Following "Boondocks" Billy Joe had a nice string of hits on Columbia, including "I Knew You When," "I've Got To Be Somebody," "Nobody Loves You But Me," "Cherry Hill Park," and – long before Deep Purple – "Hush."

Billy Joe recalled with a chuckle the "inventive marketing plan" Columbia had for "Down In The Boondocks." "Well, it's a funny story now, but they were pretty serious about it then. They figured that by the time it got out there the DJs and kids would THINK it was Gene Pitney, and by the time they figured out that it wasn't we'd already have sold a million! That's how big a star Gene was. You know what I can't figure out? Why didn't Columbia just go out and sign him and put out his records? It seems like they were sure doing it all the wrong way."

Ironically, later on in his career Billy Joe actually recorded a song called "Tulsa" written by Wayne Carson Thompson who had written "The Letter" for The Box Tops. "That was pretty much just a coincidence," Billy Joe said. "He was producing me and B.J. Thomas at the time, and he just happened to have this song called 'Tulsa.'"

Billy Joe conceded that Gene was a major influence on him right from the start of his career. "A HUGE influence. I just loved the sound of his voice and what he did with it on those records he made."

The likeable Royal said he wasn't shy when it came to infusing Pitney material into his shows from time to time. "I've always been able to sing like Gene. There must be something similar in our vocal cord construction. As a matter of fact I've used 'Half Heaven-Half Heartache' in my shows a couple of times."

He remembered one instance particularly well: "I used that song to open a Beach Boys show in Cincinnati, and it brought the house down. And I used it when I had to sing at the Columbia Records Convention in 1965. Man, I never heard applause like that from people in the business. It was thunderous. Thank you Gene Pitney."

Royal knows exactly what Pitney songs he would have liked to record given the chance. "I always loved 'It Hurts To Be In Love.' The other songs would be 'Half Heaven-Half Heartache,' obviously, 'I'm Gonna Be Strong,' Every Breath I Take,' and 'Last Chance To Turn Around.' I just wonder what it's like for Gene to get to sing them in his show. They are such great songs. Gene Pitney has been one of my idols forever."

Unfortunately, the two stars never met. They came close one day in Nashville, according to Royal. "I was in town to do *The Ralph Emery Show*, which was a big local TV show, and Gene was in Nashville to do a telethon. That was it. I really regret that I haven't formally met him. He's a musical icon of mine."

Billy Joe Royal died in his sleep at his home in Morehead City, North Carolina, in 2015. He was 73 years old.

Favorite Lyric: *"The jukebox started to play and nighttime turned into day as we were*

dancing…closely…all of a sudden I lost control as I held her charms…and I caressed her…kissed her…told her I'd die before I would let her out of my arms." Hal David was famed for his brevity in his lyrics. He certainly did it here. Many romance novels take two to three hundred pages to explore and explain passion. Hal David did it in forty six words. Genius!

Factoid: Gene was a fan of the 1970s British pop star Tony Christie, whose two biggest hits were "I Did What I Did For Maria" and "Is This The Way To Amarillo." A comment from Gene that didn't make it into the printed version of the above interview was telling. Christie's singing style was very similar to Gene's. Gene said, "I don't know why he didn't record 'Twenty Four Hours From Tulsa.' He would have done a better job than I did, and it could've been a hit for him."

Factoid: Al Gorgoni, one of the session guitarists on "Twenty Four Hours From Tulsa," co-wrote The Hollies hit "I Can't Let Go" with Chip Taylor, who wrote the title song to Pitney's *Blue Gene* album. "Blue Gene" is profiled in this book.

Factoid: Paul Hampton, who co-wrote Pitney's "Donna Means Heartbreak" with Hal David, said he sang the demo for "Twenty Four Hours From Tulsa" that was never presented to Gene. And, Hampton said in a *Gene Pitney International Fan Club Newsletter* in 1998 that he also sang the demo for "(The Man Who Shot) Liberty Valance." He recalled both experiences very clearly. "'Tulsa' I sang the way Burt had sung it to me. It had a Marty Robbins-feel to it. Kinda like 'El Paso.' It's another song Gene did a bang-up job with. He just had a great feel for it. He is a great singer and a great interpreter of lyrics. 'Liberty Valance' I did more like a Johnny Cash song. I thought my demo was great, but Paramount never had me in mind for the song. I think they always wanted Gene. He was hot, and he did a great job on the song." Hampton, who was known as "The Golden Boy of Demos" in the early 1960s, says he was paid between $100 and $150 per demo.

Factoid: While Columbia Records eagerly capitalized on Billy Joe Royal's ability to sound like Gene Pitney on "Down In The Boondocks," the company decided not to take it a step farther. In that 1999 *Gene Pitney International Fan Club Newsletter* interview, Billy Joe said there was never any thought given to him actually recording a Gene Pitney song, as a gimmick, during his days at Columbia. And, after "Boondocks" he said there was never any pressure to do more records like it. "That would have been too obvious," he indicated. "But I bet if it happened today they would have me do it. It's a whole new world out there today, and you've gotta fight for anything and everything. That's the kind of record that would get airplay now simply because of the gimmick."

Factoid: In the photos on his early Columbia Records albums, Billy Joe bears a striking and remarkable resemblance to Gene. (Google it if you don't know what Billy Joe looked like!) Back then Billy Joe was a young, thin, sultry-looking guy with wavy black hair swept across his forehead. Surprisingly, like his Pitney sound-alike hit, that TOO was somewhat planned. "I don't think I actually tried to look like Gene," he recalled. "But, I did like the way he combed his hair back then so I know I did THAT on purpose. The rest of it was just the way I naturally looked. I don't know if Columbia did that on purpose without telling me."

And, the last word goes to...Lynne Pitney: "All you have to do is hear that first trumpet and you know what song this is. And then that opening line, *'Dearest... darling...I had to write to say that I won't be home anymore.'* What a great opening for a song. I like it because it's classic Gene, and I love those trumpets. 'Twenty Four Hours From Tulsa' is another good song that Gene made great. Gene's voice suited this song perfectly. It's a catchy song that tells an interesting story of some sort of illicit romance. Somehow, he made it all sound so innocent, didn't he? Always one of my favorites."

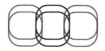

CHAPTER 31:
24 SYCAMORE

Lyrics by Barry Mason and Music by Les Reed

Fun Fact: Gene Pitney loved this song but wanted to change the title because of that other song he sang with "24" in the title.

Gene Pitney said: "Melodies like this don't come along every day. And when I heard Barry Mason's lyrics I knew it was a Gene Pitney record." Surprisingly, "24 Sycamore" is the only song Gene ever recorded by the gifted and prolific British songwriting team of Les Reed and Barry Mason, even though the types of songs they wrote were right up his alley.

Some of the huge hits the Reed-Mason team crafted were, "Delilah" for Tom Jones, "The Last Waltz," "Winter World of Love," and "Les Bicyclettes de Belsize" for Engelbert Humperdinck, "Kiss Me Goodbye" for Petula Clark, "Here It Comes Again" for The Fortunes, and "Everybody Knows" for The Dave Clark Five.

Also, surprisingly, "24 Sycamore," which was such a quintessential Gene Pitney song, was actually written for someone other than Gene Pitney. According to Les Reed, it was written for British Invasion star Wayne Fontana; Fontana needed songs in order to continue his solo career because he had split from his band The Mindbenders in 1965, shortly after "Game of Love" had gone to #2 in the United Kingdom and #1 in the USA.

Following his departure from The Mindbenders, Fontana placed three solo records in the charts, but his first real solo hit was the haunting classic "Pamela, Pamela" written by Graham Gouldman who had also penned "Bus Stop" and "Look Through Any Window" for The Hollies and "Listen People" for Herman's Hermits, among so many other hits. "Pamela, Pamela" was a very catchy and radio-friendly tune and just missed the Top 10, peaking at #11 in the UK in mid-1967. Fontana then needed a follow up.

Luck was on Fontana's side. He and Les Reed were labelmates at Fontana Records (the name is a coincidence) where Reed had his Les Reed Orchestra signed. In a go-for-broke conversation over drinks one night, Fontana pleaded with Reed for a song that would get him back "into the Top 10." Reed disclosed that he and Barry Mason had a song they had written with Fontana in mind, and they thought it would be a terrific fit for him. That song was "24 Sycamore." Reed recalled with a chuckle that Fontana's response may have been caused by having had a little too much to drink. Thinking that Reed had called the song "24 Sycamores," Fontana asked incredulously, "A song about fucking trees?" Reed explained the title and the song to Fontana, and the two agreed to work on the record together.

"Overall, that song took about a week to complete," Reed recalled. "Barry's lyrics came first as it was a personal story in his life. I added the melody a few days later. We discussed a couple of artists we should pitch it to, including Wayne, Engelbert, P.J Proby, and Gene Pitney. We thought it would have been a great comeback hit for Proby, but Wayne was really top of our mind when we wrote this song."

Reed said that after he finally had a chance to play his demo of the song for Fontana, the singer was over the moon. Fontana told him, "Let's do it right now before you give it to someone else. I need a hit." They quickly recorded it as the follow up to "Pamela, Pamela," with Reed producing.

Fontana, then twenty-two years old, had a very nice – if not distinctive – voice and did a more than competent job on his version of "24 Sycamore." To everyone's surprise (there's that word again), it didn't even chart in the UK. It did manage to hit #33 in Australia in 1967.

Barry Mason was surprised that Fontana didn't do a better job on the song. "Wayne's passionate vocal on 'Pamela, Pamela' made it a great record. That's what we were hoping he'd bring to our song. We were disappointed."

In the end, the recording needed and deserved a more unique and distinguishable voice that could sell the song while not getting overpowered by it.

Enter Gene Pitney.

Les Reed said that Jack Baverstock, head of A&R at Fontana Records at the time, had asked him – in late 1967 – to score an album for Pitney. "The album," Reed recalled, "included some lovely songs including 'Just One Smile.'" It was at this recording session that Reed says he played his own demo of "24 Sycamore" for Gene. Reed said, "Gene absolutely loved the song."

Why wouldn't he? It was right up Gene's alley: drama, pathos, love, and lost love. *"It's all over…you have lost her. Why don't you run away? What could I say? I said where's the hand that I used to hold…once so warm but tonight so cold. Now she's gone we both must share the pain…she's gone!"*

Pitney asked Reed for the sheet music, and, according to Reed, that was the last time he ever heard from the singer. "The late '60s were busy years for me, and I don't remember thinking about why Gene never recorded the song. I really wanted him to, but it was nothing I had time to pursue. Gene was busy; I was busy; it just fell by the wayside."

Gene Pitney was never one for remembering and/or collecting details on the songs he recorded. Some, however, did stick out in his mind. This one did.

"24 Sycamore" always worried him because he thought his fans would think he was trading on his huge 1963 UK breakthrough hit "Twenty Four Hours From Tulsa."

"I loved the song the first time I heard it," he said. "Les Reed played me his demo, and I knew right off that I wanted to record it."

Having said all that, Pitney did admit he still had doubts about releasing the song as a single. And that's why he sat on it for almost six years. "I always feared that the critics or the DJs or the fans would think it was a novelty thing, you know, a play on that number twenty-four." Gene said he also feared that the fans would think he put it out for that reason and only that reason: "only to score another hit."

So, he waited. "I wanted to put more distance between the two songs," Pitney admitted. He had an idea, but he never broached it with the songwriters. Change the title.

"The problem there," Gene explained, "was that the only line that repeats in the song that would work as a title is *'Where did my baby go?'* and the song was too grand for a title that 'un-grand' shall we say?"

The companion to Reed's gentle-but-bittersweet melody that soars in the chorus are those heart-breaking Barry Mason lyrics describing the heartache that love can be. Pitney's vocal was dazzling. The clincher was an elegant Gerry Bron production. In a perfect world, this record should have gone straight to #1 and become a pop evergreen.

It didn't.

Gene's version was released as a single in March of 1973 and spent seven weeks in the UK charts, peaking at #34 in May 1973.

Comparing and contrasting the two versions of "24 Sycamore" is easy but likely not fair. Wayne Fontana was not in Gene Pitney's league as a singer. Fontana's record sounds thin compared to Pitney's version. Fontana sounds as if he was in a college men's choir trying to sound like The Lettermen. It's not special, and it just doesn't grab your attention. Pitney's version is lusher and fuller. His vocal is incandescent. Fontana simply sang the song; Gene interpreted it. That was the key to making Barry Mason's lyrics work on this song.

Like Tom Jones and Engelbert Humperdinck before him, Pitney was able to jump into Barry Mason's head and feel the angst, agony, depression, and heartbreak that Mason envisioned for this song. Pitney walked the walk with this one. He sold it.

Listening to the song, you can picture, in your mind's eye, the protagonist standing in front of that home at 24 Sycamore with despair gushing out of every pore of his body as he weeps for what he lost.

Pitney's powerful – and iconic – voice allowed Bron's production to be more lush, gorgeous, and ambitious than what Les Reed had been able to do for Wayne Fontana. It sounds as if Pitney, harmonizing with himself, was challenging Bron, as the producer, to "bring it on."

When Gene was reminded of its lamentable chart position – and short amount of time on the UK charts – he wasn't shy in responding, with a little chuckle in his voice, "I was robbed."

More likely, by 1973, balladeers like Pitney were out of musical step with the times. Elton John, David Bowie, and Alice Cooper were burning up the charts in the 1970s; glitter rock and hard rock bands like The Sweet, T. Rex, Nazareth, and Roxy Music were all the rage.

The only other '60s artists on the charts consistently in 1973 were ex-Beatles Paul McCartney and Ringo Starr and The Rolling Stones.

Great songs don't always become great hits. Everyone can name dozens of songs that are their personal favorites that "shoulda been a hit." "24 Sycamore" is a great song. It should have been at least a Top 10 song for Gene in the UK, where he was considered a superstar. Why neither version of this song became a major hit is one of those mysteries of music.

Another mystery is why Gene never hooked up with the Reed-Mason team again. They wrote those great melodic songs with oftentimes sweet – sometimes heartbreaking – but always poignant lyrics that were Gene's forte. "I don't remember them pitching me any other songs," he said. "I had great fun working with Les; the man was a musical genius. It might have been because I was here – in America – and they were there – in England."

Barry Mason couldn't really pinpoint either why they never teamed up again, other than that they traveled in different circles. "After our small success with '24 Sycamore' I only came in touch with Gene a few more times," he explained. "With all of my artists, I tried to retain a close friendship, and Gene was no exception to the rule. He really was a lovely man, and, to be quite honest with you, I would have loved to work with him on further albums and singles. We certainly hit it off as buddies and good friends when he came to London! I would have been thrilled to hear him sing more of my songs."

Over the course of Gene's hit-making years, he had different hits in the USA and the UK. Some of his US hits never saw the light of day in the UK and vice versa. Four of Gene's biggest hits in the US were written by the team of Burt Bacharach and Hal David. Les Reed and Barry Mason could easily have been Gene's UK Bacharach-David songwriting team, and the three of them could have produced hit after hit after hit. Sadly, it wasn't meant to be.

The Reed-Mason resume of hit songs is eye-popping. Many of the iconic songs they wrote together were already mentioned in the beginning of this chapter. And, working with different lyricists, Les Reed crafted beautiful, sweeping melodies for songs like "There's A Kind of Hush" for Herman's Hermits and "No One Can Break A Heart Like You" for the Dave Clark Five.

On the other end of the spectrum, he also punched out the buoyant and upbeat melodies for two of the biggest hits Tom Jones ever had, "It's Not Unusual" and "Daughter of Darkness." He was also the arranger for the session in which The Fortunes recorded their massive international #1 "You've Got Your Troubles." Reed created the compelling and conspicuous – for a 1965 British Invasion band – trumpet concept on the record.

It is more than clear that, in the 1960s, Les Reed – who took his first piano lessons at the age of six and wrote his first songs at the age of ten – was one of the key go-to guys for a surefire hit melody and an aces-high production.

Barry Mason is one of the foremost lyricists of his generation. He was equally adept at writing teen-friendly lyrics like "Love Grows (Where My Rosemary Goes)" by Edison Lighthouse and deceptively realistic ain't-it-the-truth songs like "A Man Without Love": *"Every day I wake up then I start to break up...lonely is a man without love."* Ain't it the truth? That is a lifetime of wisdom in those last six words.

The legendary lyricist Sir Tim Rice *(Joseph And The Amazing Technicolor Dreamcoat, Jesus Christ Superstar, Evita, The Lion King, Aida)* said it best when he wrote, "Barry Mason can tell the story of life in three minutes."

In one of his best set of lyrics, Barry Mason told every teenage boy's painful story of lost love. That torment is laid out better than any other song ever written in The Fortunes' fabulous 1965 record "Here It Comes Again": *"When I see that girl go walking by...I know a boy shouldn't cry. Here it comes again...that feeling...here it comes again."* And then Mason drives the knife deeper into that broken-hearted teenager in love. *"When I see her look into HIS eyes...no matter how I try...here it comes again...that feeling...here it comes again."* Barry Mason was simply a master wordsmith who, in the thirty six seconds it took The Fortunes to sing those lines, took us all to a place in time in our lives where we were crushed and didn't think we would ever breathe again

Barry Mason could sum up teenage angst in as little as thirty six seconds and a life story in three minutes. Gene Pitney's interpretation of Mason's lyrics for "24 Sycamore," with the elegant Les Reed melody, illustrates what a missed opportunity it was – for Barry Mason, Les Reed, Gene Pitney, all of us – that Gene Pitney did not become their storyteller more often. Because Gene told every story on every record with absolute conviction.

Les Reed died in 2019 at the age of 84. Barry Mason died in 2021 just shy of his 86th birthday.

Favorite Lyric: *"So Mister World, look after that girl, the one that I just left behind at 24 Sycamore…"* and *"I'll take a last look and then close the book on someone that I once knew at 24 Sycamore…"* Who hasn't had to say goodbye to love? Wouldn't it be nice if we could have done it so graciously and eloquently?

Factoid: Pitney told his longtime friend, WWUH Radio host "Wild" Wayne Jones, "It's a wonderful song to do live on stage. The stuff Les and Barry wrote was just terrific, terrific stuff."

Factoid: Wayne Fontana was not with The Mindbenders when they had the huge hit with "A Groovy Kind of Love" in early 1966. Eric Stewart did the lead vocal.

And, the last word goes to…Lynne Pitney: "I haven't thought of this song in such a long time. It kinda got lost. Gene just breaks your heart with this song, doesn't he? When I hear this record, I do believe there was nobody in Gene's league. Nobody. He just sang this one so naturally; so slow, so easy. I love it. Gene's voice is so amazingly elegant on this record. While it tells a sad story, it tells it so gracefully, doesn't it? Thank you Barry Mason and Les Reed. Thank you for writing this song, and thank you for getting it to Gene."

248

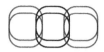

CHAPTER 32:
WHO NEEDS IT

Lyrics by Robin Conrad (Peter Callander) and Music by Len Beadle

Fun Fact: Gene Pitney got producer credit on this record because…he lost his temper at the recording session and "fired" the producer on the spot!

Gene Pitney said: "That's my Freddie & The Dreamers song!" "Who Needs It" was the B-side of Pitney's single "That Girl Belongs To Yesterday," which was written by Mick Jagger and Keith Richards. That record was a big hit for Pitney in the UK, spending twelve weeks in the charts in early 1964, peaking at #7. However, it was a different story back home for Pitney. It barely made a dent in the US charts, peaking at #49 on the *Billboard Hot 100*.

So, who is the songwriting team behind "Who Needs It"? The lyricist was Robin Conrad, a gifted and prolific English lyricist and record producer whose real name was Peter Robin Callander. We'll call him Robin Conrad for the purposes of this song. He also co-wrote "The Night Chicago Died" and "Billy Don't Be A Hero." His partner on this fun song is Len Beadle, who later wrote the theme song to a hugely popular British children's TV show.

"Who Needs It" is simply a whimsical and playful song that Gene occasionally liked to sing in his UK concerts. He said it was a great song to help pace the show and break up his string of hit ballads. And, he would say convincingly, "I have fun singing it."

"A girl is a thing that'll take all your dough. Who needs it? A girl in your arms is a terrible woe. Who needs it? She will take all your dough then away she'll go…bow wow-w-w. Who needs it? Nobody needs it as much as I need it now."

After performing this high-energy song on stage he would announce to the crowd, out of breath and with tongue-in-cheek, "that's my Freddie & The Dreamers song." Because, like most of that British Invasion band's hits, "Who Needs It" was raucous, percussion-driven, and strident.

Robin Conrad wrote songs under both his real name and his pseudonym. He was most prolific with another famous British songwriter, Mitch Murray. The two wrote the aforementioned hits "The Night Chicago Died" for Paper Lace and "Billy Don't Be A Hero" for Bo Donaldson and the Heywoods.

They were also responsible for "Even The Bad Times Are Good" by The Tremeloes, "The Ballad of Bonnie and Clyde" by Georgie Fame, "Hitchin' A Ride" by Vanity Fare," and the British #1 "I Did What I Did For Maria" by Tony Christie. The pair also produced Tony Christie's massive Neil Sedaka-penned hit "(Is This The Way To) Amarillo."

Conrad was hired to produce "Who Needs It" for Pitney. Well, sorta. Before this endeavor, he had some history with the singer. Conrad had been the record promoter in the UK on Pitney's breakthrough British hit "Twenty Four Hours From Tulsa."

When Pitney flew into the UK in 1964 for a tour to promote "Tulsa," he decided, at short notice, to also do a recording session. "I'd never produced anything before," Conrad told British music reporter Spencer Leigh in 2003, "but I said I'd do it, and it was pretty easy as Gene more or less ran the session himself."

Gene tells a slightly different story on the production of the record. He is listed as a producer on "Who Needs It," and he recalled in a 1993 *Gene Pitney International Fan Club Newsletter* interview that his temper got the better of him at the recording session. "I got that producer credit because I blew my top at the guy producing it. I told him he was doing it all wrong. So he said – you guessed it – 'If you think you can do better go right ahead.' I did…and…I did! It's a very British sounding song. Very similar to the stuff The Beatles and Freddie & The Dreamers were doing then."

Len Beadle, who provided the thumping driving melody for this song, was an English music publisher, songwriter, producer, and performer, most famous for writing the theme to the long-running (1970-1977) hit British children's TV show *The Adventures of Rupert Bear*. He was also a member of a pre-Beatles English pop group The Raindrops together with Jackie Lee (who he eventually married), Vince Hill, and Johnny Worth.

The real let down in this song is this: looking at all the aforementioned songs in Robin Conrad's catalogue, it is more than a bit surprising that such an accomplished lyricist would write such minor league lyrics for Len Beadle's major league melody. And, to make matters even worse, Conrad dressed this song up not once, but twice, with that popular phrase used in so-o-o many hit records, "Bow wow."

Pitney, obviously, knew it was a lightweight song, but he never bad-mouthed it on stage or off. It might be because he had a proprietary relationship with the song as the producer of the record. The truth of the matter is, however, very straightforward and transparent: he loved Beadle's melody. He said it reminded him of the song he had written "(I Wanna) Love My Life Away."

But, maybe, just maybe, the silly lyrics and the "bow wows" are precisely what made this such a fun song for Gene to sing.

Robin Conrad died in 2014 at the age of 74; Len Beadle died in June 2000 at the age of 68.

Favorite Lyric: *"She'll give you a date…then she'll make you wait…and how. Who needs it? Nobody needs it…as much as I need it now."* Oh my! If nothing else in this song, Robin Conrad summed up a young boy's romantic agony and heartache quite nicely here!

Factoid: "Who Needs It" was the A-side and "That Girl Belongs To Yesterday" was the B-side of the record in Australia.

Factoid: Robin Conrad also co-wrote the Wayne Newton smash "Daddy Don't You Walk So Fast."

Factoid: Later in his career Len Beadle became an important record executive with CBS Records and was instrumental in the UK successes of Billy Joel and Art Garfunkel.

And, the last word goes to…Lynne Pitney: "Freddie & The Dreamers song is right. I can just see Freddie doing that dance…and…Gene trying to do it (*laughter*). This is such a fun song. This is another one I had forgotten about. He just had so-o-o many big hits; these little records got lost. This just sounds like the kind of a song that the audience would love to sing along with…especially with the bow wows!"

As a thank you for reading this book, please enjoy these two chapters from a forthcoming historical fiction book about Gene Pitney, Twenty Four Hours From Tulsa. *It's the story of how Gene becomes involved in the careers of two rising teen pop stars and leads them to success and out of the clutches of some shady, greedy, and cagey music industry executives. With his show business and music savvy, Gene leads Hal Douglas and Jessie James to the top of the charts and the top of the music world.*

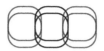

BONUS TRACK:
TWENTY FOUR HOURS FROM TULSA
CHAPTER THIRTY NINE

The phone rang in the dining room at 2574 N. Oakland Avenue at 9 o'clock on New Year's Eve morning. Hal Douglas' mom answered it the way she always did and the way her entire family was taught to answer it, "Douglas residence, Mrs. Douglas speaking. How may I help you?"

"Good morning, Mrs. Douglas. My name is Gene Pitney. I'm a friend of Hal's. It's very nice to speak with you. How was your Christmas?"

Rita Douglas may have been the fifty-three-year-old matriarch of a family of eight – and she may have been brought up on Big Band and 1950s music – but she knew who Gene Pitney was. She listened to the radio from the moment she woke up 'til the moment she crawled exhaustedly back into bed. Her favorite station was WOKY, The Mighty 92, and they played a lot of Gene Pitney records.

"Well, Mr. Pitney," she said calmly, "our Christmas was very good. We are very blessed. Hal got back home, and the entire family was together again. How about you?"

Pitney looked out the sliding doors that led from his office to his now-covered swimming pool and noticed it had started snowing. "Well, Mrs. Douglas," he said, "we had a white Christmas, and now it looks like we're going to have a white New Year's Eve, too. Imagine my excitement!"

"Were you with your family for Christmas?" she asked quickly.

"I was," Gene said.

"Then you, too, had a blessed Christmas, didn't you?" she chided in a serious tone. "And where do you call home, Mr. Pitney?"

"Gene," he said quickly.

"I never heard of that city," Rita Douglas said in all seriousness. "I've heard of Eugene, Oregon, but not a city called Gene. What state is that in?"

"Ummmm, sorry, Mrs. Douglas," he said with a little chuckle in his voice. "I meant, please call me Gene. I live in Somers, Connecticut."

"That sounds like a very nice city," she said. "Ummmm, Mr. Pitney, might I have a moment of your time?"

"Mrs. Douglas, you can have all of my time that you need," Gene said, again wanting badly to persuade her to call him Gene but thinking he was not going to get this very proper and polite lady to call him by his first name.

"Mr. Pitney," she began, "I want to thank you for being nice to Hal and helping him out. He's a good boy, a nice boy. He's been a fan of yours since he first heard that 'Liberty Valance' song of yours on the Zenith radio in the kitchen one day."

As the phone conversation continued, a very sleepy Hal Douglas trundled down the stairs into the kitchen to get some breakfast. He was going to fry up some bacon and eggs to make his favorite bacon-and-egg sandwiches and knock them back with a morning Coke.

"And every time that you put out a new record, why, he'd hop on the bus on a Saturday morning and go to Sears up there on North Avenue and use his paper route money to buy the record. It was about an hour trip. You know, he had to catch the #15 bus on Oakland Avenue then transfer to the #21. Hal knows all the bus routes around here."

The dining room phone was only one wall and about ten feet from the kitchen so Hal couldn't help but overhear some of the conversation. He wondered who she would be telling about his riding the #15 and #21 buses. It did pique his interest, so he listened a little closer.

"And then he would come home and play those records on his little Sears Silvertone record player in the playroom. He would play them over and over and over until he knew all the words."

It was becoming quite clear what his mother was talking about, but it was still unclear to Hal who she could possibly be talking to – maybe an aunt or an uncle; maybe one of his grandmas. He kept listening.

"And he would go downtown to some special store to get the *Billboard* magazines and some English and Italian magazines and newspapers every week. He could take the #15 all the way downtown and just walk a few blocks to that store."

Much to Hal's chagrin his mother still hadn't given any great clues as to who she was talking to. He kept listening.

"And, Mr. Pitney, he'd look at those pictures of you…"

All of a sudden, her voice seemed to fade away as Hal came to the shocking realization that his mother was talking to Gene Pitney on the phone.

"…and he would search high and low to find shoes and pants and shirts and sweaters that matched the ones that you wore on the covers of those albums."

Hal didn't know if he should laugh or cry. He really didn't know what to do. He was a bit stymied. Should he interrupt? That might be rude. Should he just walk into the room and let his mother see him and maybe she'd hand the phone off to him? That might be too obvious. Should he just continue eavesdropping? While it might be a bit unethical, it did seem like the best plan for him. So, he did.

At this point, Rita Douglas had been talking non-stop to Gene Pitney for a good five minutes without the singer getting a word in edgewise.

"And, in one of those teenage magazines he found the address for your Fan Club, and he joined it. Mr. Pitney, you are his hero. I just wanted you to know that – and I wanted you to know that I am so pleased that he picked someone like you and not one of those Rolling Stones boys or someone like that."

Hal was more than surprised to hear all this tumbling out of his mother's mouth and heart. It didn't ever seem to him that she really paid much attention to the minutiae of his life, such as what kind of record player he owned and which buses he took and where he went. And it certainly never crossed his mind that his mother was sizing up – and approving – his role models."

Gene finally broke into her one-sided conversation as politely as he could, "Mrs. Douglas, I don't know what to say. I'm flattered that Hal holds me in such high regard, and I'm very happy that you approve of me, too.

"That's very important because Hal has asked me to work with him on his new record, and he has asked me to help him with his next career moves. I know if you're OK with everything then Hal will be OK with everything."

"I am OK with it," Mrs. Douglas responded. "Mr. Pitney, do you know anything about money? Can you help Hal manage his money? He's still very young, and I don't want anyone to take advantage of him. You know, I was a Frank Sinatra fan growing up, and I know what happened to him. I don't want that to happen to Hal. Can you help?"

"Mrs. Douglas, I've already taken care of that," Gene assured her. "I gave Hal the name of my accountant in New York. The guy's name is Dick Naber. He's the best in the business and he won't screw – I mean take advantage of Hal."

"Mr. Pitney, I don't know how much money Hal has, but he gave all of us very expensive Christmas gifts," a very worried Rita Douglas admitted to a man she was gaining more confidence in with every minute she spoke to him. "Can he really afford that? Is he really making THAT kind of money?"

"Mrs. Douglas, your son, your very talented son, is one of the biggest stars in this country right now," Pitney said, more than a bit mystified that that apparently had not sunk in with Rita Douglas.

"He has plenty of money, and I promise you," Pitney said very softly and sincerely, "with me by his side, Mrs. Douglas, he'll become even more famous AND richer than Frank Sinatra ever was. And, Dick Naber will see to it that the money will last Hal's lifetime."

"Oh, Mr. Pitney," she said, "I am so relieved. You've made a mother very happy with those words. Would you like to speak with Hal? He just got up.

"That would be great," Pitney said. "I want to tell him my plan."

"By the way, Mr. Pitney," she added quickly, before handing the phone to her son, "I like your records a lot, especially that 'Only Love Can Break A Heart' song. That's a very pretty song. You're a very good whistler, too. Here's Hal."

Photo credit: Michael Turner

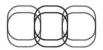

BONUS TRACK:
TWENTY FOUR HOURS FROM TULSA
CHAPTER FORTY

"Good morning, Gene," Hal said, more than a little chagrined to be party to the last minute or so of his mother's conversation with his hero and mentor. "Ummmm, you've met my mom, huh?"

"Now I see where you got all your niceness from, Hal," Pitney said with all sincerity. "She's a sweet woman. And, I'm glad to hear you're taking care of her and your family. She told me about your Christmas gifts."

"Gene," Hal retorted quickly, "my mom and dad have worked so hard all their lives to make something for us that they didn't have growing up. They're from the Depression, you know? They still fry everything in bacon fat because, essentially, it's free.

"From my mom's point of view, throwing away the bacon fat is wasteful. It's just as good as margarine to her. I'm so used to eating my food fried in bacon fat that I can't argue the point with her. It tastes pretty good to me."

"Just a little advice, Hal," Pitney said matter-of-factly. "Take care of them the way they'll let you. That'll make them happy."

"I want them to have a wonderful life for the rest of their lives, Hal explained. "I want them to relax; I want them to travel; I want them to move into a nicer house. I can afford all that, but, they're pretty frugal, and I'm not making a lot of progress."

"Baby steps, Hal," Pitney said. "Let them get used to the fact that you are wealthy and are gonna get wealthier. Let them accept that."

"I guess that's what I'll do," Hal said. "How was your Christmas, Gene?"

"White and cold and full of tea," Gene said with a laugh. "Just like my New Year's Eve is gonna be. You got a minute, Hal, to talk some business?"

"Sure do."

"I really need you and Jessie to get back here to Connecticut right after the holidays," Gene said. "I'll explain. I've got my friend, Al Kooper, working on organizing and setting up the 'A Lifetime of Love' recording session. He's got a couple of Blood, Sweat & Tears gigs to do, then he'll put it all together, probably in a week to ten days. We've got to get this done before word leaks out to Don Jon Ross and Rick Starr and they decide to stick their noses into this."

"I can get out of here by Wednesday," Hal said, remembering today was Sunday, and he was going to High Mass at 10:30 with his family at Saints Peter & Paul. Hal loved that Mass because he got to sing with the choir whenever he was home.

"Jessie, on the other hand, I'm not sure of. She loves the warmth and sunshine of California, even if it's only in the 60s. I haven't heard from her, but I'll call her and explain how important this is. I know she's looking forward to this and the UK tour, but getting her away from her home, her parents, her friends, and the weather could be tricky. I'll call her today."

"Thanks Hal," said Gene. "Then call me ASAP."

Made in United States
Orlando, FL
21 April 2022

17019117R00161